British-born investigative journalist, writer and broadcaster, Lucie Morris-Marr was twice highly commended as Young Journalist of the Year at the British Press Awards while working on domestic and international assignments for the *Daily Mail* in London. In 2006 she moved to Sydney as associate editor of *Marie Claire*, where she focused on long form investigative journalism. She went on to work as a senior writer for the *Herald Sun* in Melbourne, where she became the first reporter in the world to uncover a secret police investigation into Cardinal George Pell regarding child sexual abuse allegations. She subsequently covered the legal case for *The New Daily* and CNN. She lives in Bayside, Melbourne with her family.

FALLEN

FALLEN

The inside story of the secret trial
and conviction of Cardinal George Pell

LUCIE MORRIS-MARR

ALLEN&UNWIN
SYDNEY • MELBOURNE • AUCKLAND • LONDON

First published in 2019

Allen & Unwin
83 Alexander Street
Crows Nest NSW 2065
Australia
Phone: (61 2) 8425 0100
Email: info@allenandunwin.com
Web: www.allenandunwin.com

A catalogue record for this
book is available from the
National Library of Australia

ISBN 978 1 76087 605 0

Set in 11.5/18 pt Sabon LT by Midland Typesetters, Australia
Printed and bound in Australia by Griffin Press, part of Ovato

10 9 8 7 6 5 4 3 2

For Michael, Nathaniel, Talia and Maggie

Contents

Foreword

I'll never forget when I heard the news Cardinal George Pell had been charged by Victoria Police with multiple charges of historic child sexual abuse. He would be standing down from his post as the Vatican's treasurer and coming home to Australia to face prosecution in court. It was a devastating and seismic moment, both for Australians and the Catholic Church globally, touching the very heart of the Holy See.

There wasn't any sense of celebration or victory among survivors and families like mine who had been shattered by clergy abuse, but it was a poignant and significant development amid the backdrop of a wide-spread clergy abuse scandal that has shaken the country, and the world.

The move to charge Pell was a tipping point; everyone now had to face being held accountable, if necessary. No matter how powerful.

The subject of insidious and violent sexual abuse inflicted

by Catholic clergy, complaints of which had been buffeting the church for decades, had now involved a member of the senior hierarchy in Rome.

However, within hours of Pell being charged, a controversial court order in Melbourne ruled that media was prevented from publishing the exact number of charges and the number of complainants. We know now the media could not even explain to the public why there was missing information in its reports—it was also prevented from mentioning the existence of the suppression order itself. Later, a new suppression order created an even more draconian media blackout.

There were strong and valid legal reasons behind the order, but the case effectively went into lockdown. As a result, the public has been left largely in the dark about exactly what unfolded during one of the most important criminal cases in the world.

Lucie Morris-Marr, investigative journalist and author of this gripping and insightful book, was the first reporter to reveal Pell was under a secret police investigation regarding child abuse allegations. That experience and the challenging times that followed only annealed Lucie's resolve to pursue and relate the truth.

Riveting from the start, this expose does not let up. Lucie takes up her narrative before the cardinal reached the courts, charting his meteoric rise from his home town of Ballarat to a high-ranking position in Rome, fuelled by dogged ambition.

In the times I attended the subsequent legal case in Melbourne Lucie was always there tirelessly bearing witness, day after day, month after month, never giving up her stoic resolve to represent the public and eventually being able to share in full what they didn't yet know. Through this engaging dispatch you take a seat next to her on the front row of history.

Being ever present, among just a core group of committed journalists, allowed Lucie to bring this volume into existence as an historic marker, attesting to the details of a silenced court case that kept secret the everyday ins and outs of evidence. It was evidence that became lost in the noise of the sudden and shocking verdict, a conviction which immediately caused a polarising of the nation.

Through Lucie's precise and encompassing words, we can now learn exactly what unfolded in the courts and beyond. Her accurate, dedicated and compassionate record, stretching over many years, is not just meticulously researched, it is an intensely lived experience. She also pays sensitive homage to courageous survivors in other cases whose innocence as children was cruelly stolen by trusted clergy, but who later found the strength to come forward to try and seek justice.

There is no doubt the final outcome of the Cardinal Pell legal case will be discussed, analysed and debated for many years to come. Yet through *Fallen*, a globally important book, a harsh light has been shone within the darkness.

All the once lost pieces of the puzzle are finally in place— the unravelling of a complex legal, religious and media story shrouded in secrecy for far too long.

Chrissie Foster AM

The secret wait

Despair was winning.

We were entering day four of waiting; longing for a decision that ultimately had no timetable, deadline or decent warning that could allow us freedom to move even an inch from the courtroom door.

I was among five reporters sitting in a small interview room outside court 4.3, at the County Court of Victoria, waiting for twelve jurors to decide the fate of Cardinal George Pell, the Vatican's treasurer.

What made the wait for the deliberations so arduous was that we'd been here before; this was the retrial of what had been dubbed the 'Cathedral Trial', after the first five-week trial had resulted in a hung jury.

So it was another judicial groundhog day on 11 December 2018, as we were held hostage inside this never-ending legal quagmire from the blue skies, balmy summer air and jaunty department-store Christmas windows.

Outside, the Melburnians walking or driving past this prominent corner of William Street and Lonsdale Street had no way of knowing that within the confines of the imposing grey-tinged court building one of the most high-profile criminal cases in the world had been unfolding.

They'd learned with the rest of the world nearly eighteen months before that the cardinal had been charged with multiple allegations of historic child sexual abuse. But then the finer details became cryptic and sketchy, before the case went into total lockdown due to a strict court suppression order, brought into force by Chief Judge Peter Kidd. Rightly so, in my view, as there was a further trial, the 'Swimmers Trial', on the horizon.

As a result of the suppression order the media was prevented from publishing a word about the trial in Australia in case it influenced a future jury. We knew the world would eventually learn the full shocking allegations we'd already heard many times over. But for now, under the order, even a suggestive tweet that hinted at the details could result in a contempt-of-court charge and a jail term. So we'd sat through a secret mistrial, a secret retrial, and now another secret wait for the verdict.

The silencing of those of us who were sent to report on the case was an increasingly uncomfortable quandary. It felt as if we were betraying readers, survivors, advocates, viewers and Twitter followers by helping to facilitate the absence of public outcry over one of the biggest scandals of all time, a scandal that would reach the very heart of the Catholic Church. After all, journalists don't like to keep secrets, it's in our nature to share them. But as things stood, there was no ladder to climb out of this journalistic torture chamber; and we knew however fair it might be to tell the world about this case, that justice had to be prioritised before mass publication, no matter how frustrating.

Today, someone had kindly brought in a homemade lemon slice to share; and all of us had brought hope that the conclusion of this second gruelling secret trial would come soon, for all our sakes.

Next to us, in an equally small and cramped room, his Eminence was sitting with the door open, his black suit jacket draped over his chair, which was too small for his imposing 6 foot 4 inch stature. The ageing former ruckman turned Prince of the Church was casually turning the pages of *The Australian* and sipping on a can of Diet Coke. We'd spent so much time in close proximity to the cardinal that he'd begun to say hello each morning and awkwardly smile. With the courthouse's small businesslike rooms and office furniture, bizarrely in some ways the cardinal had begun to feel like a colleague. And though he was the sort of colleague everyone whispers about and doesn't invite for after-work drinks or lunches, nonetheless he was someone who was alongside us, bonded in part by being trapped in the same daily routine.

I heard his mobile phone ring, a sharp sound shattering the hushed chat and atmosphere of boredom. 'What? In Sydney?' he asked the caller. 'Sorry, I can't, I'm in Melbourne. I'm stuck here!'

The then 77-year-old spoke with loud incredulity, his tone suggesting he felt his predicament was a temporary irritation.

He presented like a weary traveller, as if he was ranting about having to sleep overnight in a depressing hotel room at Tullamarine Airport due to a cancelled flight; not someone who if found guilty may end up spending years in Victoria, as a long-term resident of one of the state's many overcrowded jails.

As the afternoon went on a rumour began circulating. It spiked our energy levels and lifted the spirits of the 'Pell pack', as we reporters had dubbed ourselves. The jury had a question. We would hear it in court just before 4 p.m. Finally, something. Perhaps it was news of an impasse. Or another hung jury. Whatever it was, it was better than silence.

But then, within minutes, all our phones vibrated in unison: there was an email from the media officer of the court.

We weren't going to hear a question from the jury after all.

We would be hearing a verdict.

Adrenalin surged in the sudden panic; we all wanted a seat in the front row of history, for the moment we had been waiting on. The moment that also couldn't come soon enough for editors and media outlets, totting up the huge cost of senior reporters covering the case for weeks on end.

We grabbed laptops, notebooks and bags, leaving behind power cords, water bottles and half-eaten sandwiches in the sprint to leave.

As we rushed down the corridor more reporters looked at us, confused.

'Verdict,' I said loudly. 'Check your email.'

They didn't risk wasting time, they just started jogging towards us to join the pack.

Suddenly, the scene went from something akin to a hushed library to the Hunger Games hosted by the tense electronic beats of the *Law & Order* theme tune. Friendliness and shared baked goods were replaced with primal competitiveness and a race to the best seats.

As we reached the courtroom door, Pell had emerged out of his room, still putting on his jacket, soon to be surrounded by his supporters, who were all whispering words of comfort to him. He was just nodding. Katrina Lee, Pell's loyal friend and executive adviser to the Archdiocese of Sydney, reached out and touched his hand. His niece, the willowy artist Dr Sarah Pell, offered words of comfort, telling her stricken uncle, 'It will be okay.'

Pell clearly wasn't so sure; he had turned so white his skin was almost alabaster against his black suit.

We went through the first door into a 15-foot-long corridor leading to the main doors of the courtroom. Once in, we took our seats for the next stage of this fluid, unpredictable legal drama that, for now, would be for our eyes and ears only.

What we would hear next would be both an ending and a new beginning. It would bring upset, treachery, anger and hysteria on a scale we were unprepared for.

We stood for Judge Peter Kidd and then sat down again in silence.

Pell looked ahead nervously in the dock, briefly touching his white clerical collar, alone but for a guard seated to his left. The longevity of this case, which had lasted eighteen gruelling months, had left this confident Vatican power player incredibly fragile and elderly beyond his years.

The next few moments would decide his fate, the entire trajectory of his future.

'Bring in the jury,' Judge Kidd said.

Chapter 1
A whisper in the dark

As I drove eastwards on the M1 highway through the farms of Gippsland, the expansive fields rushed past and blended into the vast grey skies. There were few travellers along this slice of rural and coastal beauty in the south-east of Victoria on this autumn weekday in 2015, and I hovered on the 100 kilometre-per-hour speed limit, confident there would be little reason to slow or stop.

I was grateful for the journey time. A long drive ahead of knocking on someone's door for a story is a gift. It's the perfect opportunity to relax and consider your approach, as you start mulling over the mindset of the person you want to talk to.

I've always been a confident reporter but a nervous door-knocker. I need thinking time. It's an uncomfortable task to ring a doorbell and then ask the person who answers to tell you their deepest secrets, or perhaps relive a buried moment of trauma, then to depart as quickly as you arrived, scoop secured on a voice memo.

It's easier to phone, of course. News outlets have digital platforms so fast, so vast, they eat stories quicker than reporters can produce them. But going to someone's home for a sensitive story, instead of calling them or sending a message on Facebook, is often the way to make a viable connection. To have a real-life conversation in person is often a better way to persuade someone to open up.

Better, definitely, but it still doesn't make the mission feel natural, or comfortable. Sometimes, after making your introduction, the door slams in your face amid expletives, threats and a report to the local police. You make a hasty, embarrassed retreat feeling shameful and small. Other times you find yourself invited in for tea and biscuits and treated like a visiting celebrity, which always comes with great relief. But you can't predict what will unfold until you knock.

Some reporters get such last-minute nerves that they 'knock the grass' as it's known in the trade, pretending to their editors the target wasn't in without even having tried to make contact. I've never knocked the grass, but I've been near enough to smell it.

As you get more experienced, you start to only want to knock on the door if it's really necessary, really vital to a bigger story or issue. I had already decided that this drive and this knock was very necessary indeed. It was critical, because behind the door was someone who may have some essential information about Cardinal George Pell.

———

The cardinal had fallen off my reporting radar somewhat until that point in April 2015. When I'd been living in Sydney, I'd known him as the city's archbishop. As my son was being born in July 2008, the streets were closed around the women's hospital in Randwick for Pope Benedict's grand visit for World Youth Day. A delighted Pell was front and centre, playing host to the whole, colourful event as over a million young people from 200 countries attended over several days.

Pell made a speech at the opening mass preaching the need for young people to practice 'self-control' in their lives.[1] 'The practice of self-control won't make you perfect, it hasn't with me, but self-control is necessary to develop and protect the love in our hearts and prevent others, especially our family and friends, from being hurt by our lapses into nastiness or laziness,' he said.

He also struck a serious note and encouraged the young people gathered to do their duty, saying: 'To the young ones, I give a gentle reminder that in your enthusiasm and excitement you do not forget to listen and pray.'

The event, controversially, cost the NSW government over $200 million. But for the Australian Catholic Church energised by the youthful PR boost, it was a huge success. With the eyes of the world's media focused on the spectacle Pell's career was catapulted to new heights as he walked alongside the Pope.

It wasn't surprising that by 2014 the Prince of the Australian Church had moved to Rome as a permanent resident and a trusted adviser to the Pope. He had already been appointed by Pope Francis the year before to a group of nine senior cardinals, to advise on the government of the universal Church and to study a plan for revising the 'Apostolic Constitution of Roman Curia'. At 73, Australia's most senior Catholic was in the inner sanctum of power in the Vatican.

Pell was the new boy in town, working in a lavish sixteenth-century tower and enjoying the lofty title of the Holy See's Prefect of the Secretariat for the Economy. There are a number of handy abbreviations for this elaborately named role, 'God's treasurer' being one of them. It was clear Dr Pell had become a very powerful man since packing his case in Sydney and getting on a plane to Italy. Very powerful indeed.

The hugely ambitious priest from the Victorian gold-rush town of Ballarat had scaled the heady heights of the Catholic career ladder: he was now in charge of his own vaults of gold; nuns brought him espressos and dainty Italian biscuits; home was a comfortable apartment at Number 1, Piazza Della Citta Leonina, just outside the main walls of the Vatican. In short, life and work for Pell in his new city was more than sweet, it was bella belissimo.

He was even being touted as a possible candidate to be the next Pope; he had participated in the conclave that elected Pope Francis over two days in March 2013 and obtained two votes in the first ballot, when one out of every five prelates got a vote. He then received one vote in the 2nd ballot and one vote in the third ballot.[2]

One glowing article from the UK's *Catholic Herald* two months later concluded that Pell was an ideal new asset for the new pontiff.[3]

'It was reassuring to observe that, as a pillar of the church he [Pell] was open, direct and also humble.' The reporter concluded, 'One can see why he will be a welcome member of Pope Francis's new committee.'

So all was going swimmingly for the son of a Ballarat publican; 'Big George', as he was known in his younger years by fellow priests and parishioners.

All except for one troubling, irritating little caveat circling Pell's impressive new life among the romantic cobbled streets, servants and Da Vinci paintings. It was a trailing cloud of scandal on his otherwise impressive CV regarding what he may have seen, heard or ignored regarding historic child sexual abuse in his homeland. Particularly, what he may have witnessed during his time living in his hometown of Ballarat, which had increasingly become recognised as the dark epicentre of clergy wrongdoing towards minors, and what he may have known regarding paedophile priests while working in the Archdiocese of Melbourne.

The anger and innuendo among survivors and advocates had followed him like an annoying wasp. No matter how many miles he travelled or how powerful he became, the questions from back home, including those from two official abuse inquiries, would follow his every step. They had started as whispered allegations and outrage, but had picked up volume, and very soon they would get even louder.

Pell's life and career were about to change direction. And so was mine.

———

Pell's name had come up completely by chance the morning before the drive to Gippsland. It was a Monday in my second week as a reporter on the *Herald Sun* newspaper in Melbourne, a top-selling Murdoch tabloid. My priority at that point was just getting stuck firmly into exciting and important stories, going back 'on the road' as a reporter as I had done in my twenties in London before moving to Australia.

'Would your prison contact be able to help with something to do with George Pell?' asked Chris Tinkler, the head of news at the time, during a brief chat by his desk.

Known around the newsroom as 'Tinks', he was a serious-minded English-born newsman whose diminutive stature was made up for by a strong and often ruthless nose for a story. He reached across his desk and pulled out a thin beige paper file. He opened it up to reveal a single piece of A4 paper inside, its edges frayed. It was a short, one-page memo and at first glance it looked like the journalists' version of a police cold case.

'Be good if your contact could find out if Gerald Ridsdale could help us with some information about Pell.'

Ridsdale is Australia's most prolific paedophile priest and is serving consecutive jail terms for abusing dozens of children in parishes across Victoria spanning several decades. One of the many aspects of George Pell's past life that has haunted his career is that he lived with Ridsdale for a year in the red-brick presbytery at St Alipius in Ballarat.

At the time they shared a residence, in the primary school and church next door, Ridsdale, and several of the Christian Brothers teachers, were raping and beating the children almost daily. Like most of these teachers, Ridsdale was in jail, and Tinks hoped he would talk about his time living with Pell.

Tinks had a thought. 'Actually,' he said. 'Maybe you could go back to one of Ridsdale's victims, a lady called Margaret.[4] Another reporter tried her last year but didn't get anywhere, she's in Gippsland somewhere I think.'

It was believed that the woman had named a mystery priest who saw her getting abused in either 1972 or 1973 in her private victim's impact statement tendered to the court. He'd failed to intervene. He simply walked past and did nothing. The victim was ten or eleven at the time.

In 1972 Pell would visit his family in the area while he was working in his first role as an assistant priest a few hours away in Swan Hill. He has confirmed in the past that he then lived as a resident at the presbytery in 1973. The dates potentially matched.

'We have reason to suspect it might have been Pell,' Tinks whispered, out of ear shot from the rest of the reporters and editors. 'But he denied it when we put it to him last year and the court won't let us have her statement so we can't confirm it was him.'

The scale and potential importance of this was obvious as soon as I heard it.

'He's number three to the Pope, isn't he?' I asked.

'Yes, very senior indeed,' Tinks replied.

'I'll go to Gippsland first thing.'

This sliding-doors moment, this chance conversation, now placed me on a path that would not just rock the Vatican but also, in time, the internal eco-system of the paper. Not to mention the course of my career and life for several years.

I had no idea of what was to come. I just felt thrilled and energised as I walked back to my desk, happy to be back in the newspaper game with a proper investigation before me.

The Pell memo was neither comprehensive nor particularly helpful, but it was a start. Other reporters had obviously tried to tackle the story but had either given up or been given other assignments.

I'd never intended to put a foot back into a tabloid newsroom after moving from London, where I'd been worked to within an inch of my life by Lord Northcliffe's *Daily Mail* for seven years.

'With tabloids it always ends in tears,' a hardened reporter on the *News of the World* once advised me wisely when I was a nineteen-year-old, wide-eyed, work-experience reporter.

But to me they are like fairgrounds. They can be high-speed roller-coaster rides of adrenalin and unpredictability, yet their thrilling allure and bright lights remained tempting. They set the daily news agenda with their confident, screaming headlines and bring governments and criminals to their knees.

Anyway, it was only my second week at the *Herald Sun* and I seemed to be proving my worth as the paper's new reporter. I'd already brought in a front-page exclusive about mining magnate Gina Rinehart and the 'Cambodian daughters' she was sponsoring through college, after saving them from the sex-trafficking trade. And I'd picked myself up and brushed off a difficult first week after an interview with the parents of deceased teen terrorist Numan Haider resulted in the paper deciding I needed bodyguards outside my family home for 72 intense hours. My suburban life suddenly became like the movie *Mission Impossible.*

I sat down at my new desk with the memo from Tinks and pulled out recent school and kindergarten photos of my smiling, gap-toothed son and daughter, then aged just six and four. I placed them on a little pinboard next to my computer. As Pell worked from his tower in Rome, I was settling into my little corner in the tall Herald and Weekly Times Building on Melbourne's Southbank.

———

The satellite navigation system was saying there were still over 10 kilometres to go to the town of Traralgon in Gippsland. Adele's 'Skyfall' song came on through the Bluetooth. I turned it up. I was getting closer to that very important door and to a potentially huge story. More fields. More sky. More of the same. The music was a distraction. But it also was a motivator, the stirring lyrics giving me a sense of purpose.

I didn't know how bleak it would get but it would involve darkness I never knew existed. Like an innocent abroad, I drove on.

Pulling off the main road, the satellite navigation system directed me through suburban side streets. I discovered rows of single-level homes with clipped lawns, pretty windows and distant views.

So far, so normal.

I found the house I was looking for. I reversed back up the street to look at the quaint single-storey cottage. It had a well-kept and well-loved garden.

I parked a short distance away, my car out of view. Then I just sat still. To gain my composure. To think about what I would actually say in the vital opening seconds when you hope, you wish, someone won't slam the door and call the police. That they will share. Talk. Trust.

Margaret's abuse by Ridsdale had been difficult reading. There had been four horrific main incidents described on the court charge sheet. She first came into contact with the priest, not as a pupil or member of the choir, but simply because she often stayed with an aunt who lived nearby. An aunt who trusted Ridsdale implicitly.

The charge sheet laid out what happened in disturbing detail:

Ridsdale caught up with her as she was near the back door in the kitchen.

He grabbed her, wrapping his arms around her in a firm hold like a bear hug.

He pulled her back near the kitchen sink area. He kept telling her to stop running away, at the same time he was, as she describes, 'mauling me and touching me.'

Ridsdale then told Margaret to bend over and touch her toes. She complied. 'I was initially resisting but then I just froze, and he pulled my pants down,' she was quoted saying.

The charge sheet then detailed how Margaret believed that another priest living in the house walked through the door to the hallway. 'She knows that this priest saw what was happening.'

How could anyone fail to help a tiny child being raped?

Could there be anything more sinful and evil? The hypocrisy and negligence were hard to comprehend.

I walked slowly down the stone path and rang the doorbell. Silence. After two minutes I knocked. Nothing.

I decided I would come back at dusk, when perhaps Margaret would be likely to have returned from work. Not that I knew she even worked.

'Hi, she's not in. But I'll wait until she is,' I texted Tinks.

I now had the best part of six or seven hours to kill. It would have been nice to enjoy this sudden luxury of time with no other task or work to attend to. But there was too much responsibility on my shoulders.

For the past three decades, cases of abuse of children by clergy from Ireland to the United States and Chile to Poland had come to the surface. There were thousands of victims. The handling of the cases was made worse by the seemingly common modus operandi to always protect the church first, no matter what; to cover up the appalling deeds by the supposed good men of the cloth; to silence victims and pay them off when necessary because reputation came above justice and the safety of children.

There were so many cases of vulnerable children being abused in church orphanages, schools and choirs. Reading the shocking reports on my phone made this visit even more vital. One door. One woman. And one potentially significant story.

As it began to get dark, I parked the car around the corner from the house, trying not to be obtrusive or bring attention to myself. I turned off my lights and saw a woman wearing a waterproof jacket and jeans walking towards me with a small dog. She looked at me briefly and walked on.

Was this Margaret?

I got out of the car and walked gingerly up to the house.

Usually a reporter would knock on a door in the company of a photographer. But often I preferred to be alone, unless I felt in danger. And I didn't now. I just needed to concentrate on getting my tone, my approach, absolutely right, to bond and not alienate.

As I knocked on the door and rang the bell, a voice startled me. A woman, with a delicate face and grey hair, stood looking at me bemused and shocked. She was the right age.

It was Margaret.

'Hi, I'm sorry to disturb you. I'm a journalist working for the *Herald Sun*.'

'Were you parked around there before?' she asked.

'Yes,' I replied.

I sensed I had very little time to explain myself. Margaret appeared calm, but her voice had a brittle edge of panic and fright.

'I don't want to name you in the paper at all but I'm really trying to find out … I'm trying to research something on Cardinal Pell.'

Her dog barked loudly at my feet. Margaret looked even more startled.

'How did you get my address?' she said.

I tried to quickly explain that I was new on the paper and that I had been sent to visit her personally as we felt it was such an extremely sensitive and important subject.

'I'm so sorry,' I said. 'It's not in my nature to upset anyone and I can't believe what unfolded in your life and in the lives of so many other victims.'

She seemed to soften, uncrossing her arms as I explained myself.

She then firmly said she had already warned the paper that she didn't want reporters to come to the house again. The police had even sent a letter to the editor on her behalf. Tinks hadn't told me that. Perhaps he thought it would have put off his new fired-up reporter from racing to the door. And maybe it would have.

But I was here now.

'I care. I'm a mother myself and I genuinely hate the idea that I might be upsetting you,' I said.

'I'm a mum too,' she said quietly, 'and I also work, and my privacy is important to me.'

'I understand,' I said. 'But if Pell saw anything happen to you and did nothing to help, he deserves to be brought to justice. That's what I care about and why I came here to see you, to see if you'd help me.

'When I read details of what happened to you, I cried. I think it's a disgrace because you weren't helped and Pell . . . well, he's right up there in Rome, he's number three, and if he's possibly witnessed anything that happened to you then he deserves to be held accountable.'

Margaret looked at me. Her dog had finally fallen quiet and was now sniffing around my handbag.

'I will have to live with that for the rest of my life,' she whispered in the darkness, her face lit up by the light sneaking behind the corners of her closed curtains.

She didn't need to say any more. There are occasions when your instinct confirms something is deeply wrong. I felt both queasy and angry at the same time.

It was clear Margaret didn't want to speak further. It was too upsetting. I didn't push it. I apologised for disturbing her and got back in the car.

I texted Tinks. He rang as I drove out of the town.

'I'll talk to the editor tomorrow,' he said. 'It's very interesting, very interesting.'

'Yes,' I said. 'We obviously need to stand it up with more sources and reassess.'

'Be careful driving home in the dark. Don't hit any kangaroos,' he said.

For the next two hours I drove through the inky darkness back to my home.

The pain etched on Margaret's face echoed in my mind and I kept hearing her words. *I will have to live with that for the rest of my life.*

It was both stoic and heartbreaking.

She had no reason to lie, but every reason to stay anonymous and not get involved; not to revisit that painfully destructive time in her life. But she'd revealed enough for me to make a decision that the allegations needed to be investigated. It wasn't all clear yet, but I would work as hard as I could on this for her. I would pursue this for the innocent, helpless little girl she once was, who was ignored and failed by a powerful adult.

There was no going back, literally, to that door or within myself. The long journey to Gippsland had ignited my inner drive to search for answers. To search for the truth. It was a drive that would, at times, turn me into both a wrecking ball and a nervous wreck. I would be both bullied and betrayed in what would be the most important and challenging journey of my life.

But for now, I was on my way back to Melbourne to plan my next move. And to learn more about George Pell, Australia's man in Rome.

Chapter 2
Big George from Ballarat

Big George, as everyone called Pell by the time he finally stopped growing at the lofty height of 6 foot 4 inches, made a decision around the age of eighteen that perplexed both his family and friends—he was joining the priesthood. The broad-shouldered teenager wouldn't marry or have children, he would devote his entire life to the church.

His father, George Arthur Pell, was beside himself. His handsome, athletic son had been playing for the reserves at Richmond Football Club and a professional contract was in the offing. He had also been considering studying to be a doctor. Those options were exciting and potentially lucrative, so the family patriarch hadn't considered that his son would end up choosing to spend his life wearing a clerical collar and giving Sunday sermons.

Committing to the priesthood just didn't make any sense to Pell senior, the colourful, eloquent, former miner and boxer who had worked in the searing heat of Kalgoorlie in Western Australia before coming to the Victorian city of Ballarat to work as manager of the Gordon gold mine. He later managed mines in Bendigo, Tasmania, the Northern Territory and New Guinea, but changed tack to become a hospitable landlord, first of the Cattle Yards Inn, followed by the Royal Oak Hotel, where he served out drinks as well as restraint. After a career dominated by adventure, travel and jovial nights at the pub, it's not surprising the idea of his son becoming a good man of the cloth was an alien concept. He'd brought up George to be a man of the world, allowing him to serve behind the bar and learn about life from weathered farmers in its full, messy glory.

Upset over his son's decision, Pell's father told a nun, family friend Sister Anne Forbes, that as George was joining the church he might as well have been a 'bloody dill', the blunt shorthand in Australian slang for an idiot. But, eventually, he came to terms with his son's vocation.

'Over the years his first reaction changed dramatically as he became increasingly sympathetic and openly supportive of Catholic views and activities,' Pell would later tell mourners at a requiem mass for his father in April 1985.[1] 'My father was a strong man, physically and personally. He was sometimes gruff and always honest. He told it how he saw it. A private man in many ways he had high principles and kept to them.'

George junior's decision to join the priesthood shouldn't have been a total surprise, however. His mother, Ballarat-born Margaret Lillian Burke, known by the nickname Lil, had been a strong Catholic influence. She was of Irish descent, the fifth of twelve children, and had instilled in him the love and devotion of the faith that ran through her veins.

It was a faith that literally sailed into Australia with the arrival of the First Fleet in 1788.[2] The Catholics on board were mostly Irish. In his book *The Catholic Community in Australia*, Robert E. Dixon charted how the new arrivals diligently kept their faith alive despite the fact that for many years priests were only sporadically available to provide them with the sacraments.

By the time baby George was born on 8 June 1941, the faith in Australia was nearing a boom period, a growth that would peak in the 1950s. Catholic education prospered and many parishes were established in the new suburbs being built across the country. As the numbers of clergy, nuns and brothers rapidly expanded, so too did attendance at mass, and in homes many families recited the rosary every night. 'The Catholic community had grown to be what the Irish bishops of the nineteenth century had worked for and dreamed of: a thriving Church based on the Irish model,' Dixon wrote.

Pell's birth also came at a precarious time during the Second World War raging. Australian forces had just joined the Allied invasion of Vichy French-controlled Syria and Lebanon. The country needed as much hope and prayer as it could muster. Times were tough, uncertain and frugal for many Australian families.

The Pell family did not escape misfortune, although its loss was unrelated to the war. Before baby George was born his parents endured a devastating tragedy, the loss of twins, a boy and a girl, shortly after they were born. The result was a spoiled and fussed upon young George.

Speaking at his mother's funeral in April 1980, Pell hinted at the painful loss of the babies. 'She knew as well as St Paul and any of the gospel writers that any human achievement meant hard work, struggle and sometimes sorrow. She and Dad worked enormously hard that their children would have opportunities not open to themselves,' he told mourners.[3]

There is a rare photograph of the cardinal as a baby in a book by his official biographer, Tess Livingstone. In a crisp white jumpsuit and matching white socks, he is captured mid-laughter. Clutching his waist, his mother, wearing a proud smile, is neatly presented with her hair carefully curled and a set of pearls around her neck. He was certainly adored and cherished by the family matriarch.

Lil would take George, and later also his siblings—brother David and sister Margaret—to mass every Sunday at Ballarat's foreboding 1871 gothic-style St Patrick's Cathedral. It was here, among the shadows, candlelight and hymns, that he would learn about the history of the Catholic Church, how the faith was built on Jesus Christ and his teachings, and that the church considers its bishops to be the successors to Jesus' apostles. He would also learn that it was a faith built on carefully structured hierarchy and that the church had a leader, who at that time was Pope Pius XII. Young George would soon understand that the Pope is considered to be the sole successor to Saint Peter, who ministered in Rome in the first century AD and is believed to have been appointed by Jesus himself as head of the church.

The Church describes the Holy Mass as the 'source and summit' of Christian life, and young George watched and learned wide-eyed as the bread and wine were consecrated to become the body and blood of Christ. He would learn too that at mass Catholics believe they are responding to Jesus' command from the last supper to 'do this in remembrance of me'. He would also be taught the four foundations of the Catholic faith, including the belief that Jesus calls Catholics to repent and believe. That is, to choose 'faith not doubt, love not hate, good not evil, and eternal life in heaven not hell'.

These early experiences with liturgical rituals must have made a strong impression on the future spiritual foundation of young George. As did the patriarchal figures around him. Much later, in 2004, he dedicated his book, *Be Not Afraid*, to his parents and 'my first bishop Sir James Patrick O'Collins, Bishop of Ballarat 1941–71'.

O'Collins, now dead, would prove to be a flawed hero; he would later face accusations of moving Gerald Ridsdale from parish to parish while being fully aware of the accusations that he'd abused children.

While Pell had a safe and loving upbringing in the family's modest weatherboard home on a corner plot on Rowe Street, his formative years also involved pain, hospitals and cruel bullying. According to Livingstone he had a nasty growth on his neck and needed over twenty operations to remove it.

'He is lucky to be alive,' his sister Margaret once commented.[4] 'When he was seven, eight and nine he had to wear a poultice tied around his head so it was pressed up against his throat . . . I would fight his battles for him when kids would sling off and laugh at him.'

When a new doctor was eventually found, the cause of the growth was diagnosed as an infection from a rotten filling that had spread down to the neck.

Perth-based clinical and forensic psychologist Kirstin Bouse believes enduring that kind of complex medical affliction and subsequent fallout with friends may be detrimental to a child's development.[5] 'It's possible that a child having to go through many surgeries could have missed out on opportunities to develop solid peer relationships and the confidence and the skills in how to do so,' she said. 'Trauma in particular has us all developing maladaptive coping skills—skills that we use to "survive" but that are often ultimately unhelpful because they don't resolve the trauma and actually tend to keep it alive and interpersonal relationships tricky.'

Life was certainly tricky at times at the Christian Brothers' St Patrick's College in Ballarat, where Pell studied from the age of twelve. The day and boarding school, founded in 1893, was about the 'making of men', according to Pell, and that meant the distribution of harsh words and frequent punishment.

In a homily at the school to mark its centenary in March 1993, Pell told the gathered staff and students that Catholic boys' schools should be about making 'real men of strength, compassion and sensitivity'.[6] 'However, I do not want to idealise any of these years,' he said with candour, referring to the unyielding regime he endured there in the 1950s. 'Few of our teachers wore their heart on their sleeves and justice, until fairly recently, was pretty rough and ready.'

Pell revealed he got a 'clip on the ears' from Brother Bill O'Malley just because he didn't stand up quickly enough when the priest came into the classroom. 'The fact that I was as tall as I am now, although certainly slimmer and more agile, and that I had to extricate myself from a tiny old-fashioned desk availed me nothing against his righteous fury.'

It isn't hard to surmise that it was his childhood bullying and tough treatment from intimidating male power figures that started to shape the often hardened character of George Pell, both the future man and cleric.

'My sense is that he's had to struggle with inner demons throughout his life, and he has openly admitted to having to tame a furious temper,' said Christopher Lamb, the well-respected Rome correspondent for *The Tablet*, who has met Pell many times. 'Could he have suffered some kind of trauma in his early years? I ask that because I have never met a senior church-man who was such a provocateur and so willing to engage in public battles.'

Kirstin Bouse agrees, saying early experiences shape every-one and that most of our personality traits are set before we even enter our primary school years. The nature of our rela-tionships as young children become life-long 'templates' in the future; 'The manner in which our primary caregiver relates to us, and later the other significant people in our lives, creates a relational template that we "lay over" all other relationships in our lives. That template determines how we relate to others, what we expect from our relationships, our worth, how we view the world and how we "are" in the world.'

While still on the stage for his alma mater's centenary, Pell asked the students seven questions, one of which was particularly blunt and sexually explicit: 'How close have you drifted to the values and practice of our condom culture, with easy access to soft- and hard-porn videos?' It would only be later that such incidents would be re-examined under a different light.

By the time Pell was invited to St Patrick's centenary, the college had already endured a litany of scandals with former staff being accused of violent sexual abuse of pupils. And there would soon be more. A number of students who attended the college between 1953 and 1983 made allegations that they had been sexually assaulted. One of the most notorious paedophiles was Brother Edward Dowlan, who was banished from the college in 1974 for abusing boys but went on to assault children at four other schools over fourteen years. He not only beat children but also often forced them over a desk and raped them, leaving them to hobble away to a shattered life of despair, depression, unemployment and suicide.

There is no suggestion Pell himself was abused at the college, but many vulnerable young boys too small and afraid to fight back were.

When young George left St Patrick's, he started his new life at Corpus Christi College, a former stately home turned seminary on one thousand acres in Werribee, 32 kilometres south-west from Melbourne's central business district. It was March 1960 and he was on his way. There would be no turning back.

———

Archbishop Bartolomeo Cattaneo, Apostolic Delegate, had opened Corpus Christi College in front of 10,000 guests in 1923.

He conveyed the personal blessing and congratulations of Pope Pius XI. It was a grand setting for the increasingly grand and confident young Pell, who entered the seminary in a class of 32 newcomers.[7]

'It was just the way he carried himself that made you feel he was going places, he had tickets on himself,' remembers Des Cahil, a former seminarian in a class two years below Pell. 'What was always the thing about Big George was that even as a teenager he had a strong presence.'

Pell was one of 177 students. His contemporaries included his cousin Henry Nolan and the studious Denis Hart, a future Archbishop of Melbourne. The first-year students slept in shared dormitories but the third-year students, and some of the second-year students, could enjoy the privacy of a single bedroom. Younger seminarians such as Pell assumed positions of responsibility, tending to the orchard, the hen house, the beehives and the gardens.

Cahil, now an emeritus professor at RMIT and a leading expert on Catholic culture, was just sixteen when he entered the seminary at Werribee. He looked up to Big George in every sense of the word. 'He was a happy, jovial, friendly person, a bit overbearing at times but otherwise good company.'[8]

'One was always aware of one's sexual desires,' he said candidly of life inside the seminary. 'We'd been brought up in an era where emphasis was put on purity and being told you weren't to "abuse yourself" was code for masturbation. We were not to entertain sexual thoughts or fantasies and stuff like that and as far as I'm aware that was followed.'

The daily routine at the seminary was strict and structured, involving early prayer, study and visits to the chapel throughout the day. The seminarians were only allowed out on Thursdays, with many choosing to walk to the beach or along the river and buying a newspaper en route. Nuns would cook fresh, hearty meals with ingredients handpicked from the garden.

So far, so civilised. Except for a disturbing legacy. The seminary would produce clergy who would go on to abuse children. And it would also host incidents of abuse within its own walls. Robert Claffey, who was just two years below Pell at the seminary, was later convicted three times for multiple child sex attacks.

'I always felt there was something amiss with Bob,' remembers former priest Eugene Ahern, who was in the same year group as Claffey.[9] 'It was just the way he interacted with some of the young Asian seminarians at one point, it didn't feel right. It wasn't anything I raised at the time, so it was devastating to later hear about his behaviour.'

Another future abuser, Paul David Ryan, also went through the seminary and later admitted to having engaged in sexual activity with other seminarians. He would tell the Royal Commission into Institutional Responses to Child Sexual Abuse that the challenges of dealing with celibacy were not formally addressed at the college.[10] He said that that celibacy was learned by abstinence and was put in a positive light of 'you give this up so you can serve'.

Ryan went on to be ordained and worked in several parishes until September 2006, when he pleaded guilty to three charges of indecent assault between 1990 and 1991.

It is clear that many offenders went through the seminary and were later convicted of sex attacks against children. One of them was priest Terrance Pidoto. Advocacy group Broken Rites revealed court documents that showed how after Pidoto had graduated he once took a young teenager, aged thirteen, back to the seminary one evening in 1972.

A report by the group said that the victim, 'Roger', stated the visit was organised on the pretext of showing him 'where priests are made'.[11] 'This is where we have mass,' Pidoto said as he showed Roger the chapel. He then took the boy to the deserted dining room. There, he grabbed Roger's private parts and performed oral sex on him. Eventually, the law caught up with Pidoto and in 2007 he was given a seven-year jail sentence after being found guilty of eleven charges involving four boys.

Professor Michael Parer, who arrived at the seminary in 1952 and left in 1959 just before Pell started, was abused by a fellow seminarian at the college and believes celibacy was part of the cause.[12] Now in his eighties Parer, who later became a non-clerical priest, married and had a family, confirmed what he told the 2012/2013 Victorian Parliamentary Inquiry into the Handling of Child Abuse by Religious and Other Organisations, that in his view celibacy as a condition of the priesthood was 'evil and will bring evil'.[13]

'I still hold firmly that celibacy as a condition of priesthood is evil and will bring evil,' he said. 'I believe that the subtle pressures by vocation salespeople who enthused me at eighteen years of age to commit myself to the priestly vocation on the condition of celibacy before I knew the joys of sex or the enrichment of a relationship with a woman was a form of deceit.'

Parer's own later research revealed that during his seven years at the seminary there were 445 seminarians. 'Out of those [267] who became priests, 21 are publicly acknowledged of child sexual offence,' he told the inquiry. 'We found all sorts of reasons to excuse them,' he said. 'I continue to be astounded that the guys I knew and the bishops I know continue to sweep it under the carpet and go from parish to parish. It remains incomprehensible to me.'

As a psychologist, Kirstin Bouse believes humans are essentially 'sexual creatures' and therefore it's 'normal' to experience sexual desire and arousal—particularly as a young man.[14] 'When it is perceived as sinful and wrong for a young man training to be a priest, then sexual desire and arousal would likely generate internal conflict and possibly attempts to disown sexual feelings, rather than own or acknowledge and appropriately manage them,' she said.

Eugene Ahern, who was in the same year as Cahil, remembers a 'very strict almost monastic regime' but one in which Pell seemed to flourish. 'In his senior years he was picked out as a prefect, a go-between for staff and students. He was conscious of his position but was always approachable, he was a decent bloke. There is no big incident I can think of that would suggest otherwise.'

There was an artistic side to Pell too, Cahil revealed. 'He had a particular love of poetry, in particular the work of Ezra Pound, the American poet and critic, and a major figure in the early modernist poetry movement.'

Despite Corpus Christi College's obvious intellectual and spiritual advantages for young Pell the seminary, and in particular his relationship with Gerald Ridsdale (who studied there before him), would form a blemish on his CV. Pell already knew Ridsdale from Ballarat. Their families were close friends, later leading some Ballarat locals, and even a priest who worked near the town at the time,[15] to speculate if young Pell himself may have been groomed by the older Ridsdale. After all, Ridsdale abused young members of his own large family.

Pell's closest friend at the seminary, Father Anthony Bongiorno, would also face two trials for abusing children. Bongiorno and Pell spent quite a bit of time together, according to Des Cahil, and they volunteered to help at a summer holiday camp at Smiths Beach on Phillip Island in 1961. What allegedly happened at this camp is something Pell would later be closely scrutinised over and would nearly derail his career. Bongiorno himself died in 2002 but has subsequently been accused of abusing Adam James, whose mother Maria James was mysteriously stabbed to death in 1980 in the Melbourne parish of Thornbury just before she was due to confront Bongiorno about abusing her son.

Pell impressed not only his peers at the seminary with his sporting prowess and diligent work ethic, but also his seniors. He was hand-picked for his next big step—studying in Rome.

Before he set off by steam ship from Melbourne to Naples, Pell went to the home of the former long-serving Irish-born archbishop of Melbourne, Daniel Mannix, then 99 years old and close to death. When Pell bent down to kiss Mannix's gold ring, as was the custom, little did he realise he would later wear the ring himself.[16]

'Not everyone got picked,' said Ahern, who followed in Pell's footsteps a couple of years later and would study theology at the Pontifical Urban University alongside his friend. 'But it was obvious to everyone that Pell was a star in the making.'

Studying and living in Rome suited Pell. He flourished in the ancient city and fell in love with the Italian culture, learning to speak the language fluently, and growing to love the heritage of classical music, including Puccini and Verdi.

It was an exciting time to be in Rome, as the Second Vatican Council, or Vatican II as it would come to be known, unfolded over several years during Pell's time in the city. The first council in nearly one hundred years, it addressed relations between the Catholic Church and the modern world and would result in changes that drew displeasure from traditionalists, including the widespread use of vernacular languages instead of Latin, the revision of Eucharistic prayers and the abbreviation of the liturgical calendar. Many of these changes remain divisive, even now, among the Catholic faithful. 'One of our masters in Rome used to get so incensed by what was going on with the council I remember him hitting the table in fury,' Cahil recalls. 'He was hugely conservative and didn't want change—I think he was a big influence on Pell.'

On 16 December 1966 George Pell was ordained as a Catholic priest in an elaborate ceremony at St Peter's Basilica, a hugely important moment in his life and career. In a service led by Cardinal Gregoire-Pierre Agagianian, Pell stood below an intricately carved window behind the altar created by Gian Lorenzo Bernini over 300 years before.

Following his ordination, Pell went on to complete a doctorate in church history at Oxford University. While studying, he also served as a chaplain to Catholic students at Eton College. The future must have looked like a glittering and unhindered road map to the top.

Dr Pell returned home to Ballarat in 1971. With his mahogany long, wavy locks he looked like the fifth Beatle. He still had an Australian accent, but one rounded off with an upper-class note thanks to his time at Oxford. 'He was literally hero worshipped,' a female family friend remembers. 'I was twelve years younger than him and I just remember my grandparents talking about him and praising him non-stop. We were all Catholics in Ballarat back then and George was viewed as God's gift.'

The former sickly boy now stood tall with Roman greatness in his blood. His family and the whole diocese couldn't be prouder; Big George was back in town and on the up.

Chapter 3
Silencing the lambs

Pell did indeed rise rapidly. Over the next decade his career would flourish but he would be living and working in an area of Victoria that was soiled by malevolent clergymen systematically carrying out the most vile acts imaginable, using their positions of power and responsibility to sexually abuse local children. Much later, the country would learn that the Catholic stronghold of Ballarat was in fact one of the epicentres of clergy abuse in Australia. It played host to manipulative, hypocritical priests and Christian Brothers teachers, in particular, who were grooming altar boys, school children, choirboys, orphans and the children of trusting parishioners. They all exploited the same golden ticket: they used their trust in communities to carry out their crimes, often quite brazenly, in dark corners of churches, presbyteries or sometimes on weekends away to beach houses and cabins on the Victorian coast. They would tell children the abuse would bring them 'closer to God' and threaten them into silence.

The sheer scale of the criminality and abuse would cause a legacy of self-harm, suicide and despair among the victims and their families that is still reverberating today. It was clericalism at its most loathsome, where loneliness, power and opportunity for sexual gratification collided with a pathological disregard for the pain and terror inflicted. It would emerge later that nuns too could be sexually abusive and brutally violent to children in their care.

When complaints were made the response of bishops was to hush, hide, move and cover up. The reputation of the church was placed far above the safety and well-being of children, a pattern that was being played out in parishes all over Australia and indeed the world. The chance that a priest would abuse more children in another church in another location was preferable to the shame of admitting the scandal and actually dealing with the perpetrator.

One police officer in Ballarat, Detective Sergeant Kevin Carson, compiled a dossier in 2012 of 43 deaths—suicides, overdoses and others—he claimed were attributable to sexual abuse perpetrated by Catholic priests and brothers in the diocese.[1] After a secret investigation, another police report, Operation Plangere, disputed this finding but many in the town believe Carson was right. And that, in fact, the figure could be far greater.

With this backdrop, Pell soon found himself working closely with his old family friend, the reigning king of the clergy abusers Father Gerald Ridsdale, who'd been attacking children almost as soon as he left the seminary. For his first posting, Pell replaced

Ridsdale as assistant priest at St Mary of the Assumption, a small Catholic parish church in Swan Hill, north-west Victoria. Some parishioners believe their roles overlapped and that Ridsdale would visit Swan Hill frequently enough to become a regular noted presence. They remember seeing the pair together taking services and marshalling the choir and altar boys.

Ridsdale himself later admitted he had abused boys in the area, with one altar boy claiming many years later he'd been attacked on several occasions by the prolific paedophile.[2]

One man who has troubling memories regarding this part of Pell's early career is a former Swan Hill altar boy called Stephen Scala. He has never revealed his haunting story to anyone until now. George Pell, he said, had a detrimental impact on his life. He describes Pell and Ridsdale's friendship as a 'double act', even though officially Ridsdale had left Swan Hill and was based at St Alipius Church in Ballarat East.

Scala, then around ten years of age, first approached Pell in the church one day after a service telling him how he 'dreamed of becoming a priest'.[3] 'I clearly remember telling him I wanted to be a priest,' he recalled. 'He said in response, "You have to be one of the special altar boys if you want to become a priest and we think you will be."'

Scala felt 'very uncomfortable' by the direction of the conversation. 'Pell then said to me, "We will invite you to come to the presbytery to have dinner one night and if things go well you will be able to sleep over". There was no need for me to sleep in the presbytery, I could get on my push bike and go home. We all could.'

It may well have been an innocent enough suggestion by Pell, but it was enough to make Scala feel awkward. After the conversation, Scala recalls Pell sending him to an upstairs room in the church to speak to Ridsdale. Later, Ridsdale said he'd had a breakdown while in his official role at the little country church, not due to abusing children, which he admitted to, but apparently because of a heavy workload.[4] It clearly hadn't stopped him from coming back to visit.

'Ridsdale sat opposite me and touched me high up on the inner thigh, and moved his chair towards me, he was telling me something about joining the special altar boys and that he wanted to get to know me better,' Scala remembers.

Scala, now an author living in Sea Lake, Victoria, felt emotionally out of his depth during the disturbing conversations with Pell and Ridsdale and found himself laughing nervously and loudly when he was in close proximity to Pell. 'It was like a reaction I couldn't control,' he explains. 'I was only young, but my instinct was Pell was quite monstrous and frightening.'

The laughter did not sit with Pell, Scala revealed. 'He sacked me and told me I wasn't good, almost suggesting I was evil.'

While it was a relief for Scala to leave the church, he would suffer a painful fallout with his highly committed Catholic mother. 'Our relationship came under great strain,' he said. 'I got the impression Pell had spoken badly to her about me and that was devastating for me. Like many people my mother looked up to Pell and he was God's representative on earth, he could do no wrong.'

After sharing his story, Scala approached Sano Task Force for guidance and in June 2019 he was offered compensation by the National Redress Scheme, along with an offer of counselling and an apology from St Mary's. An official letter from the scheme recognised that the abuse he experienced as a child 'was wrong and should never have happened'.

Soon Pell would be living in the now infamous presbytery at St Alipius in Ballarat East, where wrongdoing was a part of the daily routine. Pell was working as the Episcopal Vicar for Education in the diocese, and in 1973 he shared the pretty, single-level, red-brick property with Ridsdale, who worked as the priest at St Alipius Church next door.

Living with Ridsdale during Ballarat's dark era of clergy abuse and later being part of a committee that decided Ridsdale's new postings would haunt Pell. It formed a large part of the thunderous cloud of scandal that would follow him for his entire career.

———

I've always appreciated the emotional sustenance and sense of tranquillity that visiting churches, priories, mosques, temples, synagogues, cathedrals and other places of worship can bring. And I still do. I may not be religious in any formal way, but I admire the sense of community and belonging that religion can offer, how people can feel nurtured and cherished by their fellow parishioners and the clergy, especially in times of crisis. The uplifting music, the hymns, the values of good over evil, the friendly handshakes followed by hot sweet tea and chatter.

It reminds me of happy memories of my local parish church, All Saints' Hordle in Hampshire, England. Sitting on the edges of the ancient New Forest, William the Conqueror's former hunting ground, I would take my place near the altar and sing in the choir in my oversized blue robe and starched white collar. I remember enjoyable times singing Christmas hymns with my best friends Samantha, Jane, Sarah and Clare, the five of us giggling at the sight of brides in their 1980s' puffy satin wedding dresses sashaying down the aisle, later kissing their new husbands amid claps from their guests.

The flickering spring sunlight would beam through the imposing stained-glass windows during the Easter services, as the petals of canary-yellow spring daffodils in vases on the stone windowsills lit up like candles. It was the prettiest sight I'd ever seen as a young girl and I took it all in with wide-eyed wonder, although never quite connecting with it fully enough to become a believer.

From that young age, however, I valued the history of the building, the peace and the beauty of the art and fine craftsmanship of the ancient stained glass. I found our church to be a fascinating and tangible bridge to the past. The experience is seared in my memory and I'm often reminded through my work that I was fortunate no adult in power there ever abused my trust.

Visiting places of worship also reminds me of the grounding silence at the daily morning meeting at my Quaker boarding school, Leighton Park in Berkshire. Pupils, not teachers, would lead the assembly after several minutes of silent reflection. Independent thought was the priority and students were encouraged to stand up and share their thoughts and feelings at any time they wanted.

As a result of these experiences I couldn't think of a single place of worship in which I hadn't enjoyed the serenity, taking a moment to sit, enjoy the stillness and simply be. That is until I found myself standing alone at the top of the aisle of St Alipius Parish Church in Ballarat not long after I drove out to see Margaret in Gippsland.

I wanted to see St Alipius for myself. It was May and bitter outside, and the church, which had hosted the vile abuse of so many children in the pews and confession box all those years before, felt numbingly stark. There was none of the usual sense of beauty and peace I usually felt in similar churches. It was unsettling, and I soon felt the need to leave the building as quickly as possible.

I found myself with neatly clipped grass under my feet in the garden at the steps of the St Alipius presbytery very close to the living quarters of the resident priest, and anyone else who was lodging there, and school next door. If Pell had lived in this house while Father Ridsdale was abusing children, how could he have not seen or heard any of these events? It didn't make sense.

Ridsdale had found like-minded company among the Christian Brothers teachers at the little primary school in the grounds of the church in Brother Gerald Fitzgerald, Brother Robert Best, Brother Edward Dowlan and Brother Stephen Francis Farrell. All apart from Fitzgerald, who died before he faced charges, were later convicted and jailed over child sex crimes. Many of their victims were the children in the school and the choir.

Journalist Peter Ellingsen wrote in *The Age* in June 2002, that as Pell rose through the ranks due in part to his hardline attitude and conservative stance on sex and schooling, his Ballarat colleagues 'talked saintly and behaved sadistically'.[5] 'All through it all the church went on placing criminal clergy where they could prey on children, while at the same time frustrating police inquiries and persuading complaining families to remain silent. It was the kind of hypocrisy and manipulation that can, and did, drive victims and their families to the edge, and over it.'

Pell said later he tried hard to work well with his fellow priests but insisted he was never close friends with Ridsdale. 'I lived there with him and there was not even a whisper,' he once remarked about the abuse being carried out at the time.

Appallingly, senior figures did know of Ridsdale's abuse, as it turned out. At Ridsdale's first trial in 1994 it was claimed the church had sent him for counselling as early as 1971 and before arriving in Ballarat he had been moved around various parishes by Bishop O'Collins because of complaints. The next Bishop of Ballarat, Ronald Mulkearns, who died in 2016, was also found to have knowingly moved Ridsdale around and destroyed documents. He has since been condemned for this by his episcopal successors, Victoria Police, lawyers, the Victorian parliamentary inquiry and advocates.

As I walked around the grounds of St Alipius and its presbytery, I couldn't help but reflect on the terror the children must have felt.

Stephen Woods, a former pupil at St Alipius, tragically knew all about the intimidating and powerful Christian Brothers who betrayed him as a small boy. In painstaking detail, he recalled how he had been abused in the 1970s by two Christian Brothers teachers followed by even more serious abuse by Ridsdale.

Like Margaret, Stephen's candid testimony was an important moment in my journalistic journey. 'When you're a victim it's always there,' he explained. 'Your history, your past, is always there . . . it taints every aspect of your life including your relationships, your masculinity and your sexuality. Your whole construct as a man is challenged by the fact you were abused.

'That's where all the pain comes from, the feeling that you are bad or evil . . . because that's what we were told.'

Two of Stephen's older brothers were also sexually abused at the school. One of them, Anthony, died of AIDS in 1990. His life was dominated by drugs and alcohol. 'He called his abusers monsters. He never got over it.'

And all the time that Stephen himself was being violated, the tall and ambitious Pell would drift in and out of the scene. 'The impression I was always left with was it was like he always had somewhere else to be,' Woods remembered. 'When you were around him it made you think, "Am I good enough for him?" The arrogance was there even then.'

It was clear that when Pell was a young priest in Ballarat, he seemed to be living a happy, fulfilled life in the area where he was born. On hot summer afternoons in the late 1970s he could be spotted swimming in the Eureka pool. Children would jump on his back, asking to be thrown in the air. He obliged. 'He couldn't have been more liked or popular with the children, he was like a hero at the time,' remembers former St Alipius pupil

Julie Bibby, a mother of four who still lives in Ballarat. 'He was just so young, friendly and fun.'[6]

'The mums used to love it as they could relax for a while as he entertained the kids. I never remember a single bad word against him at the time.' But she recalls it was usually the boys Pell played with, not the girls. It would be these summers playing with children in the sun that would later come back to haunt George Pell.

Pell continued to make his mark in the Ballarat diocese as an assistant priest in Ballarat East, and then for the next ten years as director of the Aquinas College for Catholic education. He also returned to his alma mater of Corpus Christi College, by then re-located to Clayton, between 1985 to 1987 in the role of rector. Among some of the first men he ordained in this role was Charles Portelli, with whom he would form a close and life-long friendship, a friendship that would later result in Portelli being thrust into the public eye amid a mountain of headlines.

While the world continued to witness dramatic social change—change that had started back in the early sixties of Pell's time in the seminary—the man himself was becoming increasingly orthodox. As society became more relaxed on issues such as sex before marriage, contraception and abortion, Pell became more tense, more dictatorial. 'It was his way or the highway,' one former friend says. 'Even his friends were scared to cross him.'[7]

———

In 1987 Pell became an auxiliary bishop of Melbourne serving under Archbishop Frank Little. His patch stretched from the

Mornington Peninsula to the Dandenongs. It would later emerge that three parishes within the diocese in particular were run by priests who were the subject of multiple complaints to the church: Father Peter Searson in Doveton, Father Kevin O'Donnell in Oakleigh and Father Ronald Pickering in Gardenvale. All three left a trail of trauma across Melbourne, but how much Pell knew about these priests is not clear to this day. Certainly, he had none of the priests removed from their posts, potentially failing to prevent further abuse.

Pell would be asked about this in depth at various times during his career, but always denied knowing anything. He told the 2013 Victorian parliamentary inquiry into child abuse that he wasn't kept in the loop. 'When I was auxiliary bishop of Melbourne, I was not a part of the system or procedures for dealing with paedophilia,' he said.

Pell passed the blame to Archbishop Little, who he said kept his auxiliaries in the dark. However, at the time, junior bishops, including Pell, sat with Little and his Vicar General on the curia of the archdiocese—effectively its board of governors—and two men on the curia alongside Pell, Bishop Hilton Deakin and Bishop Peter Connors, would later testify that sexual-abuse cases were raised at the meetings.

Contradictions such as these would highlight Pell's possible failures during this chapter of his career and would add weight to many questions asked of him. Not just years but decades later.

———

Mentone, a pretty, breezy beachside Melbourne suburb 21 kilometres from the city, was a desirable place to plant roots. Life for Pell with his well-matched conservative congregation was remarkably pleasant to say the least. He lived in the presbytery next to St Patrick's Parish Church with a female housekeeper who tended to his every whim. He was well liked and popular. 'He used to play football with the children, so all the parents of the parish school thought he was great,' a local recalled. 'To this day, many locals won't have a word said against him due to the impression he made all those years ago.'

But Pell was on a one-way mission to the top and small parishes didn't suit his ambitions. In 1990, while still in Mentone, Pope John Paul II nominated him to the Synod of Bishops.

There was trouble ahead, however, for this up and coming conservative. In the same year as his nomination, an increasingly outspoken and confident Pell came under fire for stating publicly that while he recognised homosexuality existed, such activity was nevertheless wrong and 'for the good of society it should not be encouraged'. He also expressed his belief that suicide linked to homophobia was a valid reason to discourage recognition of a gay identity, arguing, 'Homosexual activity is a much greater health hazard than smoking.'

Controversy would soon form a pattern in Pell's life. In particular there would be the now infamous photograph taken in 1993, when he accompanied Gerald Ridsdale to Melbourne Magistrate's Court for his first hearing on child sexual-abuse allegations. His reasoning and excuse for this flagrant disregard of victim sensitivities have varied over the years. In 2002 he said defensively he had 'little idea of the full extent and gravity of his [Ridsdale's] crimes'. When it would later emerge that Pell had been asked to give a character witness reference to Ridsdale, he offered the explanation that he was just doing his duty as a man of the cloth to someone who was 'at the bottom of the pile'. Many advocates saw the decision to accompany Ridsdale to court as a mark of their deep and loyal friendship. It would certainly cause a permanent stain on Pell's reputation that could never be removed.

None of this slowed Pell's personal ambitions, however. In June 1996 he was appointed Archbishop of Melbourne by Pope John Paul II, followed by a grand ceremony three months later in the Royal Exhibition Building. Choirboys from St Patrick's Cathedral, which was undergoing renovation, sang in front of VIP guests during the ceremony.

Father Frank O'Loughlin, the parish priest at the Sacred Heart Parish, Sandringham, remembered how some of the attendees felt that day.[8] 'We all went along to the ceremony, but it was with a heavy heart and a few of us priests went to dinner to console ourselves afterwards. We knew he would soon make his mark with his orthodox conservative views.'

A few months later O'Loughlin, who had studied at both the seminary and in Rome with Pell, received a letter from the archbishop sacking him from his role as a lecturer at the Catholic Theological College in Clayton. 'He saw me as too radical and modernist in my views. I had a meeting with him but what George wanted he got. There was no changing his mind. He's a nasty piece of work in my view. He was incredibly single-minded.'

O'Loughlin and some of his fellow priests remembered Pell as having an inexplicable 'lack of empathy and connection'. 'We felt there was something wrong in terms of George's social awareness and inability to infer the thoughts and feelings of others,' he said. 'Coupled with his huge physical presence, he was hugely intimidating at the time he became Archbishop. It was quite a terrifying combination.'

One woman who remembered Pell well from this era is former publishing assistant Sophia Cosmas. In the months leading up to Pell's installation as archbishop she worked on an educational book for children, *Issues of Faith and Morals*, by Pell and his close friend Mary Helen Woods. Like O'Loughlin, she found Pell an intimidating presence to deal with. 'He used to come in for meetings and I found him quite frightening,' she told me. 'He would sweep in like Darth Vader and sort of suck the oxygen out of the room.

'I once lost a dust jacket for a book he had lent us to scan some photographs and I turned over every office in the building until I found it because I was too afraid to call him and tell him we'd lost it.'

It was certainly a busy time for Pell, who was keen to move on and up, convinced that his future lay elsewhere than in Melbourne. Within months of his appointment, political pressure on the church by the Victorian government led him to establish the 'Melbourne Response' in October 1996, a protocol for handling the increasing number of sexual-abuse cases in the Melbourne church.

When Pell announced the scheme, he stood before a panel

of reporters and apologised on behalf of the Australian Catholic Church for covering up the vile and systematic abuse of children by priests. 'I would like to make a sincere, unreserved, and public apology,' Pell said. 'First of all to the victims of sexual abuse, but also to the people of the archdiocese for the actions of those Catholic clergy.'[9] He declared himself an advocate in the fight against child abuse and announced a new compensation scheme for the victims of his religious brothers. In subsequent official enquiries he would be questioned about aspects of his time as Archbishop of Melbourne, particularly his failure to sack a number of highly questionable clergy, including Father Barry Robinson and Father Ronald Pickering, over their dealings with children.

The ancient faith was in turmoil as countless horror stories of abuse were revealed in newspapers and court cases around the world. Sexual abuse by Catholic clergy was sadly nothing new, of course. It has existed in the church since at least the eleventh century according to the infamous and controversial book *Liber Gomorrhianus*, authored by the Benedictine monk St Peter Damian during the Gregorian Reformation, circa AD 1051. The book was a tabloid exposé of sorts revealing the vices of the clergy, principally sodomy, and the consequent need for reform. St Peter Damian was especially repulsed and outraged by priests having sexual relationships with adolescent boys.

The scandals would start from there and become a regular stain on the faith over the centuries. In the 1980s, accusations of sexual abuse began to get sporadic media attention and by the 1990s cases began to cause significant public outcry. In 2002 the now famous investigation by the *Boston Globe* resulted in increased awareness of the issue and later an award-winning Hollywood film, *Spotlight*. It would be revealed that children accused more than 4000 priests in the United States of sexual abuse between 1950 and 2002, according to a report compiled by the John Jay College of Criminal Justice.[10]

In 2012, it was suggested by specialists in contact with the Vatican that there were 100,000 cases of child abuse at the hands of the clergy in the United States. Many powerful men would fall as a result, including senior church members Cardinal Bernard Law in Boston and Roger Mahony in Los Angeles.

In Europe, thousands of cases of sexual abuse against children or adolescents have emerged. In The Netherlands alone, a 2011 study found that tens of thousands of minors had been sexually abused within Dutch Catholic Church institutions between 1945 and 2010. In Ireland the number of underaged victims was estimated at around 14,500, with several bishops and priests accused and facing punishment for committing or covering up the abuse.

And it wasn't as if other faiths and institutions hadn't been touched by paedophilia in their midst. Far from it. From the Anglicans to the Salvation Army, young victims who would suffer as adults took advantage of their positions of authority.

In establishing the Melbourne Response, Pell presented himself as the saviour-in-chief to desperate and damaged victims. He was casting himself as the heroic protagonist who would help solve the god almighty mess.

———

The Melbourne Response would soon come under fire, however. There was criticism over the way it was structured, and it was accused of trying to silence victims by stopping them going to the police in a bid to protect the reputation of the church. The diocese would also face scrutiny for appointing 'independent commissioners' who were actually lawyers on its payroll to inquire into the individual allegations of sexual abuse.

Ballarat-based lawyer Ingrid Irwin, who has represented many clergy abuse victims, explained that hundreds of victims were silenced by the scheme when they were encouraged to make out-of-court settlements (these were originally capped at $50,000, but later raised to $75,000). Her view is that any scheme run with the church's oversight, including its later national redress scheme Towards Healing, is little more than a public-relations exercise. 'They were set up to steer victims towards out-of-court settlements to make it so-called easier for them. And in nearly all cases it re-traumatised those who came forward.'[11]

There was certainly huge pressure on Pell to negotiate the disharmony and anger over the abuse. Occasionally, his infamous temper got the better of him.

One woman who witnessed what she describes as 'Pell's cold-hearted and callous traits' is advocate and author Chrissie Foster, who recalls a heated meeting she and her husband Anthony had with Pell in February 1997. Pell was well aware that Chrissie and Anthony's family had been shattered by Father Kevin O'Donnell's serial and repeated abuse of their daughters Katie and Emma between 1987 and 1992. Pell also knew that the Melbourne Archdiocese had been aware of O'Donnell's abusive streak for decades but had allowed him to continue to work as a priest. Brazen and cruel, O'Donnell would regularly take the Foster girls from the playground of their Catholic primary school to the school hall or the church next door and rape them.

'At the time, they never spoke a word of the abuse to us,' said Chrissie, whose book *Hell on the Way to Heaven*, published in 2010, revealed the full, shocking details of what unfolded. As the sisters entered their teenage years, the abuse began to take an immense toll on their mental health and well-being.

In August 1995, O'Donnell was jailed after pleading guilty to multiple charges of child sexual abuse over 31 years. The resulting publicity prompted Emma and Katie to plummet into private despair. It was only then that it emerged to Chrissie and Anthony's dismay that Emma has been abused by O'Donnell. And then the nightmare resurfaced later when Chrissie read a desperate note written by Katie explaining that she too had been abused by the priest. Sadly, there was no reprieve from her pain. Katie developed a binge-drinking problem and in May 1999, when she was fifteen years old, she was hit by a car while drunk. She suffered brain damage and is now confined to a wheelchair, requiring 24-hour care. Emma continued to spiral out of control and in 2008 she tragically took her own life, overdosing on prescription medications. She was 26.

The Fosters wanted answers about O'Donnell, who had also abused other children in the parish, from their church. They also wanted to raise concerns about the way the Melbourne Response was being handled. What they experienced with Pell was 'a sociopathic lack of empathy, typifying the attitude and response of the Catholic hierarchy', as Anthony would remark.

Pell was hugely defensive and combative during the meeting. 'If you don't like what we're doing take us to court,' they reported he told them. Later, Pell said he did not think he used 'exactly those terms'. But he did concede that it was one of the 'most difficult' meetings he had ever been involved in.[12] In a written witness statement to the Royal Commission into Institutional Responses to Child Sexual Abuse many years later, Pell said it had always been his intention to treat the Fosters with compassion. 'I am very sorry for the abuse suffered by Emma and Katie Foster and for the suffering of the Foster family,' he wrote. 'I am also sorry that at least in the past I have been unable to persuade Mr and Mrs Foster of my good intentions to help.'

There were multiple witnesses to Pell's dark mood that evening. After speaking alone to the Fosters, he joined 43 parents who had simply gathered to ask questions. 'He was in a terrible mood with them all,' remembered Chrissie Foster. 'It was like he was on the war path and very dismissive and seemed annoyed that he was having to face us.' He shocked the parents when he described much of the allegations against priests as 'gossip'.

'He just seemed to want to make out it was all lies,' Foster said. 'We were all being pretty civil in the circumstances and I remember even one of the parents challenging Pell and asking, "Why are you so angry?"'

Pell carried on taking notes, not looking at them. Then he replied: 'It's the Irish blood in me.'

Pell's mood escalated, according to Foster. 'He said forcefully, almost yelling, "It's all gossip until it's proven in court and I don't listen to gossip." We were talking about a priest who had pleaded guilty to 31 years of sexually assaulting children and we believed some of our children had been abused too.'

Pell didn't deny that he used the term gossip in his later witness statement. 'I may well have used that word, because it was and is my view that while every complaint about abuse should be properly investigated, and appropriate action taken, it is not appropriate to ask priests to stand aside from their ministry simply because someone names them, for example, at a public meeting.'

Many years later it would emerge that just six days after this angry appearance, Pell was accused of a heinous crime.

———

Despite Pell's increasingly brutish and dogmatic style, in the end Melbourne did prove, predictably, to be just another stepping-stone for the ambitious cleric. He was delighted to be appointed Archbishop of Sydney by Pope John Paul II on 26 March 2001. The announcement was followed by a magnificent ceremonial liturgy on the evening of 10 May, which saw him formally installed as the new archbishop in St Mary's Cathedral.

Outside, Pell's arrival was marked with a procession of hundreds of priests and bishops. Though media reports from the time noted the jubilant atmosphere was interrupted briefly by a 'small collection of demonstrating feminists, anarchists and gays', the archbishop, apparently unperturbed, offered all 'without exception' his best wishes before entering the cathedral for the ceremony, which lasted over two and a half hours.[13]

The Pope's letter of appointment was read out by the

Apostolic Pro-Nuncio, Archbishop Canalini. It indicated an appreciation of the new archbishop's leadership qualities on the basis of his time in Melbourne, and a confidence in his 'capabilities' of promoting the faith in Sydney.

It wouldn't be long until the Right Reverend George Pell, and his increasingly conservative views, particularly on homosexuality, would find a new and regular expression—in the headlines. In May 2002 the *Sydney Morning Herald* noted he had been criticised for refusing to give Holy Communion to openly gay and lesbian parishioners.[14] Quoting the new conservative mantra of the church, Dr Pell told the congregation at St Mary's Cathedral: 'God made Adam and Eve, not Adam and Steve, and important consequences follow from this.' Pell's rejection of about twenty parishioners at this service marked the first time members of the Rainbow Sash movement had sought communion from the archbishop since he had moved to Sydney a year earlier.

Twelve weeks later, the archbishop would find himself in an even bigger media storm, one that threatened to permanently derail his future. It couldn't be more serious: Pell was accused of abusing a twelve-year-old boy at a 1961 church camp on Phillip Island during his time at the seminary all those years before.[15] 'Sex abuse allegations force Pell to stand aside,' screamed the headline from *The Age*. It reported that 'Australia's most powerful religious leader, George Pell' had stood aside from his role as Archbishop of Sydney.

With a fighting spirit passed on from his father, Pell immediately and strenuously denied the claims. 'The allegations against me are lies and I deny them totally and utterly,' he said in a statement. 'The alleged events never happened. I repeat, emphatically, that the allegations are false.'

The words 'lies' and 'false' would be used again in the future, as it turned out, but for now the senior churchman was facing a serious threat to his reputation. Church and political leaders rallied behind him, including Prime Minister John Howard, who telephoned the archbishop to offer his support, later publicly stating that he believed Dr Pell was innocent.

In the end, in October 2002, a hearing of the National Committee for Professional Standards, a body set up by the Australian Catholic Bishops' Conference, was held over four days. Archbishop of Adelaide Philip Wilson, who would later be convicted then cleared of covering up clergy abuse, and his co-chair Brother Michael Hill appointed The Honourable Alec Southwell, QC, to chair the inquiry. The inquiry heard allegations that Pell 'got a good handful' of the boy's penis and testicles on a few occasions while pillow fighting or wrestling in a tent. In another alleged incident, he was in the water, jumping in the waves, when 'from one side the respondent put his hand down and inside the complainant's bathers and touched his genitals'.[16]

The complainant's credibility was subjected to a forceful attack. By the age of twenty he had a drinking problem and later in life became an alcoholic. He also had 39 criminal convictions, mostly involving drink-driving or assaults.

As a result of questions over the complainant's honesty, Southwell said it was difficult to be satisfied about his version of events against that of Pell's. Southwell did, however, accept that the complainant had been 'speaking honestly and from an actual recollection'. But Pell also gave him 'the impression that he was speaking the truth'.

The end result was something of a confusing impasse, with Southwell ruling that the complaint hadn't been established. Questions still remain today over why the matter was dealt with by a church-appointed inquiry and not the police.

After Southwell's report was handed down, Peter Ward, the lawyer for the accuser, was interviewed on ABC Radio's *The World Today* and said he was 'delighted with the finding' and that his client felt 'vindicated'.[17] He pointed out that the judge had accepted his client was speaking honestly, but there had been a gap of 40 years.

The program presenter, Rafael Epstein, seemed somewhat confused by Ward's answer and asked if they planned to take the complaint further. 'Absolutely not,' Ward firmly replied. 'The complainant wants closure, he's had his opportunity, he has had a fair and equitable hearing, and he will now just let it go, let it go.' Ward worked for the Melbourne legal firm Galbally & O'Bryan, which would later be chosen by Pell's lawyers to represent him on another very serious matter 15 year later. He rejects any suggestion of being compromised either then or later.[18]

Soon after the Southwell inquiry it was business as usual for Pell, who by the following year had been awarded what he'd always dreamed of—a red cap. In 2003 he was elevated to the Sacred College of Cardinals by Pope John Paul II but remained in his Sydney post.

Just as Pell joined the higher ranks, however, there was trouble brewing for the church. One of London's most respected weekly national newspapers, *The Observer*, reported in August 2003 that a 40-year-old document from a secret Vatican archive instructed Catholic bishops around the world to cover up cases of sexual abuse or risk being thrown out of the church. The 69-page document in Latin bearing the seal of Pope John XXIII outlined a policy of 'strictest secrecy'. A spokesman for the Vatican denied the orders were part of any organised cover-up, claiming the document was taken 'out of context'.[19]

Meanwhile in Sydney there would be challenging years ahead for Pell in his role as archbishop. In May 2013 he gave evidence before Victoria's Parliamentary Inquiry into the Handling of Child Abuse by Religious and Other Organisations and faced heckling from the public gallery. As he spoke, he was surrounded by a strong support group including Katrina Lee and his secretary Michael Casey. 'All of them are married people with children, keen to help us in the fight against this problem,' Pell exclaimed as the hearing began.

Pell was grilled by the members of the committee on a range of awkward controversies including his dealings with the Fosters, the Melbourne Response and the cover up of abuse by prominent figures including his predecessor in Melbourne, Archbishop Frank Little, and Ronald Mulkearns, the former Bishop of Ballarat. Under tough scrutiny, Pell was firm but sorrowful.

Despite the difficult questions, Pell was an unstoppable force. On 25 February 2014 he was given the promotion of his life when Pope Francis appointed him to the newly created role of Secretariat for the Economy, effectively the third highest position in the Vatican. But before he could pack his suitcases for his new life in Europe there were yet more answers needed about his handling of clergy abuse cases. This time he would be probed by the Royal Commission into Institutional Responses to Child Sexual Abuse.

In terms of trying to hide wrongdoings within a complicated puzzle, you wouldn't want to be on the wrong end of a royal commission. Impressively forensic, royal commissions leave no stone unturned, leave no witness without a voice, and spare no expense or expertise in their hunt for the truth.

The day after it was announced by Prime Minister Julia Gillard in 2012, it was clear Pell wasn't happy with the prospect of his church being at the centre of such a comprehensive inquiry. In fact, he suggested that the sexual-abuse issue had been exaggerated, telling reporters that he believed there had been a persistent press campaign against the Catholic Church and that he objected to his organisation being singled out.[20] 'We object to it being exaggerated,' he said. 'We object to being described as the only cab on the rank, we acknowledge—with shame—the extent of the problem. One of the reasons why we welcome the royal commission is that this commission will enable those claims to be validated . . . or found to be a significant exaggeration.'

The royal commission would eventually hold an astonishing 57 formal public hearings, during which it took evidence about child sexual abuse within institutions from 1200 witnesses over 400 days across all Australian capital cities and in several regional areas. The case studies focused on how institutions—including Scouts Australia and the Australian Defence

Force among others—had responded to allegations and proven instances of child sexual abuse.

Over 8000 survivors or people directly impacted by child sexual abuse in institutions attended private sessions with commissioners, so they were able to share their experiences and recommendations without being identified or exposed to publicity. Many gave consent for their accounts to be published as short narratives. The purpose of the narratives was to give a voice to survivors, inform the community and ultimately help make institutions safer for children.

When the cardinal was questioned by the royal commission in Sydney, he had to walk past angry protesters from victim support groups. In particular, he faced serious scrutiny about his part in the Church's legal battle with former altar boy John Ellis, who was abused by Father Aidan Duggan in the 1970s. Ellis had been just thirteen and living in the Sydney parish of Bass Hill when Duggan began abusing him. In 2007 Ellis brought a case against the Catholic Church but lost when the New South Wales Court of Appeal ruled the Church was not a legal entity that could be sued. This became known as the Ellis defence.

While Pell apologised for the abuse against Ellis and admitted to a string of mistakes in how the Church responded to him over many years, he stopped short of taking full responsibility for crucial decisions of the Archdiocese regarding the matter.[21]

As the royal commission hearing was unfolding in the courtroom, anger was building outside. Leonie Sheedy, the chief executive of Care Leavers Australia Network, told reporters

Pell's legacy would be his failure towards Ellis. 'They call it the Ellis defence, but it should be called the Pell defence. He's going to go down in history as the person who denied people justice,' she told the ABC.

Called back to give more evidence a few days later, Pell admitted the church had failed Ellis and that he took ultimate responsibility for the suffering and impact on his life. 'At the end of this gruelling appearance for both of us at the royal commission, I want to publicly say sorry to him for the hurt caused by the mistakes made,' he said.

In his final mass before leaving for Rome, in front of 3000 worshippers including state and federal politicians, Pell took the chance to apologise to all victims of child sexual abuse.[22] 'I apologise once again to the victims and to their families for the terrible suffering that has been caused to them by these crimes,' he said.

Perhaps Pell believed the whole clergy-abuse issue would slowly disappear and he could begin his new influential and dynamic life away from this interfering cloud of scandal. It would be a misplaced hope. On 21 August 2014, he would be requested by the Royal Commission to appear via videolink from Rome regarding its case study on the workings of the Melbourne Response.

Initially, Pell talked somewhat proudly of the scheme, which he'd personally established in 1996, saying that it gave victims compensation quickly rather than going through a court process.[23] '. . . an attempt to lessen suffering and to help these people and to do it quickly rather than have it drag on forever—not forever, for a long time,' he said.

He was then asked to explain why victims were told that if they did decide to choose the court option and sue the church their allegations would be 'strenuously' defended. 'It's an unfortunate phrase,' Pell conceded. However, he said if the matters were taken to court the Church would certainly consider using 'defences available to every citizen and organisation in Australia'.

What came next would cause outrage and ridicule in a flurry of negative headlines. Pell said the Church was no more responsible for child abuse carried out by clergy than a trucking company would be if they employed a driver who molested women. 'If in fact the driver of such a truck picks up some lady and then molests her, I don't think it's appropriate, because it is contrary to the policy, for the ownership, the leadership of that company to be held responsible,' he claimed. 'Similarly with the Church and the head of any other organisation. If there has been—every precaution has been taken, no warning has been given, it's I think not appropriate for legal culpability to be foisted upon the authority figure.'

While Pell went on to apologise for the suffering of Chrissie and Anthony Foster's daughters, the truck driver comment overshadowed his whole appearance.

Returning to the responsibilities of his new job, Pell's Rome appointment itself drew puzzled commentary. Mike Seccombe, writing in *The Saturday Paper*, described the Pope's decision as 'odd'.[24] 'The two men are so different. Francis the reformer and Pell the traditionalist. Francis the self-effacing and Pell the self-important. Francis who ministered to the poor and powerless, and Pell, who surrounded himself with the rich and powerful.'

Christopher Lamb, a reporter who is an expert on the Vatican and who had a ringside seat to Pell's first days in Rome, watched as the Australian established a reputation as a tough, action-focused prelate who could 'knock heads together' and bring some order into the Holy See's money management. 'The Pope did not know Pell particularly well,' Lamb explained. 'But in the early period of his time in office, Pell did make some important changes. He implemented proper budgeting and set up the role of an auditor general to troubleshoot when there were problems.'

Predictably, he faced opposition from those who wanted to maintain the status quo. At one stage the expenses Pell incurred in setting up his office were leaked to the Italian media. 'This was more about a power struggle than overspending,' Lamb said. 'But there were complaints early from the Vatican old guard about Pell's abrasive and uncollegial style.'

But why was Pell appointed in the first place considering the vague result of the Southwell Inquiry and also the angry accusations over his handling of clergy child abuse at various points in his career?

'Australia is a long way from the Vatican both geographically and culturally, and sometimes stories didn't filter through,' Lamb explained. 'Pell was always good at defending himself and I think his denials of any wrongdoing are likely to have been believed.'

The cardinal, who was used to having unquestioned authority in Melbourne and Sydney, certainly drew the consternation of senior figures in Rome when he signed himself as 'Manager of the Holy See' on a contract for PriceWaterhouseCoopers to audit the Vatican. 'Pell effectively wanted to be chairman and CEO, but the Pope ruled against this,' Lamb said.

Perhaps unsurprisingly, Lamb revealed, senior figures in the Vatican now admit that appointing Pell to the treasurer role in 2014 was a mistake. 'This is not—as some diehard supporters of the cardinal have tried to argue—because Pell was uncovering financial wrongdoing, but because the cardinal brought the clerical sex abuse scandal right to the Pope's doorstep.'

This decision, made by the leader of an institution already splintering under the weight of clergy abuse cases, will be unlikely to go unnoticed in the pages of history. 'I think the appointment of Pell will be read as one of the biggest mistakes of the Francis papacy,' Lamb suggested.

As mistakes go, it couldn't have been worse.

Chapter 4
Winter Gail

By the end of my initial research on Pell's career and life I'd produced an extensive memo for senior *Herald Sun* editors, largely focusing on his time in Ballarat. Back in the newsroom, it was time to focus on Margaret's story. Tinks gave me the green light to start approaching sensitive sources. He could tell the new girl was ready to be set loose.

I had to see if this devastating story had legs. Within a day or two, I had a lucky strike. I'd gained the trust of a source who put a word in for me with someone who held the key to some answers I was seeking. I can't say who and never will. I'm prepared to go to jail to protect my sources; this is the cornerstone of journalism.

'Yes, it's true and safe to print that Pell was named in the victim's statement as the priest who saw the abuse,' the source told me. I'd also been informed that the Royal Commission into Institutional Responses to Child Sexual Abuse's forthcoming Ballarat case study would be of 'great interest' in judicial and police circles in what might be revealed about the Vatican's treasurer.

It was decided the sources were so watertight that, along with what Margaret had said, we had enough to write a carefully written, straight, yet explosive story about Pell being named by the victim as the mystery priest.

Liam Houlihan, the *Herald Sun*'s super-bright chief of staff, was as excited at the prospect of publishing the story as Tinks. A strategic thinker who has authored several books, he suggested the story would work well as a front-page splash for the following Monday. Tinks was also keen to publish the story as soon as possible.

Historically, News Corp could be brutal towards editors of its Australian mastheads; bold exclusives followed up by other media outlets were its lifeblood. A rumoured long-standing rivalry between Houlihan and Tinks, due to some complex newsroom restructure many years before, meant that both wanted a piece of this very juicy ecclesiastical pie.

I was new and just wanted to please both men but felt most loyal to Tinks, who had hired me and was giving me the time to investigate Pell.

'I think we should do a feature as well as the main news story,' I suggested to him.

'You better get writing then,' he said, smiling.

I needed to get a comment from Katrina Lee, then the media director at the Archdiocese of Sydney who dealt with all of the cardinal's media matters in Australia. Our email was firm and to the point. We told her that the *Herald Sun* would be running a story the following day that his Eminence had been named in court proceedings as the mystery priest who witnessed Gerald Ridsdale abusing a child. Would he like to make a comment?

Silence. The clock started ticking. The front-page story was being laid out, so we urgently needed the comment.

For whatever reason, I was never directly supplied a response and the story went dead that night. I went home feeling deflated. Maybe the story wasn't published for commercial or legal reasons, but nobody told me why.

Despite this, I decided to keep looking into George Pell. It was time to go back to Ballarat to speak to a person who had something to say about the Vatican's money man.

———

The childhood of Ballarat man PL, as he now wishes to be referred to, made for a chilling interview as we sat in his neat home. As a young boy he was first abused by nuns only to then be abused by four priests, including Ridsdale and Best when he was a pupil at St Alipius. But what was most compelling was his claim, told with absolute certainty, that his pleas for help after having been brutally raped by Best in the school were ignored at the time by Pell.

'I thought I was going to die,' he said of the attack. Beaten up by Best after the sexual assault, he found himself 'on the floor passed out from the pain, Best was just kicking me and saying, "Get up."' The brazen attack happened in the middle of a busy school day in a side room, when anyone could have walked in. It was sudden, violent and opportunistic.

'I tried to tell my parents afterwards,' PL recalled, 'but they didn't listen. My dad said, "Go and talk to your mum" and my mum said, "Go and talk to your dad."'

A couple of months later he bravely walked to the presbytery next door to the church. He was eleven years old. 'I desperately needed someone to talk to, I didn't feel safe at school and I had nowhere to turn.' He hoped the clergy in the house would be sympathetic and take action.

'I walked in the door and I instantly saw George Pell walking towards me, there was no mistaking him,' he remembered. 'I turned and said, "I want to talk to you." I thought he would help me—that's what they were there for, surely—to help me—but I was so wrong.'

Pell was going to be the 'boss man', the victim's father had told him. 'He was a big man and I knew he was going to be the boss one day, the Bishop of Ballarat. But Pell just wouldn't talk to me. He had his arms folded and walked looking down at me. He then beckoned over another priest and I said, "Brother Best rooted me up the arse, sir."

'His response was to ask me if I'd told my parents. I said I'd tried.'

Pell then walked off into another room, said PL, nodding to the other priest. 'Then Ridsdale walked in and said, "Do you want me to deal with him or fix him up?"'

'I was terrified,' PL recalled. 'I'd already been raped twice by Ridsdale before mass when I was an altar boy. He'd grabbed me and forced wine down my throat.'

Ridsdale then pushed PL out of the front door and threatened the young boy not to tell a soul about what happened. 'After that day I didn't see Pell for a few years. I saw him at St Alipius Church with my family in 1973.'

The man would later tell the Victorian parliamentary inquiry into child sexual abuse in 2013 about this event in an anonymous submission through his lawyer Viv Waller. When we spoke, it was the first time he was prepared to be publicly named.

It was a compelling story, but one that would come with challenging complications. As is common with historic abuse, the victim had PTSD and his recollection of the exact dates were vague. Understandably so. The man has never recovered from the abuse. He also suffers from deafness and back problems as a result of being beaten as a child.

He remembered the year of the attack as 1969 but afterwards said it could have been later. When we later ran the story, Pell discredited the man's story by producing his passport indicating that he was still studying at Oxford at the time. He insisted that we print his denial in the paper, which was abided to.

It was frustrating, but it was also a lesson learned. It was evident that any suggestion of wrongdoing by this powerful Vatican figure, who had the resources to fight back with top legal counsel, would be a precarious venture. Pell was a fighter. A tough one.

———

Any of Pell's hopes that the long-running inquiry in his homeland would find the church had somehow been wronged had been dashed for some time. What we would hear during the Ballarat case study would shock Australia. The details would be as dramatic as the shouts of the advocates and protestors gathered outside the courthouse in the centre of the town. In fact, by 10 a.m. on 19 May 2015, the first morning of the case study, Ballarat's forgotten souls would find a voice.

The Hon. Justice Peter McClellan AM, chairman of the royal commission, took his seat at court number 5 and began the proceedings. It had been over 160 years since the Eureka Stockade. While that historical event had been political and financial, this one was clearly personal. This moment was about a town whose golden past had been tarnished by abuse, a moment about truth and justice for all of those who had suffered unimaginable crimes at the hands of the trusted men of the cloth. The Ballarat hearings, Justice McClellan warned the public gallery, media, lawyers and officials, would be confronting.[1]

What would unfold in the following days would certainly not be welcomed by Pell in Rome, because what we would hear would be a pandora's box of allegations regarding his Eminence.

The first allegation was revealed during the opening address of the Ballarat hearing by extraordinary and fearless counsel assisting, Gail Furness, SC, who has been practicing law in Australia for over 30 years and had assisted other major inquiries. 'All the world's a stage,' Shakespeare wrote in *As You Like It*, and Furness had just stepped into what would become a long-running, dramatic Pell production with multiple acts. She was the leading quick-witted character who would skewer witnesses where necessary and captivate her audience.

Furness told the court that Ridsdale was discussed at a consultor's meeting with Bishop Ronald Mulkearns in September 1982. George Pell, she revealed, had been present. Quoting from the minutes of the meeting she said, 'The bishop advised that it had become necessary for Father Gerald Ridsdale to move from the Parish of Mortlake. Negotiations are underway to have him work with the Catholic Enquiry Centre in Sydney. A new appointment to Mortlake will be necessary to take effect after October 17.'

The minutes did not disclose what the bishop said about why it became necessary to move Ridsdale, but Furness explained it was expected there would be evidence that Bishop Mulkearns knew it was because the priest had abused boys in Mortlake and that he had offended in this manner in 1975. 'Several of the consultors had been present at meetings of, or were members of, the College of Consultors on each occasion in the past when Ridsdale had been moved,' she said.

This was ruinous evidence. By moving Ridsdale around he was able to keep abusing, and serious and vicious crimes were enabled, not prevented.

Furness was followed by six men—now all in their fifties— who broke down, one by one, in the witness box as they told of being abused by Christian Brothers teachers and priests, including Ridsdale, at St Patrick's College and St Alipius. It was clear the effect on their lives was ongoing and devastating.

The first to enter the witness box was Philip Nagle, who was abused at St Alipius by Brother Stephen Farrell. He held up an old black-and-white photograph of his 1973 class at the small school: smiling, happy boys in shorts and white shirts, none older than seven or eight. 'There are 33 boys in total in that image . . . I know that twelve are dead, I believe they committed suicide.'

The first shocking, emotional bomb had been dropped and there would be many more to come. Nagle then asked all in the courtroom to stand to mark a minute's silence for 'all my class-mates who are no longer there with us'.

Justice McClellan looked a little startled, but he and the rest of the courtroom stood immediately. It was a hugely moving moment as the survivors of abuse stood and looked ahead with such dignity.

Another victim of abuse, who didn't want to be named, told of the moment a few years before when, in despair, he decided to drive his car into a tree. His suicide bid failed only because his accelerator got stuck at 30 kilometres per hour.

The theme of never-ending depression, marriage break-downs, suicide attempts and difficulties with trust emerged in the evidence of all six men. Some said they couldn't get on with bosses, friends, lovers and even their own children. Others drank heavily. A few could not hold down a job. All were ruined by events of over 40 years before.

———

I had covered many child abuse stories before, including the case of notorious British singer turned paedophile Gary Glitter in England in 1999, while working for the *Daily Mail*. I watched this former pop star being led away by guards following his four month sentence after pleading guilty to 54 charges of making indecent photographs of children under sixteen.

While working in Sydney for magazines *Marie Claire* and *Madison* I'd investigated sports coaches abusing young swimmers and gymnasts in their care and the child abuse problem in remote Indigenous communities. But I had never experienced hearing first-hand testimony as wretched and traumatic as what I heard in Ballarat. Journalists are supposed to keep an emotional distance, not to get too close to the story. In this case it was already too late. This story of systematic abuse heard first hand couldn't be erased or unheard. And I wasn't alone. For one female relative watching the videolink outside the courtroom, the testimonies became too much to bear. She stared ahead, shaking.

I filed my copy for the *Herald Sun* that day back in my motel room. There was a damp foggy mist outside but only an electric blanket on offer in my room. The grimness of my surroundings after listening to a day of traumatic testimony suited the mood of the story at least.

'Maybe as the rest of their victims give evidence over the coming weeks, these once supposedly good men of God might like to be reminded of Matthew 5:5—a verse from the New Testament,' I wrote from under the covers. 'Blessed are the meek: for they shall inherit the Earth.'

It would be a quote that would later seem like a prophesy.

———

Intriguing news had just emerged—that Pell had in fact quietly visited Ballarat just six weeks earlier.[2] Apart from a visit to

St Patrick's College it was unclear where else he had gone in the area, or who he'd seen, in the lead up to the hearings. Considering his profile, it was inexplicable how Pell had flown under the radar—and why. What was clear, however, is that whatever happened during Pell's bizarre secret visit, these hearings could result in a flurry of unwanted scandal regarding the Holy See power player.

The next day, the commission would hear Gerald Ridsdale's nephew make the claim in person that he had told Pell in a phone call in 1993 of being abused by his uncle Gerald over many years from the age of eleven.

David Ridsdale, who had flown in from his home in England, alleged that Cardinal Pell asked him, 'What will it take to keep you quiet?' and then spoke about what he might need to buy for his growing family, such as a car.

David told the commission Pell had known him since he was born and continued to see him throughout his childhood, even when he was director of the Aquinas campus at the Institute of Catholic Education.

'Pell was an avid swimmer and I would see him often at either Eureka Stockade or YMCA pool,' he said. 'I called him George from since I was a kid. I never recall calling him Father. I chose to call him that for one reason, he was the only human being in the church who I believed was still a friend and that I could trust.'

David, who had been involved in a public spat with Pell since he appeared on *60 Minutes* in 2002, recalled that when he told the Cardinal by phone that he had been abused by his uncle, 'His first reaction was "oh, right" . . . there was no shock. His tone then became terse relatively quickly and I could sense anger in his voice. I started to get a sense that he was insinuating things about my story and I felt like I'd done something wrong.'

When he hung up, David called his sisters to tell them what unfolded. 'I remember saying to them both "the bastard just tried to bribe me".'

He also revealed that he'd seen Pell in the late 1990s at a Ballarat forum after the Melbourne Response was introduced. 'I called him a liar there,' David told the commission, 'but I was actually the quiet one compared to some of the other individuals present. I recall one man said that he wanted to kill Pell. I now understand this same man has committed suicide.'

The courtroom was silent.

Another survivor gave testimony that would create damning headlines. Timothy Green told the inquiry Pell was rude and dismissive when in 1974 he reported to him in the changing rooms of the Eureka Swimming Pool that Brother Edward Dowlan was abusing boys at St Patrick's College in Ballarat. Green described Pell as a 'big imposing figure', saying he 'strutted around the college when he was there as if he was superior to everyone else, because of that I just assumed that he was superior'.[3]

Green, who was twelve or thirteen when he spoke to Pell, was himself a victim of Dowlan and said Pell had rejected his claims about the abuse at the college, telling him: 'Don't be ridiculous.'

'Father Pell didn't ask any questions. He didn't say what do you mean or how could you say that? He just dismissed it and walked out. His reaction gave me the impression that he knew about Brother Dowlan but couldn't or wouldn't do anything about it.'

One of the two boys who stood alongside Green as he spoke to Pell later committed suicide by blowing himself up in his car overlooking St Alipius. 'I believe they [both boys] were aware of similar things happening in St Alipius with Brother Best.'

'I don't know why I told Father Pell about Brother Dowlan. I still don't know where I got the courage to say it, because my biggest fear was exposing myself,' Green recalled.

Another abuse victim had some words to say about Australia's man in Rome. In anonymous evidence, he told the commission that Father Gerald Ridsdale had abused him in a bedroom at the presbytery where Cardinal Pell also lived. 'I saw the back of Father Pell but did not know if he saw me and Father Ridsdale or not,' he said.

This witness echoed Margaret's claims of being ignored as she was attacked in the same presbytery in the same era.

One thing was for certain: the damning stories and allegations about Pell's behaviour all those years before were building at a fast pace.

Meanwhile, from his tower in Rome his Eminence fought back, denying the allegations that had been raised. 'Over the last 24 hours, I have been accused of being complicit in the moving of a known paedophile, of ignoring a victim's complaint and of bribery,' he said in a statement tendered to the commission. 'These matters again require an immediate response and it is important to correct the record, particularly given the false and misleading headlines.'

Pell said, however, that he was committed to 'complete co-operation with the royal commission. I will address in full all matters it wishes to raise in any statement requested from me before I make any further comment.

'I have the deepest sympathy for the victims of abuse, their families and the community of Ballarat for what they have suffered. Once again, I will answer allegations and criticisms of my behaviour openly and honestly.'

In the year before the Ballarat case study began, the Pontiff had certainly made efforts to be seen to be taking the clergy-abuse crisis seriously. In March 2014, just a month after Pell's Rome appointment, he established the Pontifical Commission for the Protection of Minors headed by Boston's archbishop, Cardinal Sean P. O'Malley. Then, a few months later, he defrocked paedophile priest Father Jose Mercau of Argentina. Mercau was sentenced to fourteen years in prison in 2011 after admitting to sexually abusing four teenagers. Many welcomed the news, but victims and advocates said the Roman Catholic Church still needed to be more determined, effective and severe when it came to punishing such crimes.

The start of the Ballarat hearing, with the Pope's treasurer front and centre, had been an exhausting few days for everyone involved. A special candlelight service would be held at St Alipius Parish Church to remember those who had suffered clergy abuse in the town, a town clearly shaken by the disturbing scars of its past being exposed in full for the first time.

I'd been profoundly moved by what I'd heard and been left with more questions than answers. When I got home, I went to my children and watched them sleeping. They were just four and six at the time. So tiny. So vulnerable. So trusting.

As I reached out and carefully held their delicate little hands without waking them, silent tears fell down my face. My soul had now been touched, both as a journalist and a mother. How could anyone harm a child?

———

On 27 May 2015, a small single-column story ran quietly in the pages of the *Herald Sun*; it was my exclusive story regarding Margaret. It was headlined: Pell claim 'emerged in court last year'.

I was bemused. It felt somewhat bizarre and a waste of the effort involved—what should have been a front-page story had now been published in a single column on page 2. This was a story about the treasurer for the Vatican, so I couldn't understand why such an explosive report wasn't given far greater prominence.

I texted Tinks. 'That was a very expensive page-two story,' I wrote jokingly, having added up all the hours and days I'd spent on it. Tinks couldn't explain it when I next saw him. Perhaps the paper finally felt pressure to run the story because it knew it was likely to come out very soon at the royal commission. And it did.

The very same day, Ridsdale's unmistakeable, clipped voice was heard by many of his victims for the first time since they were children. It was frailer and weaker than they remembered as he flickered to life on three 52-inch plasma screens in the courtroom. Forty clergy abuse survivors, both male and female, took a sharp intake of breath.[4]

'Yes, I can hear you,' he uttered by videolink from Hopkins Correctional Centre. If anyone present had ever wondered what the devil looked like, here he was in full-colour high definition; Ridsdale has been convicted of more than 140 offences concerning 54 victims.

During his five-hour long testimony, 81-year-old Ridsdale tried to distance himself from the vile behaviour of his younger self. He claimed a total of 56 times that he couldn't remember details of people, places or dates he was asked about.

It wasn't until the following day that Ridsdale was asked about the mystery priest who saw him attacking young Margaret. Could another priest have been present? 'There could have been, yes. There probably would have been,' he replied.

Asked who the priest was, Ridsdale replied: 'I don't know because I have said I don't know who the other priests were at the time, except George Pell.'

He wasn't giving certainty, but his words were illuminating. Ridsdale said other priests visited the home but agreed that it would have been unlikely for them to be in or near his bedroom when he molested children.

Justice McClellan raised the possibility Ridsdale may have been coached in his evidence, asking him repeatedly who had visited him in recent months, even mentioning the date in March when Pell had been reported to have visited the area.

'You appreciate there'll be a record of people who've been to see you in jail, don't you?' Justice McClellan put to Ridsdale, who only revealed that he made regular phone calls to his sisters and that he had been visited by Father John McKinnon, of a western Victorian parish.

With Ridsdale's evidence, Pell faced mounting pressure to reappear at the commission. He had already made two contributions by the time the Ballarat hearings began: first in March 2014, mostly regarding John Ellis, and then a few months later in August 2014 via videolink from the Vatican. But with the new allegations, this wasn't enough; even the premier of Victoria, Daniel Andrews, said he wanted to see Pell voluntarily appear to show he took child abuse seriously. The jungle drums were beating.

Meanwhile, in a suburb in the north of Melbourne, a young man reading the headlines about the Ballarat hearings was probably sleeping even less soundly. He would soon decide to make a move that would eventually shine a fierce light on this whole complicated, muddy business once and for all.

———

The cardinal may always have been thought a considerable intellect, but in many ways he also proved to be the greatest of showmen. Despite the outcry, the controversy and the headlines of the Ballarat hearings, it was business as usual for his Eminence in the following months. If he had any kind of emotional hangover from the allegations raised in his home town he wasn't showing it; instead he continued to ride roughshod over the many dissidents.

Back in Rome he was busy beating his chest and establishing

himself as a formidable force within Vatican City, even publicly criticising Pope Francis' decision to place climate change at the top of the Catholic Church's agenda. He was confidently moving forward, making waves and crossing swords with his own boss. 'The church has got no mandate from the Lord to pronounce on scientific matters,' he said grandly to the *Financial Times* in July 2015. 'We believe in the autonomy of science.'

These were certainly confident, potentially troublemaking words from a man who many expected would not want to go into combat with Francis, considering the publicity nightmare of the preceding few months. But dogmatic ambition ruled as usual, even over any sense that it might be best for an imperious Pell to keep his head below the parapet.

And in Australia, Pell's closest Catholic allies had been fighting his corner, making loud public statements offering their 'unfailing support'. A joint media statement from the senior archbishops of Australia shortly after the Ballarat hearings took place endorsed the comments already made by Denis Hart, who was then the Archbishop of Melbourne and had been one of Pell's peers at the seminary in Werribee. They couldn't be clearer: they were standing by their man in Rome.

'We know Cardinal Pell well from working with him over many years in different capacities,' the archbishops wrote. 'He is a man of integrity who is committed to the truth and to helping others, particularly those who have been hurt or who are struggling.' His style could be 'robust and direct' and 'He does not wear his heart on his sleeve,' they conceded politely. 'But underneath he has a big heart for people.'

Increasingly, however, such supportive statements would not be enough to quell the disquiet and questions regarding Pell's past in his native country. They would, in fact, prove to be an unwelcome smoking gun, dampening his Italian profile-building.

———

Even though I was busy on many other unrelated assignments, I always returned to investigating Pell in my own time, keeping in touch with the sensitive contacts I'd made. After all, there was a major development to prepare for: Pell was due to fly to Melbourne in early December to answer questions at the next hearing of the Ballarat case study of the royal commission. There was already disquiet among abuse survivors that the cardinal had retained expensive barristers for the appearance.[5]

As my notes and materials regarding Pell were so sensitive, I asked the paper if there was a spare office where I could lay out all my documents and work. I was given a key to Andrew Bolt's office. The right-wing News Corp columnist only used it once a week, I was told. He otherwise apparently worked from home.

I didn't think much about it at the time—so I laid out all my Pell articles and documents across the room.

It would turn out to be a temporary shared abode.

Chapter 5
Wake up the cardinal

In late November 2015, Gail Furness swept back into the frame, armed and re-loaded with shattering statistics and even more questions. Stage one of the Royal Commission case study of the Catholic Archdiocese of Melbourne had begun, this time in a courtroom at the County Court of Victoria, and Furness would reveal data the inquiry had collected so far regarding the conduct of Catholic priests. This had never before been made public.

As Furness explained, the commission surveyed all Catholic Church authorities in Australia and found that those clerics accused of sexual assault were overwhelmingly male, with only 8 per cent being female. Most of the complaints against the Melbourne Archdiocese concerned incidents that were alleged to have taken place between 1950 and 1989, with the 1970s producing the highest number of claims. More than 300 of the claims resulted in compensation payments to victims, with the church paying out nearly $17 million including for treatment, legal and other costs, at an average of $52,000 per claimant. It was a damning picture.

The following week the inquiry returned to the Ballarat case study once more. As expected, almost immediately the proceedings focused on Pell. The courtroom was tense and combative due to the decision by Pell's lawyers to recall two witnesses who had given evidence in Ballarat in May. The cardinal himself was not present but had promised to attend to answer questions in the following weeks.

The first was David Ridsdale. One member of Pell's legal team, Sydney-based barrister Sam Duggan, rallied hard against him. The fact that David had suffered terribly from abuse as a child and teenager didn't mean he would be treated with kid gloves by Pell's legal team. It frequently made for an uncomfortable scene.

'I want to suggest to you that George Pell never said, "I want to know what it will take to keep you quiet,"' Duggan said to David. 'Do you accept that?'

'No,' he replied.

'For completeness, I want to suggest that this conversation that you've recorded here never happened,' Duggan said.

'Oh no, utterly—that is as clear to me as the first time my uncle forced me onto his penis,' David said clinically. 'These are things that stick, they changed my life.'

David said he planned to be present when Pell was due to give evidence the following week. 'I'll be in court. It's very emotional and stressful but I'll be there.'[1]

Later, Pell's team pulled out what it thought would be a trump card. In a statement to the commission, a Mentone parish priest, John Thomas Walshe, said Pell spoke to him after the phone call with David Ridsdale.

'I have a recollection of Bishop Pell being very concerned for David and him saying words to the effect that "David is a mess" and he felt terribly for him.' Pell's demeanour was not that of a person who had been in a rude or angry conversation, Walshe said. 'My strong recollection is that Bishop Pell was concerned for David Ridsdale, who had been terribly affected by the abuse.'

But this controversial testimony led a former student priest, John Roach, to publicly reveal that Father Walshe himself had been found by church authorities to have committed an act of sexual abuse in 1982. In 2012, the Melbourne Archdiocese's Independent Commissioner accepted Father Walshe had sexually abused Roach, then an eighteen-year-old seminarian, and paid him $75,000 in compensation, the maximum available under the Melbourne Response scheme. Roach claimed he was assaulted while drunk and unconscious.

Father Walshe strenuously denied committing any abuse, characterising the incident as 'completely consensual'. Despite the adverse finding and payout, Archbishop Denis Hart and senior archdiocese officials had allowed Father Walshe to remain parish priest of Mentone–Parkdale East. Later, local parents and parishioners would become so outraged by the scandal that within months Walshe left Victoria and moved to Ireland.[2]

Timothy Green was also strongly challenged over his assertions that Pell had been dismissive when he reported that Brother Dowlan was abusing boys at St Patrick's College in the 1970s. He stuck firmly to his story.

A former Ballarat altar boy also gave evidence that in the 1980s, he overheard Father Pell telling a colleague that he thought Gerald Ridsdale was abusing boys again. The witness—only referred to as BWE because he didn't want to be identified—told the commission that when he was an altar boy at St Patrick's Cathedral in Ballarat in 1983 he overheard Pell tell another priest, Father Frank Madden: 'I think Gerry [Ridsdale] has been rooting boys again.' 'This remark shocked me to the core,' BWE said. 'It rattled me because of everything I had learned from my brothers about Gerry Ridsdale.'

The quote would be repeated in newspaper headlines for some time.

Duggan fiercely cross-examined BWE, suggesting events were 'a little hazy' after 30 years.

'No they are not,' the witness replied firmly.

Duggan, who said evidence from Pell's schedule at the time showed he was elsewhere when the alleged remark was made, suggested the whole incident was 'pure fantasy', asking, 'What do you say about that?'

'I would say you were incorrect, Mr Duggan,' BWE replied.

As much as Pell's lawyers were fighting in his corner, could he survive this? Could it all be lies and mistruths or the result of false memories? Would anyone really wish to make up false claims and put themselves through such intense scrutiny? Did everyone with a bad word against Pell have a supposed grudge against the Catholic Church?

There were so many questions building around Pell.

―――――

Back in the office a few days later, editor Damon Johnston suddenly rushed across the newsroom into Bolt's office, where I was putting the finishing touches to a feature about Pell's return to Melbourne to give evidence.

'When are you going to give Bolt his office back?' he asked jokingly, briefly glancing at all the Pell paperwork across the desk.

'It wasn't my choice of rooms,' I replied, smiling.

Johnston had just attended a lunch and had been cryptically tipped off that it was likely that Pell would make the front page the next day. 'But he wouldn't say why.'

I quickly put in some calls and found out that Pell wasn't coming back to Australia to give evidence after all. His lead barrister, Allan Myers, QC, had informed the commission that a cardiologist had advised that it was not safe for the cardinal to undertake a long haul flight due to his heart condition. The barrister then applied for his client to give his testimony via videolink instead.

Justice McClellan denied the request. Cardinal Pell would be called to give evidence before the inquiry in Ballarat.

'It is preferable that his evidence be given in person in Australia,' Justice McClellan said. 'The commission had already determined to sit in Ballarat to take further evidence in relation to the Ballarat matter, that having been listed for February of next year.

'In the hope that the cardinal's health will improve, rather than take video evidence this week we will defer his evidence to the Ballarat sitting.' If the cardinal's health had not sufficiently improved by then the commission would consider the position, which may include further delaying Pell's evidence to a date when he could travel safely to Australia.

Justice McClellan's comments were met with applause, but many, including David Ridsdale, were furious that Pell would not be giving evidence. 'It's fairly simple, he needs to come and answer some questions. It's not that difficult,' David told the ABC.[3]

'If I can make the flight and I was only premium economy, not first class like he was . . . I would implore Cardinal Pell to come and face the music like all of us men have had to do for all these years.

'I'm not disappointed, I'm furious. But having him come to Ballarat may not be the result he was expecting, so I'm pleased the commission responded as they did.'

A copy of Pell's travel itinerary was produced to the commission and made available to the media, perhaps as proof that he had indeed planned to come to Australia. It showed he was booked to depart Rome at 1440 hours on 12 December 2015 and that a private car had been arranged to pick him up at Melbourne Airport. He was then due to fly back to Rome on Monday 21 January.

Chrissie Foster's husband Anthony, who later tragically died suddenly aged 64 in 2017, said Cardinal Pell's absence did not come as a complete surprise. 'We're shocked, disappointed, [but] in a strange way, not surprised,' he told the ABC. 'This is a very, very late call for a supposedly serious ailment. I find that unlikely.'

What no one knew at the time, even within the commission, was that there was possibly a very strong reason Pell had decided to cancel his trip at the last minute. And it had nothing to do with his health.

A series of police raids had in fact been secretly carried out just nine days before by detectives from Sano Task Force, which had been formed alongside the royal commission to investigate new and historic allegations of sexual abuse at religious and other non-government organisations. Those raids included the two Lonsdale Street offices of barristers Peter O'Callaghan and Jeffery Gleeson. Both lawyers carried out work as independent commissioners for the Melbourne Response, with their invoices paid by solicitors for the Archdiocese of Melbourne.

As part of what was dubbed 'Operation Tethering', the task force detectives were there to investigate allegations regarding the cardinal and made it quite clear they were seeking certain documents in relation to him. 'There would have been no doubt whatsoever for the barristers and their staff that the raid was primarily about investigating Pell,' one inside source explained. 'The idea that the news of the Sano investigation and raids wouldn't reach the ears of either Pell's close friend, Archbishop of Melbourne Denis Hart, or directly to Pell himself at the Vatican is ludicrous. Word travels fast in Melbourne at the best of times, let alone when police raid two barristers' offices who do legal work for the Catholic Church.'

Peter O'Callaghan, who has since retired, was appointed as an independent commissioner personally by Pell in 1996 when the Melbourne Response was first founded. Jeffery Gleeson, who was the counsel assisting during the Southwell Inquiry in 2002 when Pell faced allegations of abusing an altar boy in 1961, had been working as an independent commissioner since 2012.

'A lawyer or their clerks wouldn't really be doing their job properly if they didn't inform those who they do work for, in whatever capacity, that the police had just raided their offices and taken away private documents about the most senior Catholic in Australia,' the source said.

———

Just before Christmas 2015, it was announced by Sano Task Force that search warrants had been executed on buildings linked to the church in East Melbourne, Melbourne, Maidstone and Toorak. These were the same raids that involved Peter O'Callaghan and Jeffery Gleeson's offices.

While the task force didn't offer any precise details about the raids, it did say it wanted to speak to anyone who was a victim of sexual assault at St Patrick's Cathedral in East Melbourne between 1996 and 2001. This was the exact period when Cardinal Pell was archbishop of Melbourne.

'Victoria Police encourages all victims of sexual assault and child abuse, and anyone who has knowledge of such a crime, to make a report,' Sergeant Sharon Darcy said in a statement. 'Victoria Police is committed to investigating and bringing to justice those people who prey on children no matter how many years have passed.'

I was off that day and in the city with my children. The paper wanted me to find out what I could, but when I spoke to my contacts most were nervous. I could tell they were keen to help but reluctant to put themselves at risk.

Pacing around Federation Square, I asked directly if Pell was at the centre of a police investigation regarding allegations of abuse of children at the cathedral. 'I can't say what's happening, but don't give up,' one judicial source said before my battery went flat. 'Just keep going.'

I would and I did.

It was also confirmed at this time that Pell would be giving evidence to the royal commission via videolink from Rome at the end of February due to his many complicated health issues including hypertension, ischaemic heart disease and cardiac dysfunction.

I began trying to contact those who were involved with the cathedral at the time the police specified but was soon being pulled in all directions by pressured editors who wanted me to work on other assignments. I was sent to Tasmania for the miracle story of an unborn baby who'd survived a car crash in which his mother had died, written about hoax phone calls to Australian schools and flown to the Hunter Valley in NSW to write a feature on the retired racehorse Black Caviar and her foals. There'd also been stories about the Essendon Football Club drug scandal. It all meant my hopes of focusing on Pell were decreasing. But then came Tim Minchin's 'Come Home (Cardinal Pell)'.

This protest song calling for Pell to return to Australia to answer questions at the royal commission supported a Go Fund Me campaign to pay for fifteen Ballarat survivors to attend

Pell's testimony in Rome in person. The lyrics were like getting an electric shock.

As music expert Liam Viney, associate professor at the School of Music in Queensland, wrote in *The Conversation* at the time, the song was a 'prime example of the power music has to project a political message into the public sphere'.

'There are probably thousands of ear worm-afflicted people all over the country today, each infected by the latest Minchin chorus,' he said.

He was right. I was one of them. There was something particularly courageous about the lyrics. I was fired up and knew I had to return to my Pell investigation.

I told my editors I had a new lead on Pell I needed to follow up. I had an important task lined up for the next morning: tea with a vicar.

———

I'd been left a message at the paper that a priest, who I will not name, had some 'information about George Pell'. I tracked him down to his church in a south-eastern suburb of Melbourne, where we talked at length about his time as a young priest not far from where Pell was working in the Ballarat area.

'There has been talk amongst those of us who knew Pell in those days about whether he could be being bribed because he doesn't want harmful gossip on him to come out, especially regarding his friendship with Ridsdale,' he said.

'That he's being threatened in some way to not reveal information on others?' I asked.

'Possibly,' he replied. 'A sort of "you don't tell and we won't tell" scenario.'

While the priest's story was intriguing, it was based on speculation and nearly impossible to prove. But as I drove away I decided that maybe, just maybe, this snippet of gossip could be used as a bargaining chip of sorts, something to offer one of my many 'deep throat' contacts in return for information on what was happening in terms of the investigation at the cathedral and whether Pell was the central focus.

I had nothing to lose. Or so I thought. On the way back to the office I started making the calls.

I saw Tinks and told him what was happening. 'See what happens then,' he said. 'Sounds interesting.'

Soon after, my phone rang. It was one of the many contacts I'd worked hard to keep onside for nearly ten months. Sometimes he would be forthcoming; at other times he would get spooked and wouldn't return my calls.

I told him what I had found out from the priest. Within a few minutes he was telling me that he'd heard the Sano Task Force appeal for information had everything to do with Pell. Everything. He understood that twenty full-time detectives had been investigating Pell and allegations that he abused children for the previous year. A whole year.

I could hardly believe what I was hearing from this tip off: Victoria Police had invested possibly millions in resources and staff to investigate the treasurer of the Vatican for twelve months. And nobody knew. It hadn't leaked. I was the first journalist in the world to find out.

This was at once both extraordinary and shocking. Had Pell inflicted the same pain and damage I'd witnessed in Ballarat on his alleged victims, the sort of pain I'd seen etched on Margaret's face? The full scale of what I'd uncovered was hard to comprehend.

My contact had learned about the investigation some time ago, but he needed to know that he could trust me; that I was committed to the story and wouldn't betray him or his position. I assured him that I would protect him no matter what and so would my paper.

I needed to confirm this information with other sources, of course, but I knew straight away this story was going to be the equivalent of setting off a nuclear bomb. This made all those royal commission accusations about Pell—that he had ignored, covered up and dismissed allegations of abuse—almost lightweight in comparison. This wasn't just potentially career destroying; this was prison worthy.

His Eminence was apparently under investigation, the source said, for abusing choirboys at St Patrick's Cathedral, and other boys at a Ballarat swimming pool in the 1970s. And what's more, he had heard that senior detectives at Sano Task Force were concerned; their dossier of evidence now seemed to be languishing with the Victoria Police bosses.

'They think there is enough to charge and arrest Pell, but they are worried it's come to a halt for some reason,' he said.

'Do they think there is enough for Pell to face trial?' I asked.

'Yes,' he said. 'And they are apparently frustrated because nothing seems to be moving.'

I tried to find Tinks but couldn't see him. This was so sensitive and important that I walked straight into the editor's office and asked to speak to him directly. I was worried the story would spread across the newsroom if I told anyone on the news desk. I needed to go to the top. It is very unusual for reporters to go straight to the editor with a story. It was the first time I had done so since I started on the paper.

'Can we please have a meeting later with Tinks?' I asked Johnston.

'Sure,' he replied.

'It's about Pell.'

Johnston froze and looked up. 'Okay, great,' he said, clearly guessing there had been an important development.

By the time we all met in Johnston's office a short time later I had given Tinks a quick rundown. Katie Bice, one of the news editors, had also been asked to join us. As I briefed them in detail, I sensed their tension; we all realised how significant this story was.

Johnston, clearly stunned by what I'd uncovered, was veering on the side of caution. 'If this is wrong, I could go to jail,' he said. 'We need to stand it up as much as possible. Can I meet these contacts?'

My sources were nervous and feared any potential ramifications. After all, it had taken them ten months to fully trust me let alone someone new, even if it was the editor of the newspaper.

After speaking in more depth to other judicial and legal sources who backed up the details about the Sano Task Force investigation, Johnston was happy to proceed. All being well with the paper's lawyers, the story would be Saturday's front-page splash and would go live on the digital platforms around 11 p.m. on Friday night. That gave me just 24 hours to write the story, and get it checked by lawyers and the editors.

I stayed late to write the main story. Back at home I kept waking up and tinkering with my copy. I had to be absolutely right and fair. After all, we were going to publish a front-page story basically alleging that George Pell was a paedophile who abused children in his own cathedral when he was Archbishop of Melbourne. We weren't suggesting he was guilty, but that the allegations were serious enough for a task force to devote substantial resources to the investigation.

After a sleepless night, I went back to work wearing a black suit. 'It's good you're wearing that if we have to go to court,' Tinks remarked.

'Court?' I asked.

'Yes, if Pell gets a last-minute injunction we'll have to.'

'Let's hope it doesn't come to that,' I laughed. We had a head start, but once the story was made public other journalists would be straight onto it. I would have liked longer to be able to track down the alleged victims.

But the machine—and its editors—were hungry for the story. It was going in Saturday's paper no matter what. After the lawyers gave the green light, the editors decided they wanted a feature to go with the news story. I didn't eat or drink all day. It felt like I barely had time to breathe.

At 4 p.m. I had to make the most important phone call of my career. Sitting at my desk I spoke to Katrina Lee, media director of the Archdiocese of Sydney. She didn't like me much.[4] For nearly a year I'd been asking difficult questions about the cardinal. 'We call you Lucie in the sky with diamonds,' she had once said jokingly.

I was following up an earlier email I'd sent Lee, asking her for an urgent comment on the pending exclusive front-page report. I could see Tinks and Johnston pacing the newsroom. It was clear they were thrilled, jittery and tense in equal measure. The front-page headline screamed: 'Police Probe Pell'.

I knew we had to get a response from him.

'It's the middle of the night, he'll be asleep,' Lee complained.

This was a serious matter and I cared little about what time it was in Rome.

'You better wake up the cardinal,' I told her.

———

I knew Pell would want a right of reply. And he did, rising from his bed to strongly and angrily deny the allegations.

He issued a furious statement just as the first edition was about to be sent to print. 'The timing of these leaks is clearly designed to do maximum damage to the cardinal and the Catholic Church and undermines the work of the royal commission,' it read. Describing the allegations as 'utterly false' and without foundation, the statement went on to call for a public inquiry into the 'leaking of these spurious claims'. The statement alleged the story was a result of 'various elements of Victoria Police'.

'Given the serious nature of this conduct, the cardinal has called for a public inquiry to be conducted in relation to the actions of those elements of the Victoria Police who are undermining the royal commission's work.

'The cardinal calls on the Premier and the Police Minister to immediately investigate the leaking of these baseless allegations.'

Pell wasn't just denying the allegations in the story, he wanted to shoot the messengers too. I knew he would be prepared to go into combat. But this was a fight club on a whole new level.

The story hadn't been timed to coincide with his forthcoming royal commission appearance at all; it was sheer happenstance that I had stood up the facts of the story when I did. I thought about Pell's alleged victims, who would be reading my story at home or in Melbourne cafes the next day. Grown men who could be facing a legal process that could take years. They were very noble and brave. This wasn't going to be easy. I also imagined Margaret reading the story at her home in Gippsland, wondering what she would think about the development.

Despite Pell's protestations from Italy, the story was breaking across his homeland; all four News Corp tabloids were using my story on their front page. And now it was breaking on Twitter.

'This is going off like a box of frogs,' texted journalist Samantha Maiden, who was then News Corp's national political editor. Other peers were equally as excited.

'This is the biggest story for the *Herald Sun* in ten years,' said a smiling 'Tatts', Paul Tatnell, the chief of staff, inviting me for a drink at a nearby bar.

'Are you serious, the biggest story in all that time?' I said.

'Yes, this is epic. I want you on the road reporting for the next 20 years,' he said.

Then Tinks called me. 'Where are you?' he asked

I was so overwhelmed by the unfolding speed of the story I wasn't even sure. I had to look at a sign above the bar to check.

Taking a seat next to me at the bar, Tinks looked elated.

'Well done, amazing job,' he said.

I'd been on a one-year contract until that point, waiting for a permanent job to come up. As it had been presented, it was just a matter of sorting out the paperwork. I'd been told multiple times that my position and long-term future on the paper were guaranteed.

As I sat drinking a gin and tonic with Tinks and Tatts, with my scoop being printed on the front page of newspapers across the country, I felt as if I had climbed close to the top of the *Herald Sun* ladder. It would turn out, however, that I'd just stepped on a very slippery snake.

———

I soon discovered there was a very risky—and somewhat dangerous—downside to setting off a media-and-religious earthquake. The front page the editors were so thrilled with wouldn't just be the biggest I'd ever produced for the *Herald Sun*, it would also be my last.

The next few days unfolded like a slow-moving car crash.

On Saturday I sensed that there had been a seismic shift within the paper away from the Pell scoop. Had someone higher up at News Corp shown a dislike to the story and demanded a change of tack?

I didn't know, but I felt the *Sunday Herald Sun* was distancing itself from my story when it published an article about senior church figures backing Pell. My follow-up story about a call for detectives to fly to Rome to question Pell had been given little prominence in comparison.

My suspicion that News Corp was doing a U-turn seemed to be confirmed by Monday morning, when Andrew Bolt described my scoop as a 'witch hunt' and a 'smear' in his weekly column syndicated across News Corp's main Australian tabloids.

I knew Bolt was a long-time supporter of Pell and that he'd built a whole career and brand out of his controversial statements, some of which had landed him in court. But what I read shocked me to the core; he said my report was worse than 'vicious and shameful' and the leak to the paper 'stinks'.

'It smells like an attempt to destroy a man without giving him a chance to defend himself,' Bolt said. 'Now the campaign to destroy Pell has become sinister as well, after it was joined by—in my view—elements of Victoria Police.' Bolt was even using some of the same phrasing as Pell's thundering statement.

I quickly wrote a couple of tweets defending my story, but Tinks sent me a text saying Johnston had instructed me to 'stop the Bolt tweets'. Bolt had a free hand to slam the work of his colleagues, but we were not allowed to express our views on his narrative.

It wasn't that Bolt was just expressing an opinion—he was entitled to that—it was that there were some lines in the column that greatly concerned me. He said the allegations of abuse weren't in the behaviour of the 'moral man' he knew, hinting that they were either friends or acquaintances, making me wonder if he was misusing his platform to defend the cardinal. He also speculated about my confidential sources, leaving me utterly perplexed. It was like the paper had borderline personality disorder.

Why would my newspaper throw me under the bus like this and allow Bolt to speculate on sources Johnston had vehemently promised me we would protect? It felt very odd. I had spent ten months trying to get inside what was happening around this powerful Catholic and now News Corp seemed to be turning on me. It may well have all been innocent enough, and not part of a new widespread campaign to 'save Pell', but it was totally confusing. Media commentators and bloggers even began commenting on the situation.

'A *Herald Sun* report claiming Cardinal George Pell is being investigated by police over child abuse allegations has sparked angry words between the paper's top columnist Andrew Bolt and the reporter behind the exclusive story,' journalist Amanda Meade wrote in *The Guardian*.[5]

When I'd raised my concerns about the coverage in the Sunday paper with Houlihan in a text message, he replied, 'Divine intervention?' I took it to mean he too was questioning whether Pell was wielding some kind of influence within News Corp. If the *Herald Sun*'s chief of staff, a former lawyer, suspected as much it certainly made me question what was happening behind the scenes. Houlihan's comment may not have been meant to be serious, but it certainly fuelled my curiosity. After all, he had a deeper knowledge than me about the inner workings of the paper and the company.

I was at home with my children when the situation worsened. *The Age* was reporting on its website that Victoria Police had referred my story to Victoria's anti-corruption agency, the Independent Broad-based Anti-Corruption Commission (IBAC). 'Victoria Police is concerned about media reporting alleging that police have leaked details of a sensitive Sano Task Force investigation,' a spokesman was quoted as saying.

As far as I was concerned, Bolt was the one speculating the loudest. His accusations that the story was a leak from police was published in my own paper and also repeated in his blog and syndicated column across the country. That column, in my view, had now brought trouble to my door. It was an utter debacle.

Pell had also written from Rome to the acting minster for police, Robin Scott, demanding an inquiry into the 'maliciously timed leak'.

The situation would have been farcical if it hadn't been so serious. According to the IBAC website its officers could raid my home for materials such as notebooks and tape recordings and I could be questioned and asked about my sources. If I didn't name my sources there was a chance I could be jailed for contempt.

We had been told in security training that our own safety and well-being was the priority. Becoming increasingly exhausted, I was worried about the possibility of a raid and thought it was reasonable that News Corp send a guard to my home each night. The editors weren't keen at first—I had to explain to Johnston that I just wanted to sleep soundly, knowing that I would have support from News Corp—but they did eventually agree.

As far as Pell's request for a state government inquiry went, Victorian treasurer Tim Pallas at least decided that it could detract from the other abuse investigations. 'It's a bit like a dog chasing its tail,' he told reporters. 'It's important that the substance of the issues are determined and the matters are properly before the royal commission and Victoria Police investigations.'

The next day I was asked to meet with Johnston, Tinks and two *Herald Sun* lawyers about the possible ramifications of the IBAC inquiry. I told them that I desperately needed a rest and that I didn't think I was in a good state to discuss the situation, but they insisted. I jokingly suggested Bolt should also attend the meeting, which unfortunately was taken seriously by the editor's secretary.

Before the meeting began, the columnist drifted into the room, asking 'Is this where the IBAC meeting is?' I was so angry I just put my hand out towards him and said 'no', which was probably a first from anyone—let alone a woman—in his time at News Corp.

I then picked up my handbag and left the room, with lawyer Justin Quill racing after me down the corridor urging me not to leave. When Johnston arrived a few moments later, he had the job of ejecting a rather baffled and confused Bolt from the room.

After the tense meeting, in an increasingly worried state, I put my concerns about the situation in emails to Human Resources at News Corp HQ in Sydney, stating that, in my view, Bolt had possibly broken several News Corp codes of conduct. I also pressed for answers about whether anyone in senior management was actively supporting the cardinal. In short, I wanted News Corp to investigate whether anyone was compromised. It was a 'fight or flight' stress response. By this time I had barely slept for five days.

But much later I had no regrets. I've always believed that journalists have to ask difficult questions when needed, in this case even if it meant questioning my own company. If I didn't stand up for the alleged victims and the public who would? This was about child abuse. My powerful company had to be held to account, too, in the same way it insisted governments, institutions and public figures be rigorously examined.

My bold stance came at a cost, however. Already depleted from producing the story, I struggled to sleep and started to further imagine the cars driving past my house had been sent by the Catholic Church or News Corp to assassinate me or that IBAC had come to raid the house. The only other time I had felt like this was as a young reporter for the *Daily Mail* in 2002, when I reached a point of utter delirious exhaustion covering a horrific double-murder of two small girls.

It's only now that the effects on journalists of reporting on traumatic stories—mixed with extreme pressure and lack of sleep—are beginning to be fully recognised. Journalists, like judges, magistrates, police officers and paramedics, are not bullet proof. We are human, with our own frailties. Maintaining self-care while under pressure is important. Secondary, or vicarious, trauma is a constant risk. For reporters, this is often only learnt the hard way.

According to Dr Cait McMahon, the managing director of the Melbourne-based Dart Centre Asia Pacific, a project of the Columbia Journalism School in New York, 'Research shows that between 4%–16% of domestic reporters have probable post-traumatic stress disorder.' A lack of management support and organisational treatment can compound trauma effects, she says.

What couldn't be denied is that in the days after I'd asked for the cardinal to be woken from his bed in Rome, I'd been attacked by Pell and Bolt and an IBAC probe had been launched.

As Melissa Davey, the Melbourne bureau chief of *The Guardian*, later explained to the *Columbia Journalism Review*, she believed I was being 'heavily scrutinised' in the wake of the story.[6] 'Pell has very, very high-profile supporters in the media, and just as quickly as the story broke, there were articles coming out to discredit it,' she told the publication.

The scrutiny that week certainly didn't get any easier; I was juggling two young children at home and now I was at war with my own company. To make matters worse, News Corp then emailed to say the guards were unnecessary and would be cancelled, even though it had no knowledge of whether IBAC planned a raid. I felt terribly alone.

It's not surprising that within days I began falling into a dark and frightening abyss. I needed the cyclone to stop so I could take a breath, but I was in the eye of the storm. The Saturday following my scoop, Gerard Henderson, the executive director of the Sydney Institute, wrote damningly on my story and, like Bolt, also speculated on my sources in his weekly column for *The Australian*,[7] which, like the *Herald Sun*, is owned by News Corp. Had long-time Pell admirer Rupert Murdoch, who had been awarded a papal knighthood by Pope John Paul II in 1998,[8] decided to help out Australia's most senior Catholic with a quick call to his leading commentators Down Under? I had no proof at all that the chairman was involved, but it was little wonder my bewildered, sleepless brain was starting to liquefy as I tried to make sense of the turmoil. Henderson went on to defame me, writing, 'It is unprofessional that the journalist did not mention that the royal commission is also investigating the manner in which Victoria Police handled instances of clerical child abuse in the 1950s, 60s, 70s, 80s and 90s.' Henderson was wrong in my view. This point about the police had actually been raised in Pell's statement included within my story.

But either way, I was left reeling. The company I worked for was allowing long-time Pell supporters to attack me, even in the days after an IBAC probe had been launched. They had the right to freedom of speech, of course, but who were they actually representing? Pell, their own notoriety or the public? Whichever it was, Henderson's attack was the last straw.

As Hotel Quirinale, located in the heart of Rome, was being prepared for Pell's live videolink appearance before the royal commission, at home in Melbourne the complex ramifications of my scoop were finally pushing me over the edge. I had given my heart and soul in my search for the truth; I'd listened to the most horrific stories in Ballarat to try to help and understand those haunted victims without a voice; I'd worked with sensitive sources to uncover the news of the secret Pell police operation; and now I was lost at sea and had nothing firm to hold on to amid the mayhem. I was now paying a very personal price for my passionate defence of the story; I no longer knew who to trust at News Corp and I was mentally and physically exhausted. A sleeping tablet hadn't helped.

An ambulance was called.

Chapter 6
Courting controversy

While I took time off work to regroup and recover from the mind-bending pandemonium, still unsure what moves IBAC could make and feeling protective of my family, a group of Ballarat survivors, some of whom had never been out of Australia, were landing in Rome ahead of Pell's videolink testimony to the royal commission.

David Ridsdale led the group out of the arrivals area of Rome's Fiumicino Airport on Saturday 27 February 2016, telling reporters they had travelled to Italy to make sure the process was as 'transparent and open' as it had been in Australia. 'It's extraordinary. I think everyone would agree that it's a pretty amazing thing that we're here,' he told the ABC.

The mood of the group was one of 'excited anticipation'. 'It's not going to be a holiday, although we're going to make sure we get some good times as well,' he said. 'One thing we've learned as a group together is that you have to laugh sometimes.'

One of the survivors, Peter Blenkiron, left the airport wearing a T-shirt printed with a picture of himself as a child. Blenkiron had been sexually abused by a Christian Brother when he was an eleven-year-old student at St Patrick's College in Ballarat.

The weekend before the group's arrival in Rome, photographs had appeared online of Pell tying a yellow ribbon to the Lourdes Grotto in the Vatican Gardens in solidarity with the 'Loud Fence' movement, a grass-roots movement aimed at acknowledging the lasting effects of abuse. In a statement, the cardinal's office confirmed the gesture was a show of support for the people of Ballarat. He was certainly doing the groundwork as he prepared for residents of his hometown to come directly to his door.

A day later, on Sunday 28 February 2016, Pell arrived at Hotel Quirinale three hours before the hearing, which was due to begin at around midnight (8 a.m. the next day Australian Eastern Standard Time). The hearing was held at this time so that the commissioners and lawyers in Sydney could sit during the day. Pell had been called to give evidence on two case studies—number 28 about the Diocese of Ballarat and number 35 about the Archdiocese of Melbourne.

There was no doubt it was going to be gruelling; the time frame for the case studies stretched from the 1960s through to the 1990s. It was clear Pell was preparing for a tough questioning over the next few days. Indeed, his sister Margaret, a retired violinist, told reporters he had spent the previous day resting and praying. He would certainly need every ounce of energy and strength he could muster with around 160 people expected to witness his appearance in the Verdi room, a large conference room in the hotel.

Outside, locals, wrapped up tightly against the winter weather in coats and scarves, wondered what was unfolding so late at night in their city as Carabinieri gathered to ensure the proceedings ran peacefully. Inside, survivors were let into the room, along with their Ballarat support group counsellors, to choose their seats.

Philip Nagle sat in Pell's seat and posed for a photograph. 'I wanted to see what his viewpoint would be,' he said later.[1] 'He had a big TV screen in front of him so he would see the commission in Sydney, but he could still see us if we sat at the front.'

Pell walked in looking focused and serious, wearing a black suit and his usual clerical collar. He was directed to his seat and took an oath on the Bible. His tall, suited bodyguards were close by.

He first answered general questions from Gail Furness about his position in the Vatican but was incredibly nervous. 'It was just by his body language, he was fidgeting a lot and you could see he was very uncomfortable,' Nagle remembered.

What may have made the cardinal uneasy, apart from the fact that he was under a serious police investigation, was that it was clear from the beginning that Furness wasn't going to go gently on him due to his ill health, or that she would operate in nothing less than her usual forensic manner. They were soon in combat.

Within the first few minutes, Pell tried to water down the suggestion by Furness that child abuse had been an issue in the church for centuries. 'I'm aware that this has been a problem right across society and unfortunately also in the church for centuries, as you said,' he replied.

Furness pressed on, reminding the cardinal there had been many inquiries around the world in relation to child sexual abuse and the Catholic Church. 'There appears to be a consistency in their findings in respect of the response of the Catholic Church to allegations,' she said. 'And that consistency seems to be in relation to those in more senior positions not taking the action that a reasonable person thought should be taken in respect of those allegations. Now, are you familiar with that?'

'Let me just say this as an initial clarification, and that is, I'm not here to defend the indefensible,' Pell responded. 'The church has made enormous mistakes and is working to remedy those, but the church in many places, certainly in Australia, has mucked things up, has made—let people down. I'm not here to defend the indefensible.'

It was a welcome admission but the use of the words 'mucked up' would be the first controversy of many in his testimony. Advocates felt that his vernacular was too casual, considering the grave and devastating subject at hand.

Survivor Paul Levey told *The Guardian* afterwards, 'It was disgusting the way he said the church "mucked up", like he was talking about naughty little kids at school.'

Every word mattered to those watching in Rome, traumatised as they were by their past experiences. At age 14, Levey was sent to live with Gerard Ridsdale at the Mortlake presbytery. His Catholic parents put their trust in the priest to care for their son after the breakdown of their marriage. But what unfolded for Mr Levey was eight months trapped in a living hell, in which he was subjected to daily sexual abuse by Ridsdale.

Furness was keen to know the cardinal's thoughts on why the Catholic Church had operated in a similar way all over the world, in terms of its tactic of covering up abuse and moving offenders to different parishes.

'Unfortunately, original sin is alive and well; the tendency to evil in the Catholic Church too, and sometimes it's better, sometimes it's worse, but for good or for ill the church follows the patterns of the societies in which it lives,' Pell replied.

He refused to concede that it was the structures themselves that were the cause of abuse, saying, 'There are many levels of structures, and we'd have to be specific. I don't think it calls into question the divine structure of the church, which goes back to the New Testament, the role of the Pope and bishops. I think the faults overwhelmingly have been more personal faults, personal failures, rather than structures.'

Regarding his time working in Ballarat, Pell agreed that he had been critical in the past of Bishop Mulkearns destroying documents ahead of the Victorian Parliamentary Commission. He also attacked Mulkearns for the way he handled Ridsdale, calling it a 'catastrophe'. It was a 'catastrophe for the victims and a catastrophe for the church', he said. 'If effective action had been taken earlier, an enormous amount of suffering would have been avoided.'

Furness then firmly questioned Pell on whether he himself was aware of Ridsdale's offending when he was working in the

Ballarat diocese and when he served on the consultor's committee led by Mulkearns. 'I did not know at the time,' he replied clearly.

There would be other strong denials and revealing admissions during this first session. Pell admitted that in the early 1970s, when he first heard allegations of priests sexually abusing children, he was 'strongly inclined' to believe the priests' versions of events.

The questioning then moved on during the first session to the haunting case of prolific paedophile priest Monsignor John Day. In 1971, John Howden, deputy headmaster at St Joseph's College, Mildura, informed a local detective, Denis Ryan, that a twelve-year-old female student had been fondled by Monsignor Day. Desperately alarmed, Ryan would soon risk his career as he started doggedly investigating Day. In the end, fifteen victims testified to police that the monsignor had driven them to Melbourne, where he abused them in various locations including in his car, hotels and even his sister's house.

Ryan's courageous investigation was opposed by the head of his unit, Detective Sergeant James Barritt, who was a friend of Monsignor Day. Barritt, who died in 1997, ordered Ryan to drop the investigation. Ryan and Howden were also ostracised by fellow parishioners for speaking out against Monsignor Day.

In 1972 Ryan was ordered to move to Melbourne, but as he needed to stay in Mildura for his family he was effectively forced to resign from the police force, giving up his superannuation entitlements and his career.[2] He later wrote a book, titled *Unholy Trinity*, about his experience and in 2018 was awarded compensation of an undisclosed sum.

Monsignor Day was never prosecuted and was instead rewarded with an appointment by Bishop Mulkearns to the rural parish of Timboon, near Warrnambool in Victoria, where he remained until he died in 1978.

During his testimony, Pell agreed that in 1972, while at Swan Hill, he became aware from newspaper reports of allegations that Day had been sexually abusing children. He was also aware, however, that Day had denied the allegations and that he had some very passionate supporters. 'One such view that was quite influential with myself was a wonderful woman in Mildura who I knew insisted that he was innocent, and I remember being impressed by that,' he said to murmurs of irritation among the crowd.

Pell was also interrogated on that first day over his knowledge of offending by Christian Brothers at St Alipius Primary School and St Patrick's College in Ballarat. Shockingly, the boys who were abused by brothers Fitzgerald and Dowlan were referred to by other students as their 'bum buddies', the commission was told. Pell had never heard that term, he said, but he was made aware Fitzgerald had swum naked with male students. 'I had heard, at the break-up at the end of the year, they did swim naked.' The incident was an 'imprudent' act but 'no improprieties were ever alleged to me'.

There was a surprise observer of the proceedings. Sitting in the Verdi room and taking notes was my colleague Andrew Bolt. He was there as a contributor for Sky News and to conduct an 'exclusive interview' with the cardinal later in the week, it was announced.

Yet, in the previous days and weeks, there had been no mention that he would be covering Pell's royal commission testimony in Europe. He was also an unusual pick considering his supportive stance of the cardinal and the fact that he was rarely sent to cover stories in the field. It was certainly interesting timing, considering the questions I'd raised with HR about Bolt's motivation and whether he was compromised.

It was a move that perplexed commentators at the time. 'Miranda Devine defending George Pell and Andrew Bolt reporting from Rome. What kind of fresh media hell is this?' tweeted presenter and comedian Emma Rusciano.[3] Journalist Bevan Shields tweeted 'Whaaaaat? Andrew Bolt is in Rome reporting on the George Pell hearings? He's on Sky right now. Breathtaking bias.'[4]

———

If Pell has a core skill, it's staying on message. The following days would bring yet more meticulous and exhaustive questioning of the increasingly weary cardinal in the late-night live sessions to Sydney. He insisted many times that he was in fact lied to on multiple matters—by Bishop Mulkearns and Archbishop Frank Little.

Pell's most controversial, headline-making statement, however, would come on day two when Furness asked if it was common knowledge that Ridsdale had offended against children in the parish of Inglewood.

'I didn't know whether it was common knowledge or whether it wasn't. It's a sad story and it wasn't of much interest to me,' Pell replied among gasps of those watching in both Rome and in the commission hearing in Sydney. Instead he laid blame on Mulkearns, saying his superior had known of the complaints about Ridsdale interfering with children but had lied to Pell about them.

Author and journalist David Marr wrote in *The Guardian* that it was a 'devastating admission', suggesting Pell had chosen his career rather than step in and take action at the time. 'Had young Pell made it his business to find out why the paedophile Father Gerald Ridsdale was being shifted from parish to parish in the 1970s—in later years by a committee on which he himself sat—he might well be living the twilight years of his career not in Rome but the seaside parish of Warrnambool,' Marr wrote.

'From Pell's evidence on the second day of his Roman cross-examination there emerged a picture of an ambitious and capable young priest who decided, early on, to steer clear of this dangerous issue.'

Outside the hotel Ridsdale's nephew and victim, David Ridsdale, angrily said Pell was 'either culpable or an ignorant buffoon'. 'I don't believe he's the latter and we have no evidence of the former, so we have to wait for the commission to do its job,' he told reporters in Rome.

Even Bolt, at first at least, seemed outraged by Pell's comments, describing them as 'damning'. But by the next morning he'd made a rather bizarre backflip, saying it was an exaggeration to interpret Pell's evidence as proof that he didn't care about children. 'What he [Pell] seems to have said, meant to say, was that he had no reason to look at what was happening in that parish of Inglewood by Gerald Ridsdale and as a result, those things slipped his mind,' he said.

After four days of evidence, Pell told the inquiry that he hoped his appearance contributed to a 'bit of healing'. 'All the leadership of the church in Australia is committed to avoiding any repetition of the terrible history of the past and to try and make things better,' he said. 'It has been a hard slog. I'm a bit tired.'

It was clear the cardinal was as exhausted as the survivors sitting in that hotel room in Rome, but it was arranged they would have a private meeting together. Philip Nagle, however, was granted a brief one-on-one audience with the cardinal ahead of the group meeting. 'I just wanted him to remember what we went through,' Nagle said later.[5] 'It was a short chat and it was obvious he was uncomfortable.'

Pell remained stiff, eyes downcast during his meeting with all fifteen survivors in Rome. When survivor Andrew Collins, whose family had been close to Pell for years, gave the cardinal a hug, he seemed to soften and later delivered an emotional statement promising to help them and others who were struggling with the crushing memories and associated side effects by building a special centre in Ballarat.

'But that never happened,' Collins reflected later in a *New York Times* story. 'I've had four survivors that I've known personally take their own lives this year. That was part of what we were trying to get through to people in Rome,' he said. 'We need help and assistance.'

Following their experience in Rome, the close-knit group would never quite be the same again, shattered by a dark secret from the past. It emerged not long after the trip that David Ridsdale had not been exactly transparent about his own past as an abuser.[6] It emerged that in 1995, when he was eighteen, he was charged with two counts of indecently assaulting a twelve-year-old victim.

He pleaded guilty and was placed on a twelve-month good-behaviour bond, but members of the group said Ridsdale misled them about the extent of the abuse when they first learned about it before the Rome trip. Furness would also conclude that there wasn't sufficient evidence that Pell sought to bribe him in the 1993 phone call regarding allegations against his uncle. David Ridsdale has largely remained out of the public eye ever since.

As for his exclusive Sky News interview, Bolt said he wanted to make clear that he wasn't a friend of the cardinal. 'We met socially, briefly, on four occasions before I came to Rome,' Bolt claimed. In truth, though, their association went deeper than that, with Bolt later confirming in the interview that he had launched one of Pell's books. It is probably fair to say they were friendly acquaintances at the very least.

At the end of the interview Pell spoke about how tough the four days of giving evidence had been. 'When I wasn't on at the royal commission I was just resting and trying to get myself together for the next performance.'

A performance? So was everything Pell said all part of a show? Asking Australians to give both him and the church a 'fair go', Pell admitted that he may have previously put the reputation of the church first. 'I'm a Christian, I'm a priest. Now, I might have put the church first, for a while, rather than the victims, but I'm certainly not into putting myself first, I'm not into that.'

In the weeks and months that followed, after the survivors and reporters had left Rome and returned home to Australia, Pell settled back into his role in the Vatican, perhaps hoping the distracting roadshow from his homeland wouldn't darken his door again.

But he soon found himself in the headlines again, this time when the *Daily Mail* published a photo of him tucking into a plate of steak and chips and drinking beer on an outdoor terrace of a Rome restaurant.

'Heart condition improving then, George?' the headline read. The accompanying story questioned whether he really was as unwell as he'd claimed. 'Cardinal Pell submitted a two-page medical report in February which stated a flight to Australia to give evidence would severely impact his health and possibly lead to "heart failure",' the article read.

Another dinner at about the same time would prove to be just as revealing. Melbourne couple Gerald and Jill Byrne had been travelling through Europe on holiday when they decided to see if Pell was free to spend an evening with them during a short stay in Rome. Gerald was an old friend from their seminary days, although he had rejected a life in the priesthood and instead married and had children.

They were invited to meet Pell before dinner at his apartment just outside the Vatican. 'It was pretty simple, nothing too ostentatious,' remembered Gerald.[7] 'I was quite surprised about that actually.'

'He seemed to be feeling good. He commented a few times that a lot of the survivors had come up and hugged and kissed him and he seemed very touched by that. He felt he had been exonerated.'

Certainly, there had been no further news regarding the Sano Task Force probe, and he told his friends that his impression from the Ballarat victims was that there was a new level of peace between them; that they'd been satisfied with his answers during his royal commission interrogation.

'Pell seemed pretty much at ease with his life and work when we saw him and didn't think he would get in any trouble from the issues raised in recent months,' his friends remembered. His Eminence was optimistic. He still had the finances of the world's biggest church firmly in his grasp and could look forward to a warm summer in Rome. Nobody would know for some time that it would turn out to be his last as treasurer.

———

In Melbourne, shaken by what had unfolded in the wake of my scoop, I just wanted to put the whole chapter behind me and get back to doing what I loved best: working as a journalist.

I'd received an official letter from News Corp saying there had been a review of my complaint to HR and it found that Andrew Bolt had not breached the News Corp editorial code of conduct. I still wasn't entirely sure what to make of it all but felt that at least I'd raised my concerns. My view was if Bolt was still writing for the paper then I should too. I missed my colleagues and wanted to keep breaking important, high-impact stories.

To help smooth things over before my return I decided it was best to apologise for sending the emails, even though I felt deep down they should be apologising to me for causing the toxic, unhealthy situation I'd been caught up in. It was my right by law to raise workplace concerns. I said I was committed to my role as a senior writer for the paper. I was advised by HR to write a personal note to managing director Peter Blunden, apologising for any upset my communications, while under severe pressure, may have caused. I had presumed that management would understand the great stress I'd been under due to the weight of the ramifications of the Pell story. I believe reporters are the soldiers sent into war, so if they emerge covered in blood and sweat they need to be supported, not punished.

I had only been back at work for six weeks when I was told by chief-of-staff Paul Tatnell that I had to meet with Tinks and Rick Pruckner, a senior HR partner. My mouth went dry. I could feel what was coming.

'I expect I'm going to get my head chopped off,' I said to Tatts.

'No, I'm sure you won't,' he said, smiling.

But my sense of foreboding was right. Tinks, the man I considered a mentor, couldn't look at me when I walked into Pruckner's small office on the floor below the *Herald Sun* newsroom. Johnston had left his henchmen to carry out the execution.

My one-year contract was ending, and I was due to sign the permanent contract I had been promised many times before I pulled off the Pell scoop and the many other exclusive stories and investigations.

'Due to redundancies I'm afraid there are no jobs . . . but we'd like to have a relationship with you, and for you to be a freelance contributor,' Pruckner said.

'So do I get to keep my desk?' I asked, trying to stay composed.

'Um no, it's more of a hot-desk situation,' he said, looking rather embarrassed.

As I viewed it at the time, the freelance contract with its strict confidentiality clause would silence me on the way out of the door. There was no salary or superannuation either. They clearly didn't want to say it out loud, but I was being fired. The next day, they confirmed, would be my last in the newsroom.

I walked out of the room absolutely devastated. I made it to the toilets and wept. This was made worse when I learnt immediately afterwards that a permanent contract had been given to another journalist and that newsroom production positions were being advertised on a jobs' website, belying the excuse of lack-of-budget. I had been whipped into the News Corp machine, broken a hugely important story, been smashed into tiny pieces in the political fallout and then unceremoniously spat out.

The sense of despair and betrayal by my bosses I felt was immense, but most of all it felt sinister; I had only just made it back to the surface, recovering my well-being after the nightmare following the Pell scoop. This felt as if I was being cruelly pushed back under the water again. The psychological impact of their decision would be severe, my thoughts dominated for months by constant rumination over what had happened.

I felt wrongly and cruelly bayonetted while still probably under an IBAC probe—I was out and Bolt was in. The day after the meeting, the columnist wrote another blog post damning my story and supporting Pell.

I had decided not to sign the freelance contract but did not let my decision be known at News Corp. This gave me time the next day to gather all my personal items, documents and notebooks. It was distressing and humiliating to pull down the pictures of my children from my desk, walk through the newsroom carrying my overloaded bags and go down the lift for the last time.

The next day an extended news feature I had written about the inquest into Sydney's 2014 Lindt Café siege was published over three pages. 'What went wrong?' the headline read. I could say the same about my career at News Corp.

———

Over some weeks, the company chased me with phone calls and a letter to sign the freelance contract, extending its 'offer' to working as an 'intermittent casual reporter'. Despite desperately missing my role on the paper and my colleagues, I just couldn't agree to be demoted—or silenced—over what had unfolded. I wasn't going to set myself on fire to appease its needs or wants. I knew I had to be free. I would later be glad I trusted my instincts. Unlike my editors, I was closely aligned with and connected to the story and trusted the judgement and experiences of my sources.

I was devastated that I seemed to have been poisoned in the fall-out from my own scoop, but as my Quaker school in England had instilled in me so many years before, I had the confidence to trust my own independent thoughts. Maybe it had been my destiny to be the rogue outsider with the sheer nerve to question the system and the status quo. A destiny that resulted in parting ways with Australia's biggest media employer without a backstop.

Soon afterwards I was sent a note from a trusted senior judicial source, who said they believed 'powerful figures were trying to crush those seeking to expose the truth' regarding Pell.

And just as I left News Corp, I discovered the head of Sano Task Force had been stripped of his post. Sources told me Detective Senior Sergeant Michael Dwyer, whose own hunch had sparked the investigation into Pell, believed 'outside pressure' had been to blame for his sudden move to another post. Were we both victims of powerful forces trying to shut us down, or was it all an innocent coincidence?

I didn't know it yet, but in time I'd be back inside the Pell story again. I'd have to endure many difficult, depressing and lonely months trying to process what had unfolded, but leaving News Corp wasn't the end; I sensed something else was waiting for me. The story that briefly destroyed my career would reignite it.

A media and judicial tsunami was on its way that would dramatically wash away any of the positive steps Pell had taken to try and amend the public fallout following his Rome testimony and interview.

First, ABC journalist Louise Milligan had been asked to follow up my exclusive story about the police allegations. 'It was a bold move by the paper and, undeniably, what's known in the business as "a good get",' Milligan later wrote of my story in her book *Cardinal: The rise and fall of George Pell*.

Initially, Milligan said, she didn't believe the story. 'I felt in my bones this story would go nowhere,' she said. 'My bones lied to me.'

Just a month after I left the *Herald Sun*, in July 2016, a *7.30 Report* story by Milligan followed up and explored my story in full, including interviews with some of the victims of the alleged swimming-pool incident. I was still crestfallen and dispirited about my sudden departure from the paper, but I also felt a sense of relief; I was no longer the only journalist who had reported on the allegations. They were now being taken seriously by the national broadcaster.

'You're not on your own out there anymore,' *The Guardian*'s Amanda Meade tweeted to me.

I was glad to see that two men, Lyndon Monument and Damian Dignan, had been brave enough to waive their anonymity and speak about their claims that Pell had allegedly touched them inappropriately in the summer of 1978–79 when he was playing a throwing game with them at Ballarat's Eureka Pool.

Monument told how he'd made a statement to Sano Task Force that Pell would touch his penis, testicles and bottom before throwing him up into the air in the pool.

'I tried not to think about it,' Monument told the program about the incidents. 'He was always just the godly figure. We all had to look up to him. We would get told in class that George Pell is coming today, so brush your hair and tuck yourself in.'

When asked why he hadn't come forward earlier, he said it was too traumatising to discuss. 'Because it was a lot of pain for not only me but for a lot of other people. And I learnt to deal with things by just keeping them close to me, I suppose.'

Monument also alleged in his police statement that Pell had invited him into the changing rooms after they went swimming. 'He would undress. And then he would say to us to undress. So we would undress. And then he would teach you how to dry your testicles and in between your bum and stuff like that,' he told the program.

When asked if he was wearing any clothes at the time, Monument said, 'No'. It was certainly chilling viewing.

Dignan explained that he'd told police about the throwing game in the pool with Pell. He was scared of Pell as a child. 'It's sort of hard to explain,' he said. 'To sit in the confession box with a very, very strong scary man sitting on the other side. We were very, very scared as little kids.'

Another man, Torquay resident Les Tyack, went public with the allegations he submitted to the royal commission and to police that he had seen Pell expose himself for many minutes to three boys at the local surf lifesaving club in the 1980s. Tyack had walked into the Torquay Surf Life Saving Club changing rooms to discover a naked George Pell behaving in a manner in front of three boys he estimated to be aged between eight and ten years old that caused him concern. 'I thought that was not on,' he said. 'Very strange situation for an adult to be full frontal to three young boys.

'I said to the young boys, "Finish doing what you're doing, off you go." When they left, I then said to George Pell, "I know what you're up to. P*** off, get out of here. If I see you in this club again, I'll call the police."'

The publicity from his television report was a huge blow to Pell. What he thought had drifted off over the horizon had just exploded above him like fireworks; the scandal was growing, not shrinking. It emerged later that two men watching the program at home in Victoria came forward to police to allege that they too had been touched as boys while playing at the same pool with Pell.

Yet he hit back as strongly as he had done in response to my story. In a statement, his office discredited the contents of the ABC program, saying: 'The claims that he has sexually abused anyone, in any place, at any time in his life are totally untrue and completely wrong.

'He denies the allegations absolutely, and says that they, and any allegations of them by the ABC are nothing more than a scandalous smear campaign which appears to be championed by the ABC.

'If there was any credibility in any of these claims, they would have been pursued by the royal commission by now.'

Importantly, regarding my ongoing worries about the IBAC probe into my original story, Graham Ashton, Chief Commissioner of Victoria Police, told reporters that the investigation had been abandoned. 'I got a letter from Cardinal Pell some time ago regarding a complaint around that,' he told Melbourne radio station 3AW. 'I sent it to IBAC and IBAC had a look and wrote back to me and said they dismissed the complaint.'

This was the first time in five months I'd had any news of the IBAC investigation and it came as a huge relief, but it still didn't ease the daily grief I felt about losing the job I loved. I was in a very sombre and uncertain place.

But there were two men who had a few questions for Pell who would soon fly to Rome and change everything. For Pell, for me, for everyone.

———

At the time we were told very little, but it had leaked to the media that detectives from Sano Task Force had flown to Rome in October 2016 to interview the cardinal regarding the historical sexual-abuse allegations. Only much later would we witness the explosive scene that unfolded when Pell was confronted by detectives Chris Reed and Peter Sheridan in a hotel at Rome's Fiumicino Airport with the details of what he stood accused of.

What was clear to me at the time was that sending the police across to the other side of the world meant that this investigation was more than alive; detectives were possibly close to making an arrest.

We would also find out later that a new character in the saga was being lined up to begin furiously working away behind the scenes trying to stop police from charging Pell: Melbourne criminal defence barrister Robert Richter, QC. A popular choice among the unpopular, the gambling-loving self-described atheist is no stranger to controversy. He represented Julian Knight, who committed the Hoddle Street massacre, on a pro-bono basis in 1998 and defended underworld figure Mick Gatto in 2005. Such was Gatto's joy at eventually being acquitted, he later had Richter's name tattooed on his chest.

The barrister was born in 1946 in the former Soviet State of the Kirghiz Republic, where his parents met after being displaced during World War II. His father Berek was a Polish Jew and his mother Sofia a Ukrainian. 'Richter has an affinity with outsiders, mainly because he was one,' wrote Tim Elliot in a profile on the silk for *Good Weekend*.[8]

Still working as hard in his early seventies as he did in his forties, Richter is forensic in his approach and theatrical and bold in his style; he would reveal later that he had presented detectives with his own thick dossier of evidence in December 2016, two months after the cardinal was questioned, including testimony from many witnesses, aiming to prove that his client was innocent of all allegations.

While Richter worked away, I was asked by various media commentators why I had left the *Herald Sun*. At first I was fearful of burning bridges, but eventually I decided I had no reason not to explain what had unfolded. It had felt wrong and frustrating to stay silent. This would prove to be a surprising yet vital turning point in my journey. The support from the public and many respected media figures, amid a viral rush on Twitter, followed by an interview with *The Guardian*, was tremendous, appreciated and unexpected. I no longer felt so isolated and alone.

When Andrew Bolt was asked by *The Guardian* for a comment about my departure from the paper, he not only denied he had a hand in it but said, 'I did not know she had made any HR complaint.'[9] Despite having an official letter saying News Corp had conducted a formal review into my concerns, it seems the organisation had not mentioned it to, or questioned, the star columnist at the centre of the complaint. It felt like a cover-up.

The revelation didn't impress experts in the HR industry. In an article published in the *Canberra Times* and the *Sydney Morning Herald* Peter Wilson, chairman of the Australian HR Institute and president of the World Federation of People Management Associations, wrote about my saga, saying HR complaints should be communicated properly.[10] 'The tendency for chief HR officers to side with those in power, and to move people on who make management uncomfortable, is an old game not a new game,' he said. 'HR's job is to work for the good of the company, which isn't always served by simply pleasing the boss.'

———

Meanwhile in Rome, Pope Francis was showing increasing determination, publicly at least, to deal with the global clergy-abuse crisis. He exhorted Catholic bishops worldwide to do what was needed to ensure children are protected.

The Vatican released a letter from the Pope, who wrote about the injustices to children including slave labour, malnutrition, lack of education and sexual exploitation, including abuse by priests. He decried 'the sufferings, the experiences and pain of minors who were abused sexually by priests. It's a sin that shames us all.'

In what appeared to be an honest acceptance, the Pope also denounced the sins of local bishops around the world who covered up child sexual-abuse cases. He expressed the church's regret and denounced the 'sin of what happened, the sin of failing to help, the sin of covering up and denial, the sin of the abuse of power'.

As for the future, he called on bishops for complete commitment to ensure that 'these atrocities' will no longer take place, saying that they needed to adhere to a 'zero tolerance' approach.

Unfortunately for Pope Francis and the Catholic Church, news from Australia's ongoing royal commission would make headlines around the world. Gail Furness was back in the hot seat with some shattering details from a report containing the latest statistics collated by the commission. She told the inquiry that 7 per cent of the nation's Catholic priests had allegedly abused children between 1950 and 2010.

The sheer scale of the scandal was hard to comprehend. In one Catholic religious order, St John of God, over 40 per cent of church figures were accused of abuse. Furness described the victims' accounts as 'depressingly similar', saying, 'Children were ignored or worse, punished.'

After reading that the archbishops of Sydney, Perth, Brisbane, Adelaide, Melbourne and Canberra–Goulburn would all soon be giving evidence as part of case study 50, Institutional Review of Catholic Church Authorities, I decided to undertake a special project that would allow me to immerse myself in a subject I'd become so passionate about. I began working with Byline Media, a London-based crowd-funding media platform, to live-tweet the proceedings. This would enable me to travel to Sydney to cover the key days in which the archbishops were giving evidence.

Anthony Foster was one of the first to contribute to the crowd-funding appeal and to greet me as I arrived at the hearing in Sydney. 'I'm so glad you made it,' he said, leaving me incredibly touched and honoured.

The testimony of the archbishops, who sat awkwardly in their clerical collars in the witness box, proved to be fascinating. They were quizzed by Furness about how they might deal with a fictional child called 'Sally' reporting abuse to them in a confessional. Their responses were mixed.

Sydney Archbishop Anthony Fisher said he would never be prepared to break the holy seal of the confession. 'Even little children have spiritual rights,' he said. 'If they come to confession and it all tumbles out, whatever is in their heart, they know whatever they've said, they've said to God, and it won't be repeated. I know that for people that aren't part of the Catholic tradition ... this sounds strange but to us it would be like bugging the confessional.'

Archbishop Fisher said he would try to persuade 'Sally' to talk to authorities outside the seal of the confessional, but if he could not persuade her, her discussion would remain confidential.

His controversial stance was also supported by the Archbishop of Melbourne, Denis Hart. On the subject of celibacy Archbishop Hart, who was then the president of the Bishops Conference, asked that potential priests avoid joining the church if they could not embrace the concept.[11] 'Celibacy seen as a burden runs the risk of turning in on oneself and would feed any immaturity or lack of balance in the person,' he said.

However, together with his four colleagues, Archbishop Hart admitted that celibacy was a factor in the child sexual abuse seen in the church, although he would not say it was the cause. 'In a person who hasn't got the capacity to embrace celibacy ... where there are weaknesses there then I'd have to admit that the capacity or probability of abuse is certainly increased,' he said.

What would also soon increase were the rumours that Pell was about to be charged. In February, the Senate called on the cardinal to return home 'to assist the Victorian police and office of public prosecutions with their investigation into these matters'.

Pell dismissed the parliamentary resolution as 'an interference on the part of the Senate in the due process of the Victoria Police investigation'. But there was nothing he could do to stop the might of Sano Task Force. The dossier of evidence, which had been sent back by the director of public prosecution to Victoria Police without a decision on whether to proceed, was submitted again and the green light had been given for officers to charge the cardinal. The media was running breathless stories about an imminent development but was left frustrated that no dates or timeline were being released.

The news, in the end, was sudden and swift. It was 4.30 a.m. in Rome on 29 June 2017 when Victoria Police announced that the sleeping cardinal would be charged with 'multiple allegations of historic sexual abuse'.

This stopped me in my tracks. The charges were served on Pell's legal representatives in Melbourne and were also lodged at Melbourne Magistrates' Court. After everything that had happened Pell would soon have to fly home, after being ordered to appear at the court on 26 July.

'Cardinal Pell is facing multiple charges . . . and there are multiple complainants,' Victoria Police's deputy commissioner

Shane Patton said in a media conference in Melbourne. The charges were 'historical sexual assault offences'.

Pell's response was typically confident and outraged. In a statement released by the Catholic Archdiocese of Sydney 90 minutes after the charges were announced, Pell said he would 'return to Australia, as soon as possible, to clear his name'.

'Although it is still in the early hours of the morning in Rome, Cardinal George Pell has been informed of the decision and action of Victoria Police,' the statement said.

'He has again strenuously denied all allegations.

'Cardinal Pell will return to Australia, as soon as possible, to clear his name following advice and approval by his doctors who will also advise on his travel arrangements.'

After the sun rose in Rome, the cardinal himself emerged to begin the biggest battle of his life. He told a news conference at the Holy See: 'I'm looking forward finally to having my day in court.'

Pell could have claimed diplomatic immunity in the Vatican and refused to fly home, but he vowed he would be in court for his first hearing on 26 July.

And so would I. I was hired by CNN to report from inside court for the whole case and by Bruce Guthrie at *The New Daily* to lead its coverage and write a regular column, 'Pell's Day in Court'. The story that had disrupted my career was putting me back in the middle of the most sensational legal case in Australian history and the Catholic Church was right on my doorstep.

What I didn't know then was just how thick the veil of secrecy would be over the case. Just hours after Pell was charged, a suppression order was granted by the court, preventing the media from reporting the number or nature of the charges against Pell. We could still report the hearings at this stage, but we had to carefully omit certain details or face fines and even jail terms.

Reporting from the court was certainly going to be as challenging and technical as it gets, but despite being bruised by the story in the past I was determined to take my seat in the front row and share as much as I could without breaking the order.

Covering this case to the finish line now felt like my calling; I would see it through to the end. After all the cover-ups by the Catholic Church, the public, advocates, survivors and their families deserved to know as much as I could share.

Chapter 7
Belinda's burden

It wasn't the usual way the cardinal liked to start his morning. On a normal weekday he could be found working inside the grand confines of Saint John's Tower, the mediaeval building on the western tip of Vatican City that is the official seat of the Prefect of the Secretariat of the Economy. Here assistants would bring him coffee or run errands across the ancient Roman cobblestones. It was a place he could work in peace.

There was nothing peaceful about the scene that greeted Cardinal Pell on Wednesday 26 July 2017 at Melbourne Magistrates' Court, where he arrived just before 9 a.m. for his first hearing on multiple charges of historic sexual abuse.

At 5 a.m. and in the darkness, I had been the first in line at the doors of the court to ensure a seat inside, and to help lead the eight-strong team working to cover the hearing for CNN. Advocate Julie Cameron had also appeared out of the shadows clutching a framed print of Madonna and child. 'I'm a Christian and I'm just looking for truth and justice,' she told me. Julie would be a witness to the proceedings until the bitter end along with several others, who were determined to watch the case unfold for themselves.

Very soon the William Street court building was under siege, with an army of over 150 local, national and international journalists and TV crews. We all morphed into one huge, breathless, heaving and agitated pack. In truth, as I wrote for my *New Daily* column later that day, we were all hungry for breakfast as well as the story as we stood shivering in the queue as dawn broke.

The huge media interest, of course, wasn't surprising: Cardinal Pell was the most senior Catholic to ever face criminal charges—charges that he had by then strongly and consistently denied. This wasn't just a routine filing hearing. This was history in the making. Everything was now at stake for Cardinal Pell. The possible ramifications for the worldwide Catholic Church were endless, already battered as it was by ongoing abuse scandals that continued to grow.

As the cardinal entered the court nobody needed a ladder or a bunk-up to catch a glimpse of this Ballarat-boy-turned-Vatican-superpower ascending the steps. His imposing frame meant his steel-grey hair stood out like a lonely skyscraper above the clouds of chaos. He was guided and guarded by an armful of police and walked into a roaring soundtrack of media argy-bargy and a handful of protesters shouting 'shame on you'.

When I saw him for the first time, I was already inside standing outside the tall pine and glass door to court 2, with a pack of reporters lined up behind me. After everything that had happened over the previous two years, I knew I was exactly where I was meant to be. I was witnessing this incredible moment on behalf of a global audience and writing my own personal column on the case. It was as if my often treacherous journey with this story suddenly made sense. 'News Corp threw you to the wolves and now you're back leading the pack,' a reporter remarked in the queue. I hadn't given up on myself—or the story.

Pell looked deathly white, poker-faced and noticeably more fragile than his confident, fearless appearance at the Vatican press conference the previous month. No doubt the long-haul flight, ongoing health issues and intense meetings he was likely to have endured with his legal team had taken their toll. Head mostly bowed, ignoring the survivors' shouts and support-ers' claps, he was whisked into a private room after facing the standard indignity of being told to stretch out his arms for a security-wand check.

Pell strolled into the small, packed court about fifteen minutes early. The thick gold ring on his little finger, a badge of high clerical office passed down from Archbishop Daniel Mannix, the most powerful and controversial Australian cleric of the twentieth century, was the only lightness on his otherwise sombre palette of black suit and shirt.

Apart from a few mumbled conversations with members of his legal team he sat in silence, staring dead ahead. He was surrounded by 50 reporters and some well-known advocates including Chrissie Foster and Philip Nagle. It must have been his worst and most feared nightmare.

The magistrate, Duncan Reynolds, began the businesslike hearing—eight minutes of mostly routine administration and date setting.

The wheels of routine were broken, however, by Richter, who rose to his feet grandly, saying with a flourish that 'for the avoidance of doubt . . . Cardinal Pell would be pleading not guilty to all charges'. He wasn't required to say this, but in doing so he ensured his defiant quote claimed the headlines for the next 24 hours. It was a PR battle as well as a legal one.

The date for a committal mention was set for 6 October. Pell walked out of the doors with a tight ring of police officers surrounding him and headed towards his barrister's office nearby. In a slow-moving, frenzied clerical sardine sandwich, he was swamped by the press pack and protesters holding small placards. 'I will pray for you, Cardinal Pell,' shouted a male supporter as he disappeared from view.

———

What would soon become clear was that the conclusion of this case, whatever the outcome, would be not just months in the future but possibly years, with experts predicting it may involve split trials. With two months until the next hearing, this wasn't going to be a short assignment. The wheels of Victoria's legal system were moving so slowly. It would be an epic saga the public would not be fully party to until the very end. I feared for the mental health of the victims waiting to give evidence, imagining how the case would be hanging over them, filling their thoughts.

At Pell's second court appearance in October 2017, we learned that it would be a full five months until the committal hearing that would ultimately test the evidence and decide if the case should proceed to trial at a higher court. Lasting four weeks, over 50 witnesses would be cross-examined.

The reloaded media bait ball rolled around the corner following Pell, accompanied by armed police officers in black baseball caps and bulletproof vests, to Richter's office.

———

For a case surrounded with so much publicity, in retrospect it was perhaps fortuitous that there would be a lengthy lull between proceedings. Other aspects of the clergy-abuse scandal could be aired and given the attention they deserved.

In early December 2017 the royal commission released two final reports on the Melbourne diocese and Ballarat case studies. They were damning, but among the worst revelations was a letter written by Frank Little, the Archbishop of Melbourne who would be succeeded by the ambitious Pell.

Dated 20 August 1984, he told parishioners that he would not be investigating allegations of abuse by the notoriously violent Father Peter Searson as requested. He felt it was 'improper', he wrote.

The commission singled out Archbishop Little, who died in 2008, for 'abjectly failing to protect the safety of children' and leaving them at risk of 'catastrophic human consequences'.

'Complaints were dealt with in a way that sought to protect the Archdiocese from scandal and liability and prioritised the interests of the church over those of the victims,' the royal commission's report said. It also said that Archbishop Little, who headed the Archdiocese from 1974 to 1996, dismissed or ignored serious allegations of child sexual abuse against a number of other priests who terrorised children.

Despite the long list of allegations against Searson, Archbishop Little appointed him as the parish priest at Doveton in 1984, where complaints continued to be made including torturing animals in front of children and abusing a small girl, Julie Stewart, while she was seated on his lap. There had also been a serious complaint from Year 12 boys who were cleaners at the school. 'The boys told him [Little] that Father Searson had held a gun to them when they were in the school cleaning the toilets at 8 p.m. and had told them to get off the property,' the report said.

Commissioners concluded that Archbishop Little 'abjectly failed to protect the safety and wellbeing of the children within the parish' by not removing Searson, who remained at Doveton until 1997 and died in 2009, before any charges could be laid.

Although the reports were available in their entirety, it was clear that over 15 pages had been fully redacted because they referred to Pell. What had Pell possibly seen or ignored? We would have to wait for the conclusion of his legal case before we could read what had been blacked out.

Meanwhile, as we prepared for Pell's committal, a global phenomenon was unfolding. Major public figures were now being held to account for their sexual harassment of both men and women, both inside and outside the workplace. This would spark the #MeToo movement.

The behaviour of Hollywood producer Harvey Weinstein towards up to 80 women would be the catalyst for the responses from celebrities and the public around the world. Other major names would soon fall from grace including Bill Cosby and Kevin Spacey. It was a wounding time for the world. Who could anyone trust now?

———

In Melbourne itself, the very city where the Pell case was unfolding, a scandal emerged in December 2017 involving the Lord Mayor of Melbourne, Robert Doyle. A city councillor, Tessa Sullivan, had made allegations of sexual harassment against Doyle and had resigned, leading to a formal investigation. Other women had come forward with further allegations. The *Herald Sun* ran a series of negative stories about Sullivan, seemingly backing yet another powerful male figure.

'When something like this happens, you lose so much confidence and you feel so dirty and ashamed and humiliated,' Sullivan explained in an interview at the time.[1] 'You think [it's] the most disgusting thing that ever happened to you and that everyone's going to know about it.'

'There is absolutely no benefit to coming forward with something like this,' Sullivan said, 'I'm not getting a payout. I lost my job. I'm getting nothing. All I want is the truth.'

Against this backdrop, another time bomb was about to explode for the Catholic Church. The royal commission had finished its five-year inquiry and had handed down its final report and recommendations, the most radical of which was that the Vatican should consider allowing Catholic priests to be 'voluntarily celibate' and change many of its canon laws to help prevent child abuse. The commission also asked for the Australian Catholic Bishop's Conference to call for the Vatican to overhaul the confessional.

Resistance was almost immediate among senior ranks of the church, with Archbishop of Melbourne Denis Hart reiterating his stance that the sacred seal of the confessional should never be broken—even to report a crime. 'I couldn't report the abuse from what I heard in the confessional,' Hart said, but he 'would do everything' he could to get the confessor 'to go to the authorities'.

Hart didn't think the commission had damaged the credibility of the church. 'We are a humble church,' he said.

The royal commission's report covered five years of testimony and the harrowing accounts of thousands of survivors. It called for methods to make it easier to prosecute institutions that have failed to protect children. Other recommendations included the creation of a national office for child safety, and a website and telephone helpline for reporting abuse. Together with the three final reports already released—Criminal Justice, Redress and Civil Litigation, and Working with Children Checks—the commissioners made a total of 409 recommendations.

Gary Bouma, Professor of Sociology at Monash University, was not surprised that 'pushback' began immediately from senior figures such as Archbishop Hart.[2] 'I think there will be enormous pushback from the Catholic Church on this in a variety of ways—it will be a defence of a thousand years of tradition or more,' he said. 'In terms of asking the bishops to scream at the Vatican to end celibacy it's interesting that the commissioners made that recommendation. The pushback on that will be enormous, but that does not mean it's impossible.'

In his final sitting address, on 14 December 2017, Justice Peter McClellan pointed out that it was important to remember that the number of children abused in 'familial or other circumstances' far exceeds those who are abused in institutions.

The final report also contained 3955 de-identified, moving narratives based on survivors' personal experiences of child sexual abuse, told during private sessions and shared in written accounts.

In Rome, the Pope promised to read it all, but advocates and experts were sceptical change would follow. He seemed to be taking one step forward and one step back in his handling of the clergy-abuse crisis, and he didn't always get it right.

During a visit to Chile in early January 2018, on a trip that was meant to heal the wounds of a sexual-abuse scandal that had cost the Catholic church its credibility in the country, Pope Francis accused victims of the country's most notorious paedophile of slander. Until he saw proof that high-profile bishop Juan Barros had been complicit in covering up the sex crimes of another cleric, Reverend Fernando Karadima, the accusations against Barros were 'all calumny', he said.

The Guardian reported that the Pope's remarks drew shock from Chileans and immediate rebuke from victims and their advocates. They noted the accusers were deemed credible enough by the Vatican that in 2011 Karadima had been sentenced to a lifetime of 'penance and prayer' for his crimes.

Very quickly, however, the spotlight returned to Pell. One of the Ballarat swimming pool accusers, Damian Dignan, had tragically died following a long illness. He had shared his deepest, most personal memories on ABC-TV six months earlier, but he would never get his day in court.

Dignan's partner, Sharon Rixon, confirmed his death on Facebook, describing him as her 'best friend and the father of my children'. 'It's hard to say goodbye, but [you're] pain free now and that's the best thing we could hope for,' she wrote.

A former Melbourne magistrate, Nicholas Papas, told *The Australian* that Dignan's death could have ramifications for Pell's court case. 'Normally it requires that the person who has given evidence to be there, and so normally it would be the case that without them there, the prosecution can't proceed . . . but you can't be absolutely sure.'

Pell learned of the news in a seminary in Sydney, where he was being well cared for among 40 trainee priests.[3] He was spending his days quietly in prayer, reading emails from supporters, having visits from friends and eating meals prepared by cooks.

A spokesman for the seminary said the cardinal had no official role there. 'The seminarians are very comfortable with Cardinal Pell's presence. He [Pell] does not take part in ministry for the seminary, nor is he involved in mentoring or liturgy. Cardinal Pell is now very much looking forward to the March hearing and his day in court.'

It would be a day that would reveal just how much of a fight Pell was prepared to put up to save himself.

———

It emerged that Pell's defence team was one of the most experienced and most expensive ever seen in Australian legal history. Led by Richter, it included Ruth Shann, who had already appeared as junior counsel in murder, manslaughter, police corruption and sexual offences matters in the High Court, Supreme Court and County Court. Also on the team was Pell's principal solicitor, Paul Galbally, and other junior solicitors and clerks. It was speculated that Richter's fee alone could top $2000 per hour and the total cost of the entire team per day was potentially an eye-watering $30,000.

This was a force to be reckoned with. They were across every detail, and diligently looked into every angle and opportunity as they rapidly built their defence case.

Pell's team would go head to head with lead Crown prosecutor Mark Gibson SC, a highly experienced barrister. He would be supported by Fran Dalziel, who had been appointed as a Crown Prosecutor in 2012 and has contributed to the Court of Appeal process and practiced in criminal law and personal injury at the Victorian bar. They would both later be made QCs.

The case had only just started but Pell's team was already showing its ruthlessness. During an earlier legal argument hearing before the committal, and without the cardinal present, they were accused of going on a 'fishing expedition' to get medical records from Pell's alleged victims. But such accusations would be water off a lawyer's back to the impenetrable Richter, who was on the most important mission of his career and one he must have hoped would prove to be his glorious swan song.

Court subpoenas were also planned for the complainants. The defence team had successfully gained materials via court orders from Victorian lawyers who had represented Lyndon Monument and Damian Dignan as well as the surviving choirboy in the Cathedral matter. As we would learn later in much more detail, the other choirboy had tragically died in 2014. Richter had already won his bid during the previous two months to raise undisclosed materials from victim's advocacy group Broken Rites, Victoria Police and Louise Milligan.

By day one of the committal case we had been shown all the signs that the battle ahead would transcend one man and one case in a small Melbourne courtroom.

Pell looked determined yet weary as he arrived by car just before 9.30 a.m. into a scrum of reporters, TV crews and photographers from around the world. A female protester screamed at him, 'Go to hell, George Pell' as he was swallowed up by the crowd.

Overseeing the case now was well-respected legal figure Belinda Wallington, the supervising magistrate of the sexual-assault portfolio.

The sharp-tongued Richter was in fighting form during the initial 23-minute hearing, which dealt with legal administration and legal argument. He alleged Victoria Police had breached a protocol reserved for high-profile defendants by failing to presume the Vatican treasurer's innocence. 'We say that wasn't followed because of a presumption of guilt,' he told the court.

Crown Prosecutor Gibson had previously applied for parts of the hand-up brief of evidence against Pell to be withdrawn, but with a Shakespearean flourish Richter leapt to his feet and strongly argued it should all be heard before the magistrate. 'If there is exculpatory material in the brief it should be tendered,' he said.

Thirty reporters gathered in the packed courtroom, including from the *Wall Street Journal*, *New York Times* and the BBC. Many of them quickly Googled the word 'exculpatory', discovering it meant 'freed from blame'.

Richter accused the prosecution of saying Pell should not have a priest as his support person. They hadn't. And he didn't.

He was even sniffy about the support dog, a black labrador named Coop, the magistrate ruled could sit at the feet of complainants as they gave evidence from a remote location during the two weeks of videolink testimony. In the end, Richter said he would not object to the canine 'as long as he doesn't comment. Whatever comfort the dog can give we don't object to the dog.'

Amid the sound of frenetic typing from the reporters, Pell, who now faced one less charge after the death of Dignan earlier in the year, sat motionless throughout the hearing. The magistrate allowed the cardinal's application to have a male friend as a support person with him in court due to his age and poor medical condition.

Extra chairs had been moved into the court to accommodate all the reporters, but we were only allowed in the courtroom for a short time before Wallington closed the court for video evidence from the accusers. In Victoria the media are not allowed to be present in court when alleged victims of sexual abuse give evidence, so they do not feel embarrassment or shame and alter their evidence as a result.

Judy Courtin, a lawyer who specialises in representing victims of historic sexual abuse, was concerned, however, about the pressure on the complainants being cross-examined by the famously thorough Richter. She believed no parts of the case should be in closed court. 'The power differentials will create a vast chasm,' she told me. 'They should have their own legal representation to support them through such a process; the high-profile nature of the case creates unreasonable expectations.'

Other experts agreed with her, including Professor Jeremy Gans, who specialises in criminal law at Melbourne. 'It should be open to the public as with any other criminal trial or commit-tal, the use of a videolink already helps reduce the stress on the complainants. While I realise that intrudes on witnesses' privacy, I think openness reflects the public nature of courts and prosecutions.'

Only the prosecution team, Pell, his male 'support person' and his counsel were allowed seats inside the courtroom along with the magistrate and clerk.

From our vantage point outside the door, the media could keep an eye on the proceedings from as close as we could legally get without actually putting a glass up to the wall and listening in. We watched as legal clerks pushed two trolleys through the doors of the courtroom, each holding approximately 30 thick white files bearing the words GEORGE PELL, such was the scale of the proceedings.

What we also discovered by waiting outside was that Pell himself seemed to be struggling as his accusers gave their testimony for the first time. At one point I saw him wipe his eyes with tissues as he emerged from court for a short break during one of many adjournments.

———

As the week went on, Pell's general state seemed to worsen. By Friday he looked exhausted and seemed quite unwell. We could hear his cough echoing through the stairwell when he left the courtroom.

Walking with a worsening stoop, neck leaning forward, he shuffled awkwardly to and from the small private interview room where he ate lunch and took breaks. He was trailed everywhere he went by a court security guard.

The courthouse was like something out of the Wild West. Prostitutes puffing on cigarettes lined up with drug addicts at the front entrance. And six floors above was the room where those charged with domestic violence had to report. Sometimes there were loud shouts as guards rushed to break up an altercation. This was a far cry from the exquisite interiors of Pell's Vatican workplace in springtime Rome.

Pell's team was working hard to support him during the challenging days of the accuser evidence. Richter showed great comfort and offered reassurance to the cardinal, patting him on the back on more than one occasion as they went into the private room for breaks.

———

On the afternoon of 14 March 2018, the media was finally allowed back in to report on the proceedings. Just as we took our seats, there was an angry exchange in the witness box between Richter and a high-profile advocate who had carefully documented Catholic abuse for 35 years.

Bernard Barrett, a retired academic and volunteer for Broken Rites, had been praised in the past for investigating cases long before the media. Raising his voice and banging his fist on the table, Richter claimed that Dr Barrett was 'big-noting himself' by making accusations against Australia's most senior Catholic.

Dr Barrett, somewhat shaken at times, denied all of Mr Richter's accusations, saying he was simply offering support and information to the mother who first made contact with him by email in December 2014 with allegations that her son had suffered abuse by a now deceased Maltese priest while he was an altar boy. We were not able to identify the son, who was referred to in court as J.

In June 2015 the mother then sent a further email to the advocate making allegations that her son had also revealed that he'd been abused by Pell while a choirboy at St Patrick's Cathedral. 'He [J] has made further disclosures about his time as a choir boy . . . he's feeling quite desperate and confused and would like to speak with you when he finishes work today,' the mother's email to Barrett was quoted as saying. The son then called Barrett directly.

'It would have been a considerable feather in your cap if you had tried to pin something on Cardinal Pell, wouldn't it?' Richter asked the witness. 'You would have considered it a considerable victory if you could pin something on Cardinal Pell as doing something wrong?'

Dr Barrett denied this, saying he did not report the matter to Sano Task Force himself and did not mention Pell when he spoke to a detective. He had simply asked a detective, when they were speaking about another matter, which phone number the complainant should call. He also confirmed he suggested contacting lawyer Vivian Waller, who specialises in clergy-abuse cases.

Demonstrating his famously sharp manner during cross-examination, Richter raised his voice and told Dr Barrett he was using the witness box to rally against the Catholic Church. 'Look, do you know what it means to answer a question that you are asked, rather than advocate from the pulpit yourself,' he demanded.

But that wouldn't be the end of the unedifying stoush; Richter also criticised Dr Barrett for failing to take notes of the initial phone call with the accuser.

Pell mostly looked down and took his own notes, occasionally chatting to the Sydney Archdiocese executive advisor Katrina Lee, who was seated next to him.

The atmosphere tensed again when the father of the second choirboy allegedly attacked by Pell in St Patrick's Cathedral told the court by videolink of his son's fatal descent into heroin addiction. The young man, identified as R, died on 8 April 2014, just 24 hours after being released from jail. He was 30 years old. 'I believe he was used to taking a lot more [heroin] and he thought he could do that but it was just too much for his body,' his father said.

The father revealed that a CD of his son singing with the choir of St Patrick's Cathedral was played at his funeral. The father had been unaware at the time of the alleged attack on his child there.

R's addiction to heroin began when he was introduced to it by a friend while still a pupil at St Kevin's College in Toorak, an independent Catholic boys' school. Giving a painful insight into his son's addiction, R's father said it was so severe 'he tried to enter rehab seven or eight times'. Whenever they met up with him for dinner over a period of many years, his son was 'always high'.

Pell's junior counsel, Ruth Shann, asked if R had ever claimed to have been abused. 'At no time did he ever tell me that and we had quite a few discussions,' he replied. 'I'm aware of that sort of thing and I never saw or hinted there was something going on.'

The father confirmed the choirmaster at the cathedral told him his son was no longer welcome in the choir at some point later in 1997 and he lost his scholarship at St Kevin's as a result. 'He was not happy with . . . the general behaviour of coughing and disrupting the choir and bending music sheets.'

Giving weight to the notion that the alleged attack by Pell may have caused his change in behaviour, the father said his son had previously enjoyed singing in the choir. 'It was quite a chore to do, but he—he certainly was enjoying it, yes.'

The next day we would learn of another allegation against Pell, that he had abused a ten-year-old boy at Lake Boga, at nearby Swan Hill, in December 1975. The incident was being included in the case not as a specific charge against Pell but to prove 'tendency and coincidence', a legal term used when evidence is given to prove or disprove one of the elements of the case, or to make one of the elements of the case likelier or not.

The father, who also alleged to police his son had been abused by Father Ridsdale on several occasions when he visited Swan Hill, was questioned via videolink. He said Cardinal Pell had arrived with another priest at the picturesque lake just after lunch and enjoyed some water skiing behind the family speedboat before joining them for afternoon tea. What we couldn't include in our reports at the time was that during a game in the water, the boy was said to have slipped off Pell's shoulders and made accidental contact with the priest's erect penis. Pell was alleged to have told the boy, 'Don't worry, it's only natural.'

The father said in evidence that his son, who had been an altar boy at St Mary's in Swan Hill, struggled to talk about the incident, which is why his other son told him. 'I think he was protecting me from it because of health concerns.'

Richter didn't hold back in attacking the father, suggesting he'd made up that Pell had been named as the offender. He said that in his first statement to police, the father had only accused Father Ridsdale of abusing the son in another location.

'. . . that is an insult,' the father responded.

'Yes, it may be an insult, but it's true, is it not?' Richter said.

'Absolutely not,' the father replied.

The barrister suggested the father never mentioned the incident at the lake, only to tell people he had once given Pell a water-ski ride.

'I was proud because he was such a big man . . . and as a challenge to the driver of a ski boat,' the father hit back.

The court also heard from the brother of the surviving choirboy, J. The witness had overheard his brother say in a drunken 'emotional outburst' that 'some f—ed up stuff has happened to me'. It wasn't until June 2015, when J made a statement to police, that the brother was told of the allegations against Pell.

After the examination of the witness on 15 March 2018 concluded and the court opened after lunch, a visibly distressed Wallington announced the court had received some 'very devastating news' and would not be sitting for the rest of the day, or the next day. Reporters speculated if the news concerned the Pell matter, but it soon emerged that the well-respected magistrate Stephen Myall had tragically taken his own life, due to an unrelenting case load. It was a stark reminder of the pressures judicial staff were under on a daily basis.

By this point, journalists were also feeling the strain navigating the case in the Victorian court system; reporting the committal had become like trying to piece together a jigsaw while wearing a blindfold. When we did hear something new, we were often restricted by the court order. We heard from multiple witnesses, but often it was impossible to include their evidence as we were unable to publish the location where the alleged offences took place or the nature of the charges. It was a legal minefield. The group of reporters who attended every day—we dubbed ourselves the 'Pell pack'—worked closely together as we checked quotes and discussed what we believed could and could not be reported. The responsibility was huge. None of us wanted to be blamed for a possible future trial collapsing, let alone risk a fine or a jail term for breaking the order. Some media outlets had in-house lawyers but many of the others, including my own media clients, were relying on the court reporter to decide what was legally safe.

Soon our task became even trickier; it would emerge the full allegations against Pell were more serious than anyone had realised. It wasn't just the cathedral, the swimming pool and a lake that formed the backdrop to these allegations. There was something else.

———

It was 19 March, after a weekend break from proceedings. A mobile phone rudely went off in court 22. As the sound echoed around the small, airless room Cardinal Pell jolted up from his A4 notepad. The noise was not coming from the pack of reporters; it was in fact coming from his own beige jacket pocket. He quickly passed the offending device to his friend and supporter Katrina Lee to stop the ringing. It would be less easy to control the noise from the allegations against him, which were becoming increasingly grave.

Before lunchtime, it emerged that Pell had been accused of attacking a small boy from St Joseph's Boys' Home on multiple occasions.[4] We would learn in detail later that the man, known in court by his initials as SG, had first alleged he'd been the victim of two sexual assaults by Pell at the YMCA pool in Ballarat. These were said to have occurred in 1976, when he was in grade four. He had no further interaction with Pell until he was around 12 years of age, although he claimed he did spot Pell at St Joseph's in the company of nuns.

The next time he met Pell, he said, he was unexpectedly told by a nun that he was going out for the evening to see a screening of the hit Hollywood movie *Close Encounters of the Third Kind*. He believed it was March 1978. What unfolded next would turn out to be one of the most heinous and brazen descriptions of child abuse I'd ever heard.

They had been watching the film for about 20 minutes when Pell allegedly pulled SG onto his lap and slid his pants and underpants over his knees. He was then said to have lifted the terrified boy up and down on his penis so that he was anally penetrated. This went on for about three minutes and the pain was apparently so severe that SG screamed. We learnt later how SG recalled in his closed court witness testimony that there were not many people in the cinema and so his cries went unnoticed. Afterwards, he said, he bled heavily from the anus.

However, during cross-examination of John Bourke, a former projectionist for a cinema in Ballarat, Richter swiftly stepped up a gear. Under his concise questioning, the witness soon conceded that he would have noticed the 'distinctive looking' Pell if he had attended the cinema. He also explained how his ushers were employed to lead people to their seats as well as deal with 'any trouble'—and none had been reported at the time. 'They would investigate [if they saw trouble] then they'd take whatever necessary action they required,' Bourke told the court.

Most importantly, Richter said, Bourke and the accuser had got the dates of the screening wrong. Senior detective Jason Rowles had been charged with searching old editions of the *Ballarat Courier* to check where the movie was shown. His enquiries revealed the film was shown at the Regent cinema for two weeks from Thursday 21 September 1978 and not March as SG believed. A member of Pell's legal team also checked the dates.

Credibility and concise facts were vital in a case where it was the word of an accuser against a defendant.

———

We soon discovered that during the media lockout Richter had been defending Pell on other horrific attacks alleged by the boy. On an evening three or four months after the cinema incident SG claimed he was told by a nun that he was going out on a trip. George Pell was at the front door. When SG saw Pell he 'bolted', but the sister grabbed him and marched him back.

According to the man's testimony, later relayed in court by Wallington when she handed down her decision on whether the cardinal would face trial, Pell 'grabbed his arm and threw him in the back of the car'. 'He was driven to a playground where he was anally raped on a slide, after which he was carried back to the car and returned to the home.'

The next time, SG wasn't sure how much later, Father Pell came to his dormitory in the middle of the night and took him to the chapel, where he was 'anally raped at the altar'. 'There was further bleeding,' Wallington said.

About two months after this, the man alleged the mother superior came to him in the recreation room of the home one evening and told him he was going out. This time there were two men at the door who he did not recognise. They allegedly grabbed him by the arms. 'One sat in the back seat of the car with him and the other sat in the driver's seat. George Pell was in the front passenger seat,' Wallington said, recounting SG's testimony. The boy claimed he was then taken to Mount Buninyong, an extinct volcano in western Victoria, where the three men took turns to anally rape him.

The disturbing image of the unthinkable and cruel incident, if true, was beyond comprehension. We would hear that about two months after the last rape SG was still bleeding from the anus. He was living with his foster mother and father on a farm near the orphanage and claimed to have shown his foster mother blood in the toilet from his injuries. The court heard she took him to her GP, who referred him to a specialist who, he claimed, examined his rectum.

However, when the foster mother gave evidence she said she was never shown any blood by the boy and never discovered the reason why SG was unwell. The specialist said he had no memory of the consultation and that after 40 years the medical records had been destroyed. He did agree he would probably remember a child with anal injuries causing bleeding.

The lack of evidence to back up the accuser's claims allowed Richter to argue strongly that it was 'impossible' Pell carried out the abuse.

This was supported by the evidence from the foster mother

and the doctor and the recollections staff who were present at the orphanage, who could not recall Pell ever being seen at the home, except for one official visit.

The defence team was gaining in confidence. At one point Pell tapped Richter's arm and whispered, 'Well done.' Richter was certainly earning his fee. He had surely made it very difficult for a future jury to be sure beyond reasonable doubt regarding this accuser at least.

———

Stepping in from stage left the next day would be a witness vitally important to the defence case who claimed that Pell could not have attacked two choirboys while he was Archbishop of Melbourne.

Monsignor Charles Portelli, the former seminarian who first met Pell when he was rector of Corpus Christi in Clayton and remained a close friend, had worked as master of ceremonies at St Patrick's Cathedral. He always accompanied Cardinal Pell, he said, during his time in his robes before and after Sunday mass services. When asked by Richter whether there was any chance of some 'errant choirboys' being in the priest's sacristy at the time the archbishop still had his vestments on, Portelli agreed it was impossible.

Describing the usual routine, Monsignor Portelli claimed he always waited for Cardinal Pell at the door of the cathedral, helped him undress out of his heavy robes, and then usually took him for a cup of tea or lunch in the kitchen. They would often leave together to attend an afternoon function.

But just as Pell's team seemed to be marking up another winning point, there would be another blow. The following day, the court heard that when Pell was newly installed as Archbishop of Melbourne he was considered to be a 'bully'. In particular, the choir felt the cardinal was a 'stickler' for discipline.

Under questioning from Richter, David Mayes, who had previously sung in the choir, quoted from his police statement: 'I have no love for the man. As I said earlier, he was a bully . . . I have a very distinct memory of one of the rehearsal spaces . . . he's was a very prominent figure and shouting at the choir,' he told the court.

Richter argued that Pell never went into the choir rehearsal rooms, either the previous one used by the choir or the new one when the Knox Centre next to the Cathedral was built. Mayes disagreed. 'I do recall Pell in some capacity coming into that older room,' he said.

With the absence of a jury in the committal, Richter clearly wasn't afraid of clashing forcefully with witnesses. Under cross-examination, the mother of former choirboy J started weeping after Richter suggested she had purposely added a further detail into her police statement that was harmful to Pell's defence. The mother rejected the accusation, saying she had only recently recalled the fact she had often waited for her son for long periods after mass in the car outside.

Richter asked the witness repeatedly if she realised the relevance of what she had changed in the statement.

'I do know what the relevance is—that if I was waiting there was time for things to occur,' she replied.

Richter's brutal run went on. In a heated exchange he accused journalist Louise Milligan of trying to 'poison the public's mind' with her book *Cardinal: The rise and fall of George Pell*. He also went so far as requesting for the magistrate herself to be disqualified and stood down, alleging that she was showing 'bias'. His request was ignored by an incredibly calm Wallington, who simply sighed and said, 'Your application is refused.'

His call came during cross-examination of Detective-Superintendent Paul Sheridan, head of the serious crime division, Crime Command, Victoria Police, who had travelled to Rome to interview Pell with Chris Reed. Sheridan revealed that in March 2013 Sano Task Force had set up a secret investigation, 'Operation Tethering', then led by Michael Dwyer, to try and establish allegations against Cardinal Pell when he was still Archbishop of Sydney. The operation was effectively dormant, the court heard, until March 2014 when a statement was taken from the man who accused Pell of inappropriate behaviour when he was a boy at Lake Boga. The operation then swung properly into action when Damian Dignan came forward in January 2015 with allegations about being groped by Pell at the Ballarat swimming pool in the 1970s. Dignan had also been abused by a teacher as child, the court heard.

'. . . Operation Tethering wasn't a "get Pell" operation, was it?' Richter asked.

Standing calmly in a dark suit in the witness box, the detective-superintendent did not deny the accusation. 'Operation Tethering, as I understand it, commenced as an intel probe around what offences the cardinal may have committed,' he said. '. . . I guess you could term it the way you did, but I wouldn't term it that way.'

Richter later questioned David Rae, a detective senior constable who worked on Sano Task Force, about the apparent failures of Victoria Police to carry out a proper investigation. The barrister suggested proper procedure was not followed in terms of interviewing potential witnesses, failing to seek Cardinal Pell's diaries, improper note taking and failing to look into the psychological history of the accusers. He argued that officers had also failed to ask 'the most obvious questions' in regard to allegations involving St Patrick's Cathedral.

But it was confirmed in court that day for the first time that Victoria Police had planned to arrest and question Pell after he had attended the royal commission hearing in Melbourne in November 2015, before ill health apparently kept him in Rome.

By the end of the explosive committal hearing in mid April, it was perhaps predictable that Richter argued passionately for the case to be dropped, saying a trial would be a 'waste of public time, money and effort'. He also argued the fact that Pell did not seek diplomatic immunity in the Vatican, and had answered all police questions willingly, helped show his innocence.

The credibility of complainants was always important, and in this case Richter suggested in his closing remarks that all the allegations were possibly the product of 'fantasy or the product of some mental problems that the complainant may or may not have . . . in order to punish the representative of the Catholic Church in this country for not stopping abuse by others of children', he claimed. The accusers were simply trying to 'destroy' the cardinal. 'What we say is, it ought to be difficult to destroy and lock up a citizen unless there has been a proper investigation that has produced sufficient evidence which is so persuasive as to allow for the destruction of such a person.'

A trial would be unfair to Pell, a man who has 'given distinguished service to his church', Richter argued. 'There is suffering to be undergone, not just by him, there is additional suffering to be undergone by people who have made complaints where there is no prospect of the complaints getting up, because they are wrong,' he said, dismissing the complaints as 'lies' made amid an unfair 'backdrop of innuendo'. The 'undertone' generated by evidence from the royal commission about Pell supporting Ridsdale during his court case 'generated feelings of hatred for the man as representing an organisation, and that hatred became greater and greater as he ascended in [that] organisation', the cardinal's barrister declared.

Following Richter's two-hour long submission, Gibson rejected key areas of the defence arguments and the 'attack' on the credibility of the complainants and the way the police operation was conducted by officers from the Sano Task Force. 'It does not fundamentally impact on the reliability of the complainants' evidence,' Gibson told the magistrate. The trajectory of this high-profile case now rested solely in her hands.

On the eve of Good Friday, the final day of the committal hearings, court artist Fay Plamka expertly captured Wallington's somewhat pained and weary expression as she looked down at the voluminous amount of paperwork in front of her at the bench. Her decision would take two weeks.

As the Vatican started preparing for Easter Sunday Holy Mass in Saint Peter's Square with up to 80,000 worshippers, George Pell was trapped on the other side of the world starting a long car journey back to the seminary in Sydney, where he would face a tense wait. Would he make a triumphant return to Rome in time for the northern hemisphere summer or face sitting in the dock for one of the most sensational trials in Australian history? Belinda's burden could not be greater.

Modest beginnings: Young George Pell with his sister Margaret, a future violinist, mother Margaret Lillian Burke and his father George Arthur Pell, a miner turned publican. (His younger brother David, born in 1951, is not pictured.) A keen footballer and academic, he later shocked his family when he declared he wanted to become a priest.

Going places: In 1987, after two years as rector of Corpus Christi College, Father George Pell, then aged 46, was named as a new assistant bishop for the Archdiocese of Melbourne to assist Archbishop Frank Little. Pell was considered a rising star among senior ranks of the Australian Catholic Church. (Simon Corden/Fairfax Media)

Friends in low places: George Pell never shook off questions and controversy over why he chose to accompany his former Ballarat housemate, paedophile priest Gerald Ridsdale, to his first court appearance regarding child sex offences on 15 August 1993. Pell later said he was not aware of the full extent of the accusations against Ridsdale and was supporting him purely out of duty in his role as a priest. (Geoff Ampt/Fairfax Media)

King of the castle: The new archbishop, George Pell, alongside the retiring archbishop, Frank Little, outside Melbourne's St Patrick's Cathedral on 18 July 1996. The cathedral and its staff, routines and inner workings would later be extensively examined and argued over during the legal case against Pell. (Sebastian Costanzo/Fairfax Media)

Cloaked in ambition: In his full vestments, a confident Cardinal George Pell, Archbishop of Sydney, walks onto the stage during the opening mass on 15 July 2008 in the lead up to World Youth Day. Despite facing the Southwell Inquiry six years earlier regarding allegations of child abuse at a beach camp in 1961, Pell's determination to reach the higher ranks of the church never waned. (Rick Rycroft/AP)

Power player: Pell with Pope Benedict XV in Sydney on World Youth Day 17 July 2008. Cast by the world's media as a new and recognisable senior figure in the global Church, within six years he would be working in the Vatican's inner sanctum as its treasurer. (Andrew Brownbill/AP)

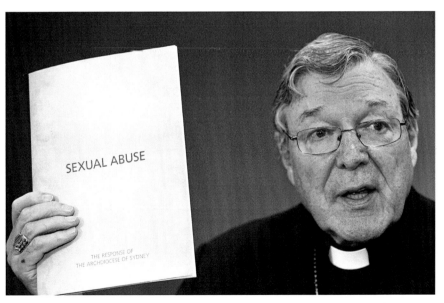

Uncomfortable spotlight: As Sydney's archbishop, Pell spoke defensively at a press conference shortly after the Royal Commission into Institutional Responses to Child Sexual Abuse was announced in November 2012. Statistics gathered by the enquiry later established 60 per cent of all survivors of abuse were from faith-based institutions. Of those, nearly two-thirds concerned the Catholic Church. It also found that 7 per cent of Australia's Catholic priests had allegedly abused children between 1950 and 2010. (Paul Miller/AAP)

Eyes wide shut: On 17 May 2013, Cardinal George Pell appeared in front of lawyers, advocates and members of the public to answer detailed questions from the Victorian parliament's Inquiry into the Handling of Child Abuse by Religious and other Non-government Organisations. Despite growing disquiet over what Pell may have seen, heard or ignored regarding abuse by Catholic clergy, he would still be invited to move to Rome the following year. (Arsineh Houspian/AAP)

Notes on a scandal: Pope Francis signs a cricket bat he received from Cardinal George Pell on 29 October 2015, the year before the allegations against his trusted advisor and treasurer were first made public. The unusual gift was aimed at boosting relations between the Catholic and Anglican churches. (*L'Osservatore Romano*/Pool/AP)

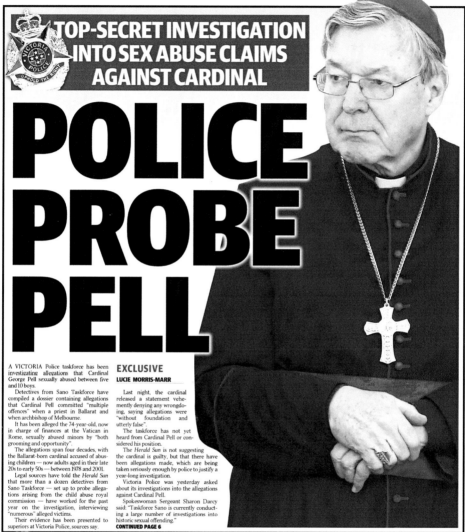

SATURDAY, FEBRUARY 20, 2016 $2.20 (inc GST)   HERALDSUN.COM.AU   WE'RE FOR VICTORIA

Herald Sun

TOP-SECRET INVESTIGATION INTO SEX ABUSE CLAIMS AGAINST CARDINAL

POLICE PROBE PELL

A VICTORIA Police taskforce has been investigating allegations that Cardinal George Pell sexually abused between five and 10 boys.

Detectives from Sano Taskforce have compiled a dossier containing allegations that Cardinal Pell committed "multiple offences" when a priest in Ballarat and when archbishop of Melbourne.

It has been alleged the 74-year-old, now in charge of finances at the Vatican in Rome, sexually abused minors by "both grooming and opportunity".

The allegations span four decades, with the Ballarat-born cardinal accused of abusing children — now adults aged in their late 20s to early 50s — between 1978 and 2001.

Legal sources have told the Herald Sun that more than a dozen detectives from Sano Taskforce — set up to probe allegations arising from the child abuse royal commission — have worked for the past year on the investigation, interviewing "numerous" alleged victims.

Their evidence has been presented to superiors at Victoria Police, sources say.

EXCLUSIVE
LUCIE MORRIS-MARR

Last night, the cardinal released a statement vehemently denying any wrongdoing, saying allegations were "without foundation and utterly false".

The taskforce has not yet heard from Cardinal Pell or considered his position.

The Herald Sun is not suggesting the cardinal is guilty, but that there have been allegations made, which are being taken seriously enough by police to justify a year-long investigation.

Victoria Police was yesterday asked about its investigations into the allegations against Cardinal Pell.

Spokeswoman Sergeant Sharon Darcy said: "Taskforce Sano is currently conducting a large number of investigations into historic sexual offending."

CONTINUED PAGE 6

Trouble ahead: The explosive front-page story broken by the author, Lucie Morris-Marr, for Melbourne's *Herald Sun* in February 2016. The story, which would be condemned by the cardinal and his right-wing media supporters, revealed how a secret police investigation in Victoria had resulted in a damning dossier of allegations, including abuse of choirboys at Melbourne's St Patrick's Cathedral and boys at a Ballarat swimming pool in the 1970s. (Newspix)

Testing times: Senior counsel Gail Furness stands in front of a screen in Sydney while Pell holds a bible at beginning his videolink testimony to the Royal Commission into Institutional Responses to Child Sexual Abuse from a hotel in Rome on 29 February 2016. Giving evidence over several days, he acknowledged the church had made 'enormous mistakes' regarding the handling of abuse complaints. (Jeremy Piper/Royal Commission/AP)

Hear no evil: When asked if it was common knowledge about Gerald Ridsdale's offending in the parish of Inglewood, Pell replied: 'It's a sad story and it wasn't of much interest to me.' (Courtesy Cathy Wilcox)

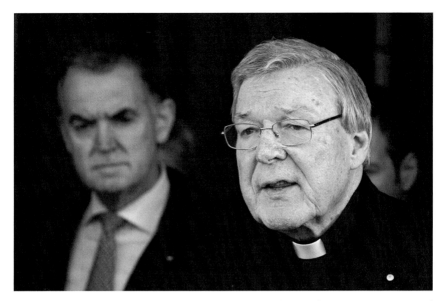

Homeland promises: The cardinal leaves the Quirinale Hotel in Rome on 3 March 2016 after giving evidence to the Royal Commission and meeting members of the Ballarat Survivors Group. He described the meeting as 'hard, honest and occasionally emotional', and gave his support to the idea of a research centre in Ballarat to help combat suicides and to 'enhance healing' for survivors. (Riccardo De Luca/AAP)

Shy support: A woman makes her faceless views known outside Melbourne Magistrates' Court during Pell's lengthy committal hearing in March 2018. Protestors and supporters would regularly wait outside the court for his arrival and departure. (Lucie Morris-Marr)

No exception: George Pell may have been a top-ranking cleric but he still had to endure strict security checks at Melbourne Magistrates' Court during his committal hearing just like anyone else entering the building. Arriving by car at least 45 minutes early, he would go to a small private interview room with his supporters and legal team for coffee and to prepare for the day ahead. Due to security concerns the cardinal was unable to leave the building for lunch. (Luis Ascui/AAP)

Key witness: George Pell's close friend Monsignor Charles Portelli, the former master of ceremonies at Melbourne's St Patrick's Cathedral, would be thoroughly cross-examined while giving evidence at the committal hearing, the mistrial and retrial. He would be later described by Pell's appeal barrister Bret Walker SC as a vital 'alibi' because he claimed to have always been by Pell's side after mass thus making an attack on the choirboys 'impossible'. (Lucie Morris-Marr)

No expense spared: The cardinal's legal team of leading criminal defence barristers Robert Richter and Ruth Shann leaving Melbourne Magistrates' Court during his committal hearing in March 2018. Despite a heavy workload, Shann had a baby between the committal hearing and the first trial in August 2018. Richter's fees alone were speculated to be $2000 per hour, paid out of a trust fund advertised in multiple Catholic publications. (Lucie Morris-Marr)

via Skype
Melbourne, Australia
5:17 PM

Melbourne, Australia

NEW DEVELOPMENTS
CARDINAL TO FACE TRIAL ON HISTORICAL SEX ABUSE CHARGES
Lucie Morris-Marr | Journalist

LIVE
CNN
Nikkei ▲ 40.16
CNN NEWSROOM

Global news: Reporting for CNN on 1 May 2018, the author explains how Pell would soon become the highest ranking senior Catholic ever to face trial for child sex offences. Magistrate Belinda Wallington's decision rang loudly through the Vatican and the Catholic Church globally.

Alleged crime scene: The juries for both the mistrial and retrial were taken to the priest's sacristy of St Patrick's Cathedral where Pell was accused of abusing two choirboys in 1996. The room would become a central issue in the case with the defence team arguing it was too busy and too public for Pell to have carried out the attacks without being noticed by cathedral staff. (County Court of Victoria/AAP)

The advocate: Chrissie Foster AM attended many days of Pell's mistrial and retrial. She realised during the case that she and other parents had had a combative meeting with the cardinal just days before he was alleged to have carried out a second indecent assault against a choirboy in the corridor of St Patrick's Cathedral in February 1997. (Lucie Morris-Marr)

Before the retrial: Ribbons continued to be tied to the fence around St Patrick's Cathedral in Ballarat. The Loud Fence movement, which began in Ballarat in 2015, has spread worldwide with members of the public tying ribbons to the fences of religious buildings as a show of support for survivors and victims of childhood sexual abuse. (Dylan Burns/Fairfax Media)

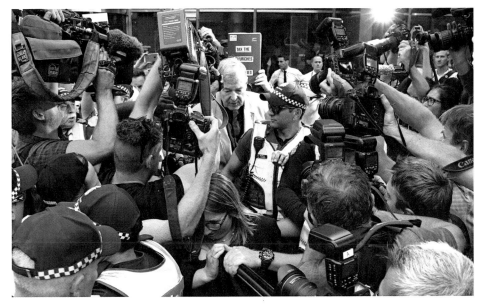

The secret's out: George Pell leaving the County Court in Melbourne on 26 February 2019 shortly after the planned 'Swimmers Trial' collapsed and the strict suppression order regarding the case was lifted. For the first time the shocking news that the cleric had been found guilty in December 2018 of abusing two choirboys when he was Archbishop of Melbourne could be reported. (David Crossing/AAP)

It's not over yet: Crown prosecutors Mark Gibson and Angela Ellis leave the County Court after Pell was remanded in custody on 27 February 2019. They would soon help in preparing the Crown's case against Pell's bid for freedom at his appeal hearing in June 2019. (Erik Anderson/AAP)

The Sydney Morning Herald

Wednesday, February 27, 2019   **$3.20** (inc GST)   **INDEPENDENT. ALWAYS.**   First published 1831   No. 56,591

TAX THE CHURCHES

CHARITIES

Police

GUILTY

| **Victims see justice in guilty verdict at last** NEWS PAGE 4 | **Nation's leaders shocked and disgusted** NEWS PAGE 9 | **He got a fairer trial than many victims** EDITORIAL PAGE 24 |

Cardina
George Pel
leaving the
court in
Melbourne
yesterday
Photo: Justin
McManus

---

sa Cunningham,
1 Cooper and Tony Wright

nal George Pell is expected to
led today after being found
of sexually abusing two
boys after Sunday Mass at St
ck's Cathedral in Melbourne
1990s.

jury reached its unanimous
ct in December but the media
prevented from reporting the
due to a suppression order
n place because Pell had a
er sex abuse trial pending.

THE PELL ROME INTERVIEW TAPES REVEALED

George Pell sat in the conference room of a hotel near Rome's airport on October 19, 2016, arms crossed, as he first heard the charges against him from Australian police.

When told he had found his

That trial, on charges of abusing boys in a Ballarat swimming pool in the 1970s, did not go ahead because of lack of admissible evidence, meaning the suppression or-

victims "poking around" in the sacristy of St Patrick's Cathedral, he responded: "It's an unfortunate term, poking around, but what do you do when you are poking around?" When the allegations were put to him in more detail, he

der could be lifted. Pell was found guilty of orally raping one choirboy and molesting another in the sacristy 22 years ago.

The cardinal was the archbishop

said: "In a sacristy after Mass? Completely false."

As other aspects of his crimes were detailed, he described them as "a load of garbage". He was charged eight months later.
FULL STORY PAGE 5

of Melbourne when he abused the two 13-year-old boys and was managing the Catholic Church's response to widespread child abuse by priests through the "Melbourne

Response", which he had design

Pell's lawyer, Robert Richt
QC, launched an appeal last w
but the cardinal is expected to
behind bars by day's end af
County Court Chief Judge Pe
Kidd earlier flagged that he wo
jail Pell when he returned to co
for his pre-sentence hearing.

The cardinal is likely to be s
tenced in the fortnight after
pre-sentence hearing. He is exp
ted to apply for bail today.

Each of the five charges of wh
Pell has been found guilty carrie
Continued Page 4

Last night of freedom: The front-page photograph in the *Sydney Morning Herald* captures the shattered and weary cardinal as he is escorted to a waiting car by police and his close friend Katrina Lee, executive advisor to the Archdiocese of Sydney, on 26 February 2019. Pell knew he would be taken into custody after a remand hearing the following day and be driven to the nearby Melbourne Assessment Prison. He would be held in segregation for his own safety and only be allowed to mix with prison staff. (Fairfax Media)

Hand of friendship: Powerful pubic figures and media supporters rallied around the cardinal after news of his guilty verdict was finally reported, sparking anger from survivors and advocates. Former prime ministers John Howard and Tony Abbott both made public remarks of support, with Howard being among ten people to give a character reference. (Courtesy Cathy Wilcox)

Words that stopped a nation: Chief Judge Peter Kidd delivered his powerful sentencing remarks on 13 March 2019 in a rare live broadcast. 'As I directed the jury who convicted you in this trial, you are not to be made a scapegoat for any failings or perceived failings of the Catholic Church . . .,' Kidd told the cardinal. 'I am not sitting in judgement of the Catholic religion or the Catholic Church— it is George Pell who falls to be sentenced.' The broadcast was a notable contrast to the cloak of secrecy that had dominated much of the legal case due to the strict suppression order.

Living history: Protesters, including members of Care Leavers Australasia Network, gather outside the County Court to listen to the live broadcast of Pell's sentencing to six years in prison (with a non-parole period of three years and eight months) for the alleged attacks on the two choirboys in St Patrick's Cathedral. (Andy Brownbill/AAP)

Fallen cardinal: In an extraordinary scene, the once powerful cleric is escorted to a waiting prison van in his clerical collar and wearing handcuffs after the second day of his appeal hearing at Melbourne's Supreme Court on 6 June 2019. He was taken back to Melbourne Assessment Prison where he was spending 23 hours a day in his cell. (Erik Anderson/AAP)

Chapter 8
The Cathedral Trial

Like much of the extraordinary narrative involving Pell during the preceding years, reporting on the decision over whether he would face trial was an unpredictable task. The court was packed with reporters, lawyers, survivors and members. Pell's loyal friend Monsignor Charles Portelli, considered an important witness in the Cathedral matter, had taken a seat but was asked to leave in case he was a witness in a future trial.

Belinda Wallington was at the bench. The court hung on to her every word. In the opening minutes of her hour-long decision, she confirmed the first six charges had been dropped. We'd previously heard that the accuser had been deemed 'medically unfit'.

The magistrate then went on to dismiss the eight charges regarding SG, the Ballarat orphan who made the allegations of being raped by Pell on multiple occasions. Wallington ruled that the 'inconsistencies' in his answers created a 'fundamental defect' in the evidence. Archived records from the boys' home along with a letter from his grandmother showed he left the home in January 1979, making abuse spanning 12 months in that time frame 'impossible'.

Wallington revealed, however, that during his testimony SG had insisted the records were wrong and he lived at the home throughout 1979, leaving an open-ended question over the allegations among the reporters in court.

It wasn't down to Wallington to declare Pell innocent of the charges she was striking out, of course. Her job was to decide if the evidence was of 'sufficient weight' to support a conviction.

With the initial and most serious charges being dropped, could this really mark the moment when this case screeched to a halt? It seemed Pell already had one foot on the steps of the plane taking him back to Rome. 'Heads up: I think the whole case might collapse,' I wrote in a group message to my key editors at CNN.

Pell sat emotionless in the front row with Katrina Lee and his artist niece Sarah Pell by his side. He must have been confident the whole legal ordeal was all over as the magistrate then went on to drop a further charge regarding one of the many men who'd claimed to have been abused at Eureka Pool in Ballarat in the 1970s.

It emerged the accuser, who was referred to as MB and who had come forward after watching his old friends Lyndon Monument and Damian Dignan make allegations of being abused at the same pool by Pell on ABC-TV's *7.30* in July 2016, didn't perform well during his closed court videolink testimony.

He demonstrated what was described as a 'cavalier attitude'. Whether it was nerves, stress or a change of heart, it was never explained.

'When cross examined MB had a poor memory not just of the events 40 years ago, which is to be expected, but also of two years ago when he gave his statement and even of his answers given shortly before in his evidence,' Wallington said. 'MB's lack of recall was often a non responsive way of avoiding answering the questions. When clarity was sought, he said variously, "Just whatever mate, whatever. I'll leave it up to you. Whatever you think works", and "no comment".'

The softly spoken Wallington then offered the plot twist that would race around the world in a breaking news alert: the cardinal would face trial after all. She was committing him on charges involving the other alleged sexual offending at the swimming pool in Ballarat in the 1970s. Even though the defence had argued that some of the accusers were not credible, as they had led lives blighted by criminal offending and mental health issues, the magistrate ruled there was enough evidence for the cardinal to stand trial. She then announced that Pell was also committed to stand trial on the alleged abuse of the choir boys in St Patrick's Cathedral. Regarding these allegations in particular, Wallington noted the evidence of the sole surviving accuser, as a matter of law, was 'capable' of a guilty finding.

Pell kept his composure. Just. He put his hand to his mouth, let out a small cough and quickly glanced around the court, knowing the decision would ring loudly through the Holy See and the Catholic community.

As the reporting pack was busy tweeting and emailing the news that the cardinal's fate would be decided by a jury after all, Wallington asked Pell to enter a plea. Remaining in his seat, he said in a loud, clear voice: 'Not guilty.' I was shocked. This was the first time we'd heard Pell's voice in the case so far.

A media barrister representing several outlets applied for the final number of charges Pell was now facing to be published. However, Wallington rejected the submission, saying suppression orders were not 'thrown around like confetti' and that ensuring a 'fair trial' had to be the priority.

As she left the bench, a group of advocates and survivors at the back of the courtroom clapped.

Pell descended the steps outside through a wall of cadet police officers making a safe exit for him. 'Three cheers for Mrs Wallington,' shouted advocate Julie Cameron, clutching her mother's small, tattered missal in her hands and waving it in the air.

There was something rather feudal and primitive about the spectacle of this powerful church leader being jeered and booed by angry onlookers less than a few kilometres from the cathedral where he once reigned as archbishop. It was hard to comprehend the legal case had now reached this remarkable point.

Pell's solicitors, Galbally & O'Bryan, quickly released a defiant statement reminding the public that Pell was denying the allegations. 'Cardinal George Pell has at all times fully co-operated with Victoria Police and always and steadfastly maintained his innocence,' the statement said.

'He has voluntarily returned to Australia to meet those accusations.

'He will defend the remaining charges.

'He would like to thank all of those who have supported him from both here in Australia and overseas during this exacting time and is grateful for their continued support and prayers.'

As I went live outside the court for CNN, broadcasting news of Wallington's decision to 200 countries, I was asked what the news meant for the Pope. 'Well, if the Pope thought he was having a bad week, then it just got a lot worse,' I replied.

The Pope had just hosted three victims of Chile's sexual-abuse scandal in Casa Santa Marta, his primary residence within Vatican City. The three men, Juan Carlos Cruz, James Hamilton and José Andrés Murillo, had been among the most vocal survivors of abuse by priests in Chile. They were outraged that the Pope had defended Juan Barros Madrid, the bishop who had witnessed and covered up abuse by the Reverend Fernando Karadima. But a damning 2300-page report had prompted Francis to swiftly issue an apology admitting errors in how sexual-abuse cases had been handled in Chile.[1]

Just as the Pope was making amends with the Chilean survivors and attempting to manage the outrage, he now had to face a scandal reaching right to the heart of the Holy See.

The Vatican could easily have turned its back on Pell at this point but instead it issued a short, non-committal statement saying the Holy See had 'taken note' of the decision to commit Pell to trial. 'Last year, the Holy Father granted Cardinal Pell a leave of absence so he could defend himself from the accusations,' the Vatican statement said. 'The leave of absence is still in place.'

The news would get even worse for Pope Francis, however. The next morning, after Wallington's shock decision made global news, a short hearing was held over the road from the magistrates' court at the County Court of Victoria. It was there we learned there would not be one trial as we had thought. There would be two.

———

Before a hearing presided over by fast-talking Judge Susan Pullen, both the defence and prosecution had agreed that two trials were needed to split the allegations. The first matter, the 'Swimmers Trial', would involve the allegations Pell groped boys at the Ballarat swimming pool in the 1970s, and the second, the 'Cathedral Trial', that he attacked two choirboys two decades later.

Richter told the court he hoped the trials would be 'expedited'. 'That's for various reasons . . . my client is 76 years old, and number two, everyone needs to get on with their lives,' he said, clearly worn down by the drawn-out legal case.

As a reminder of the huge costs at stake, Pullen asked if there were any funding problems for the Vatican treasurer, to which Richter replied: 'No problem with funding.'

But how was Pell paying his fees? Even prosecution sources had been quietly speculating, 'Who is paying for all this?' So the Crown didn't seem to know where the rivers of gold were flowing from either.

There were now two trials to fund and all the preparation involved, which would easily cost in the region of millions of Australian dollars. Was the Vatican helping? Or was Pell being supported by wealthy friends? Surely Pell did not have the personal savings to afford the bills coming his way. It was time to lift the veil of secrecy over how the Vatican's treasurer was funding his defence.

———

The question of where Pell was receiving funding had intrigued me for some time. I started investigating.

Across the globe, from cities in the United States to the tiny Victorian hamlet of Hall's Gap, I discovered discreet advertisements had been placed in newsletters, parish notices and Catholic publications. They all started with identical wording: 'A number of people are wanting to know where they can contribute to assist Cardinal George Pell with his defence costs.' They included bank account details of a special trust fund overseen by a law firm and an email contact address.

I was able to confirm, for the first time, that the Vatican was not contributing to Pell's legal bill but leaving one of the most senior figures in the Holy See to seek funds from supporters right down to pensioners in rural parishes. Anyone could contribute to this fund, yet the names of the donors would not be released. It was not known how much had been donated so far from supporters around the world, other than that it was sufficient for Pell to engage his top legal team. Was this a way for the church to quietly fund Pell's defence without a public backlash?

The Archdiocese of Sydney's Katrina Lee insisted that wasn't the case, telling me in a statement that 'many people asked how they could assist with his legal costs' and the fund was not 'set up by or overseen' by the Archdiocese of Sydney. 'The Arch-diocese has not contributed to this fund nor has the Vatican provided any funding,' she said. This was the first time that the cardinal's representatives had confirmed that the Vatican was not contributing to the legal fight.

Ferdinand Zito & Associates Pty Ltd, the lawyer firm in charge of the defence fund, operated out of a small office in the Melbourne suburb of Ivanhoe East. When asked about the fund, a spokeswoman said the firm was unable to assist as anything relating to the cardinal comes within the 'ambit of legal profes-sional privilege'.

Ingrid Irwin, who has represented many victims of clergy abuse, told me at the time that she had received a payment from the fund after she submitted an invoice for supplying documents to Pell's legal team as demanded by a court order. In her view, the Catholic Church did not want to be seen to be paying directly for the cardinal's legal fight. 'He's more than fortunate to have a trust fund paying but who's really paying and who's organising the distribution of the adverts for the fund?' she asked. 'The big issue remains that the accusers have no right to a lawyer no matter how rich they are and he's entitled to the best money can buy.'

Unfortunately, as a result of the exclusives I'd written for *The National* and *The New Daily* and subsequently posted on Twitter, on 7 May 2018 a very damaged and broken survivor of clergy abuse graffitied St Paul's church in Coburg, a suburb of Melbourne. (He also damaged the law firm in Ivanhoe East.) The following morning school children were greeted with his offensive remarks about Pell. I made my feelings clear on Twitter about the incident, condemning the graffiti attack.

The man responsible for the incident sent me a message admitting the crime and apologising for the damage. 'I'm sorry, I was just really angry,' he said, leaving me no choice but to inform Victoria Police.

The man's painful past was later taken into account by the magistrate. He was ordered to pay a fine and given a twelve-month good-behaviour bond in what would turn out to be one of many legal sideshows related to Pell's case.

As the graffiti was cleaned away, we would soon be introduced to a new leading character in this long-running saga, Judge Peter Kidd.

———

As Chief Judge of the Victorian County Court, Kidd, then aged 52, would be presiding over the Pell trials. Adelaide born, his CV is extensive, wide-ranging and exemplary.

In the late 1990s Kidd appeared in the high-profile prosecution of Leslie Camilleri, who is now serving a life sentence for the horrific abduction, rape and murder of Bega teenagers Lauren Margaret Barry and Nichole Emma Collins. Then, after studying a Masters of Law in Switzerland, Kidd was appointed an International Prosecutor of the War Crimes Chamber of the State Court of Bosnia Herzegovina. As lead counsel, he prosecuted the commander and guard shift-leaders from the Omarska and Keraterm concentration camps, in what must have been harrowing and disturbing work. Returning to Victoria, he became a senior crown prosecutor, leading the case against drug kingpin Tony Mokbel before eventually being appointed as chief judge. His working style is characterised by 'intense concentration and single-mindedness'.[2] Those characteristics were soon evident as we witnessed him operate in the pre-trial hearings on the Pell case.

One of Judge Kidd's early tasks was to deal with a comprehensive suppression-order request put forward by the Crown prosecutors; they said a media blackout on reporting the first trial, which had now been decided would be the Cathedral Trial, was necessary to 'prevent a real and substantial risk of prejudice to the proper administration of justice'. We learned that the prosecutors wanted the order to apply to publications in all Australian states and territories, including any website or broadcast format accessible within Australia.

The reason for the Crown's concern was to ensure the jury of the second trial would not be influenced by knowledge of the details of the first. This would mean that we would be able to report the second trial as it unfolded, but only when that jury reached a verdict would we be able to publish the details of the entire case.

A number of media outlets and commentators were dismayed by the prospect of being prevented from reporting on the high-profile case as it unfolded. While they didn't dispute the ban of publication or broadcast within Victoria, a media barrister representing outlets including the ABC and Channel Seven argued that the media in the rest of the country should be able to report the matter.

Kidd disagreed, saying that the geographical borders would

not prevent Victorians reading about the case on social media or picking up newspapers when they were travelling interstate. 'The daily coverage would be at saturation point,' he said.

As debate raged inside and outside the courtroom it was argued that Victoria was too heavy handed with the use of suppression orders, especially considering at the heart of the court system was the principle of open justice.

Very soon, however, almost nothing on the cardinal would be published for quite some time. Kidd had finally ruled that there could be no reporting on the matter until the start of the second trial. We weren't even allowed to say an order had been made; the media was in lockdown.

The order was made for good reason, but it didn't make it any easier to accept that this globally important case had just been plunged into darkness and silence. It was as if we were being forced to take part in a secret conspiracy. This didn't sit well amid the backdrop of the extensive abuse cover ups that the church had carried out in the past. Journalism is about sharing information with the public as fast as possible, not witnessing it and letting it sit in notebooks and laptops for months on end.

The Pell pack would still take its seats in court, but we had to accept our new truth: we wouldn't be blindfolded like Lady Justice—but we would be gagged.

———

While the Pell case fell into a deep well of secrecy, another in the NSW city of Newcastle was causing headlines around the world: that of one of the cardinal's close clerical allies, the Archbishop of Adelaide, Philip Wilson. In an overflowing courtroom, I watched from a seat in the jury box with other reporters as he became the highest-ranking Catholic official to be sentenced for covering up child sexual abuse.

It was alleged that in 1976 Peter Creigh, a 15-year-old altar boy, went to Wilson on two occasions and told him that four years earlier he had been abused by a fellow priest, James Fletcher. When police investigated other allegations against Fletcher many years later Wilson was accused of failing to disclose what he knew.

The 67-year-old Wilson, who had strongly denied any wrongdoing and would immediately launch an appeal, showed no reaction as Magistrate Robert Stone told him that subject to assessment, he would spend six months of the sentence in home detention, with the further six months spent on parole. For health reasons he was spared jail.

'It's basically a holiday,' one female member of the public in court said loudly, as the hearing concluded.

Like Ballarat, the Maitland–Newcastle Catholic Diocese had become known as one of the epicentres of abuse in Australia. A number of paedophile priests had been jailed during two decades of scandal and a dedicated strike force laid more than 170 abuse charges. Joanne McCarthy, one of the *Newcastle Herald*'s senior reporters, had spent years doggedly documenting paedophile clergy cases and the paper had launched a hard-hitting campaign, dubbed 'Shine the Light', urging the government to announce a royal commission into the abuse scandal.

In August 2012, Prime Minister Julia Gillard was in New-castle on the day of the funeral of local man John Pirona, who had taken his life unable to cope with the dreadful memories of abuse by a priest in 1979.[3] In her book, *My Story*, she wrote of the significance of speaking to *Newcastle Herald* staff on the day of the service and understanding the depth of the child sexual-abuse crisis in the area. On 12 November 2012 she announced the royal commission into child sexual abuse. 'I think it got into my head, and got into my language because of the campaign,' Ms Gillard told the paper later.

As fast as the Wilson headlines started disappearing, another scandal emerged for Pope Francis, this time about a well-known American cardinal. Theodore McCarrick, the former Arch-bishop of Washington, DC, became the first cardinal in living memory to lose his red hat and title after church officials in the United States said allegations that he sexually abused a sixteen-year-old boy almost 50 years ago were credible.

The American Broadcasting Company subsequently reported further incidents of abuse that started when another accuser was eleven and continued for two more decades. Several other men have also come forward to allege that McCarrick had forced them to have sex with him at a beach house in New Jersey in the past, when they were adult seminarians studying for a life in the priesthood.

The Wilson and McCarrick scandals did not exactly make a good few weeks in the papacy of Pope Francis; and now one of his closest advisers was about to face a criminal prosecution in his homeland. It made me wonder if there ever was a time when, apart from leading worship, the Pope wasn't spending every moment trouble-shooting the child-abuse matter. It literally appeared to be a full-time job.

———

It was a long time in the coming, and not without drama, but on 15 August 2018 George Pell became the most senior Catholic figure in history to stand trial. The Cathedral Trial—or 'The Trial of the Century' as heralded by *The Australian*—had finally started nearly fourteen months after the cardinal was first charged for multiple allegations of child sexual abuse. Yet as I stood with the large media pack gathered at the security queue to get into the County Court of Victoria, it was odd to realise that locals walking past were unaware of the significance of the moment.

We watched the initial phase of the jury selection unfold on video screens as Judge Kidd, in the jury room downstairs, spoke to the group of over 200 members of the public who had been called for jury duty. As he carefully informed them that he was selecting for the Pell case, I saw one man in the crowd lift his hand to cover his mouth in shock. Others shared surprised glances.

Bridie Kelly, Judge Kidd's young senior associate, stood in court 3.3, the main courtroom, and read out five charges so Pell could enter a plea for each one as the potential jurors watched via videolink in the special holding room. They mostly stared ahead, poker-faced.

The charges involved two counts of sexual penetration of two choirboys, R and J, in the sacristy of St Patrick's Cathedral, and three counts of indecent assault on J—two in the sacristy and one in the corridor a month later. It was the first time the exact charges had been read out in open court.

Wearing a black suit, white clerical collar, gold ring and metal-rimmed glasses, Pell firmly said 'not guilty' in a loud and dramatic voice in response to the charges. His humiliation, played out in front of the group of everyday Victorians, could not have been greater.

After a series of questions about any conflicts of interest, bias and their ability to commit five weeks of their lives to the case, the potential jury group was reduced by half. Clearly a number of them had taken the chance to run as fast as they could from this difficult trial. The media was then asked to leave the main courtroom to allow the remaining potential jurors to come in for the ballot that would decide who would take up a seat in the jury box.

As the court rules dictate, each juror walked from their seat and did a loop of the courtroom, walking past Pell standing in the dock. As is his legal right, the lofty cleric inspected them for approval and checked that he didn't know them.

Fourteen jurors—eight women and six men—took their seat instead of the normal twelve. On important cases such as this, judges like to have spare jury members. Nobody enjoys a retrial.

As the jury was being selected in Melbourne, news was breaking regarding two new clergy-abuse scandals, one in the United States and the other in Chile. In the United States a shocking grand jury report said that internal documents from six Catholic dioceses in Pennsylvania showed that more than

300 'predator priests' had been credibly accused of sexually abusing more than 1000 child victims. 'We believe that the real number of children whose records were lost or who were afraid ever to come forward is in the thousands,' the grand jury report said.[4]

'Priests were raping little boys and girls, and the men of God who were responsible for them not only did nothing; they hid it all. For decades. Monsignors, auxiliary bishops, bishops, arch-bishops, cardinals have mostly been protected; many, including some named in this report, have been promoted.'

The grand jury described the church's methods as 'a playbook for concealing the truth' after FBI agents identified a series of practices in diocese files.

In Chile, authorities had raided the headquarters of the Catholic Church's Episcopal Conference as part of a widespread investigation into child sexual abuse committed by members of the Marist Brothers. It emerged that the country's equivalent of the FBI was looking into more than 35 accusations of abuse committed against students at schools run by the order.

As news outlets reported on these scandals, Judge Kidd in Melbourne was instructing the jury in detail about its role, warning it sternly not to read anything on the internet about Pell, or to speak to friends or relatives about the case. 'Don't get on Google,' Kidd instructed, 'don't do any searching.' He made it clear that even if they were aware of sexual-abuse scandals involving the Catholic Church it was critical that Pell was judged only by the charges brought against him and on the evidence presented in the trial. 'This trial must not make George Pell a scapegoat for the failures or the conduct of the Catholic Church more generally,' he told them.

It was clear this exemplary judge would oversee this case with utmost diligence. But not everything would be in his control. Before the end of the day, a juror asked to be excused from duty. The length of the trial would mean too much time away from a family member.

'I'm concerned that we're down to thirteen and we haven't started,' Judge Kidd sighed.

———

If the jury was wondering exactly what the case was all about, they soon discovered in fine detail when, on day two, the prosecution and defence gave their opening addresses.

Crown prosecutor Mark Gibson outlined in disturbing detail the allegations of what had unfolded in the first incident in the cathedral late in 1996. It would make disturbing listening. Pell, emotionless, largely looked down and wrote notes as the allegations were described.

At this point, there wasn't an exact date when the alleged incident took place. Only later would it be concluded that the first incident could have occurred on either Saturday 15 or Saturday 22 December, a few months after Pell had been installed as the Archbishop of Melbourne in August 1996. He had led Sunday Solemn Mass in the cathedral, as usual, the jury was told. After mass two choir boys (R and J), both thirteen-year-old scholarship students at the prestigious St Kevin's College, broke away from the choir procession as the 40-strong group rounded the side of the cathedral, and took the opportunity to have 'some fun'. 'After all, the role of the chorister within St Patrick's Cathederal Church Choir carried with it much responsibility and there was an expectation by the adults for the performance to meet the hight standard . . . and so you'll hear following mass and singing duties they decided to have some fun,' Gibson said.

Instead of going to another room in a back building where they were supposed to get changed, or take part in a rehearsal or CD recording, they returned to the cathedral through a side entrance. Roaming the corridors, they went into the priest's sacristy, where they were said to have discovered sacramental wine after opening a wooden bi-fold door covering an unlocked cupboard. As they were each having a 'few swigs' from the bottle of what they described as red wine, Pell entered the room and caught them in the act, Gibson explained. 'You'll hear the boys were told by Cardinal Pell they were in a lot of trouble,' he said.

Pell was still wearing his formal church robes and started to move something underneath his robes. He then approached both boys. 'He proceeded to manoeuvre his robes so to expose his penis to the boys,' Gibson said. Pell then stepped forward and 'grabbed' the first boy, R, by the back of his head with one hand, and then placed his head and face in close proximity to his genital region. The archbishop was standing, and the boy was crouched in front of him, Gibson said. As R squirmed and flailed around, J was said to have seen his face and he was terrified.

According to J, at one point R said, 'Can't you let us go? We didn't do anything.' We would learn in a later court hearing that R had also called out 'help' and 'no' during the attack.

A short time after the assault on R, Gibson explained, Pell then allegedly sexually penetrated J, pushing his erect penis into J's mouth. J later remembered how he was pushed down crouching or kneeling and that he was 'freaking out' for the two minutes he was being assaulted. At a later hearing we would learn that both boys were crying and sobbing. They did call out, but it was 'at a level of whimpering and whispering'. Pell was alleged to have told them to be quiet.

But the horrifying attack, as alleged by the Crown, didn't end there. Gibson told the jury how Pell was also accused of instructing J to take off his pants before touching the boy's penis with his hands, while masturbating his own penis at the same time. When Pell stopped after another minute or two the boys fled the sacristy, rejoining the choir in the rehearsal room.

J was driven home, Gibson said, but didn't say anything at the time about what had happened.

After another Sunday Solemn Mass around a month later, Gibson said, Pell allegedly pushed J up against a wall in a corridor and squeezed his genitals before letting go and walking off. They were both in their robes at the time.

Gibson conceded that much of the evidence from staff at the cathedral and the other choirboys may contradict the evidence of the accuser—but it was up to the jury to decide the facts. 'The last thing the prosecution would want is for a determination to be made in this case by you based on a bias or prejudice against the accused man, Cardinal Pell, because of his position within the Catholic Church,' Gibson said, looking at the jury box.

In his opening address, Pell's counsel Robert Richter told the jury that it was an 'extraordinary case' in the 'sense that Cardinal Pell is the most senior cleric ever to have been charged with actually committing sexual offences'. The core of the defence case, Richter said, rested on the fact 'the incidents did not happen, period', suggesting the allegations were the result of 'fantasies or lies'. 'It is possible, ladies and gentlemen,' he said with his unique flourish, 'that a meteor will come out of space and strike this court while we are sitting here . . . it's possible physically. The physics make it possible. But do you plan your life around that basis? No.'

The jury should find Pell not guilty. 'So, probabilities, ladies and gentlemen. If it's not probable it's not likely to be the truth . . . the simplest explanation is likely to be the truth . . . in the end we will be arguing to you that the simplest answer to this is it did not happen. It most probably could not have happened and if it was even a possibility that it happened you will be finding him not guilty.'

Following the opening arguments, the jury was taken by bus for a private viewing of the cathedral. When I'd visited some weeks before, I'd noticed Pell's legacy in gold lettering on polished wooden plaques stating the dates of his term as archbishop. Largely, I was taken by the sheer size and scale of the building; it was uncomfortable and almost impossible to imagine the evil that may have played out within such beautiful, historic confines.

Not only was the media not allowed to visit the cathedral with the jury, by day three we would be barred from hearing the videolink testimony of the surviving choirboy, J, despite an official request to be allowed into court to hear the testimony on public-interest grounds. Just because Pell was the third most senior Catholic in the world, we were told, didn't mean the rules would change.

The surviving accuser would soon find himself being grilled by the ferocious Richter. A few months earlier Carole Stingel, who was cross-examined by Richter as part of her civil rape case against then Aboriginal leader Geoff Clark, described how the experience had felt like a 'public vivisection'. 'You start to feel like you're at fault, I was in a mess after that, I should have gone to hospital,' she said in an interview with Tim Elliot for *Good Weekend*.

Her words didn't bode well for the surviving choirboy, but the Pell pack wouldn't have the chance to witness the spectacle for ourselves. We packed up our notebooks and laptops for the evidence to begin without us.

———

When we did return four days later a problem was emerging. A female juror had asked for the rest of the day off as a family member was sick and she couldn't concentrate. As usual, Judge Kidd took guidance from both Richter and Gibson on the matter, deciding in the end to let the whole jury go for the day, hoping the juror would be back the following day.

The next morning, we learned the juror had called to say she was 'unable' to return. Had something in the testimony from the choirboy disturbed her? Or did she feel she had some kind of bias either for or against Pell? Or was the family member really very unwell? We will never know, but she was discharged by Kidd, who was clearly unhappy with the second disruption to the jury line-up.

There were only twelve jurors left. If one more juror dropped out, there would have to be a retrial. But the wheels were in motion and the case had to proceed with a long list of all-male witnesses, including former cathedral staff and ex-choirboys.

The following days and weeks would be a constant battle between the Crown and defence teams over several key points. It had already been established in the committal that there were no witnesses who actually saw or heard the sacristy or corridor attack at the time, or who were even told of it by the boys, so the defence was on a mission to prove the incidents simply could not have occurred or unfolded in the way they had been described. It was trying to destroy the very foundation of the allegations and bring doubt and uncertainty to everything the Crown had put forward as the context to the attacks.

The Crown probed witnesses in order to prove that Pell had indeed found himself robed and alone sometimes after mass and that he wasn't always accompanied by another priest. It also tried to prove that it would be possible for two choirboys to dash away from the procession unnoticed, and that the sacristy could be unattended long enough for the attack to have taken place.

The questioning from both sides would be probing and detailed. As during the committal, it was clear that Pell was very much engaged and involved in helping the defence case: making notes on an A4 notepad, clarifying points with Richter during the breaks and taking questions that may help their examination of witnesses.

The first witness in the box after the trial was reopened was John Mallinson, 84, the organist and choir director at St Patrick's Cathedral at the time of the allegations. He was responsible for the training of the choir, having first started at the cathedral in 1976.

Mallinson told how he would play the organ between four to nine minutes after the Sunday 11 a.m. mass had ended. Many parents stayed to listen to the music and talk while waiting for their sons from the choir to return. 'Sometimes people would come and speak to me after,' he said, giving the impression of a somewhat hectic and busy scene following the service.

Richter suggested there was an awareness of the problem of clerical abuse. Mallinson agreed, saying great care was taken to monitor all the choirboys.

It was suggested that after Mallinson himself finally returned to one of the back rooms to disrobe somebody would have had to wait in the cathedral if one or two children were missing and hadn't returned their robes.

'That did not happen, as far as you can recall [having to wait for missing children]?' Richter asked.

'As far as I can recall,' he replied.

'That's all we can ask for,' Richter said.

Richter later suggested that while Mallinson was playing the organ after the mass, he would have spotted two young choristers in their red-and-white robes walking back into the cathedral after the procession out of the main doors.

'No, I wouldn't see them,' explaining that he would have been unable to see over the console of the organ.

Later the same day, Dr Geoffrey Cox, the academic and musician who had been assistant organist and choirmaster at St Patrick's, remarked that Mallinson 'didn't have eyes in the back of his head' when it came to keeping the children in order. He told how one of the adult singers, former Christian Brother turned school teacher Peter Finnigan, was made a designated choir marshal. 'I was often busy playing . . . and it was very useful to have one other adult who had the sort of disciplinary responsibility, I suppose.'

When the choir procession left the cathedral after mass the boys walked out two by two but soon it would become more 'chaotic' as they dispersed. On their return to the choir room they 'had to be watched like hawks', Cox told the court.

A clear picture of the culture of the choir and how it was run was emerging. There was clearly an aim of enforcing strict discipline but in practical terms it was akin to looking after a group of young wild horses easily excited by the breezy prospect of freedom.

In continuing his evidence, Cox explained how the 'work sacristy' was a 'messy' room where the florist would arrange flowers, candles would be trimmed, while the clergy would get robed next door in the priest's sacristy. Pell was also using the priest's sacristy to change as the archbishop's sacristy further along the corridor was being renovated.

When Peter Finnigan took to the stand, he explained how he became responsible for the pastoral care of the boys a few years after joining the choir in 1990. 'It was essentially the role of what a school teacher would do in managing large groups of children . . . any problems arose, any squabbles between the boys; sort that out.'

After a break over the weekend, on Monday 27 August, the judge called the missing grandmother juror who had discharged herself in order to care for her granddaughter. 'You have caused an inconvenience, you need to know that,' Kidd told the woman sternly. 'We do the best that we can but at the end of the day, as the judge of the court, it's a decision that I make as to whether a juror leaves the jury and that was not your decision to make last week.'

After the woman apologised and was allowed to leave, Finnigan returned to the witness box. He was shown the long and elaborate robes Pell wore at the cathedral to confirm they were indeed the former archbishop's. A court usher was asked to pick up the 'alb'—Pell's long, white liturgical vestment, which was worn as an inner garment.

Richter stated that the alb was a gown that has 'no splits down the side', conceding however that the one being shown in the courtroom had a pocket. He then held up the long ornate outer garment, known as the chasuble, made of creamy gold with a deep purple neckline, gold-stitched swirls and pea-sized buttons.

Finnigan explained how Pell would wear the robes and a mitre, a ceremonial hat, and carry a crosier, a stylised staff used by high-ranking Catholic clergy during the processions at mass.

Had there ever been an occasion when Finnigan was conscious of the archbishop being fully robed and alone in the sacristy, Richter asked.

'Not that I ever saw,' he said.

'It would be something that would stick in your memory, if it'd happened?'

'Not necessarily,' Finnigan admitted.

After Finnigan had finally finished giving evidence, he walked out of the box and suddenly stopped by Pell, who was seated in the dock nodding. 'Thank you,' the cardinal mouthed. Finnigan moved forward and shook Pell's hand.

This was extraordinary; he was a prosecution witness.

Judge Kidd said later, without the jury present, that he understood the issues concerned with 'church hierarchy' made it difficult for some witnesses not to acknowledge the cardinal but said 'it's best that it just not be done'.

'I'm just telling you that's what happened,' Judge Kidd said, 'the jury saw it.' Witnesses would now no longer be allowed to walk directly past Pell.

Would this behaviour have already made the jury think the witness had done his former archbishop a favourable turn in the box? We would never know. But it was clear Judge Kidd was going to be keeping a close eye on the conduct of the witnesses. And rightly so. Fairness in all trials had to prevail.

———

Soon, another important witness would take to the witness stand. Max Potter, the sacristan of St Patrick's Cathedral between 1963 and 2001, had effectively been the caretaker of the building. He also prepared the liturgies and would busily bring items such as chalices and missals to the priest's sacristy from the sanctuary after mass.

Potter confirmed that the sacramental wine was kept in a

special 'safe' in the form of a large walk-in vault in the priest's sacristy. It was labelled 'Sacramental Altar Wine', sometimes in green and sometimes in gold. But most importantly for the defence, he was adamant the wine itself was *white*, and not red as the accuser had described.

The reason for the change from red to white, he explained, was that in 1996 Monsignor William McCarthy, the dean of the cathedral at the time, was only able to drink white wine for health reasons. McCarthy would not be giving evidence confirming this fact; the police had deemed old age had left him too senile to be a reliable witness.

Potter explained how either he or Father Charles Portelli, the master of ceremonies, would walk with Pell after mass had finished because the sacristies were closed.

'He [Pell] didn't have a key to enter those rooms . . . it was our responsibility to open those rooms for him to go in,' Potter claimed.

Asked by Gibson whether it was possible Pell was ever alone after mass, Potter replied that it was 'very rare'. 'Because we knew he'd be walking back into the cathedral . . . we'd then greet him and open up the doors for him.'

Asked what exactly he meant by 'rare' Potter answered: 'I'm working on something in the sanctuary, moving something to the back of the sacristies.'

This point was vital. Was there then the occasional window when Pell was alone in the sacristy, as the accuser had told the court?

Under concise questioning from Richter, Potter then seemed to contradict himself by saying Pell, then referred to as 'His

Grace' due to his status of archbishop, was never alone in his robes and that either he or Father Portelli, or both, would accompany the cardinal after mass and help him change.

'So, once Archbishop Pell went back into the sacristy area, first of all, he would be accompanied, would he not?' Richter asked.

'Yes, yes,' Potter said.

'And sometimes there were other priests who were co-celebrants?'

'Who were assisting, yes.'

'So one of you would let him in [to the priest's sacristy] and one of you would go in with him?' Richter asked.

'Yes, to help him disrobe, his mitre, pass things he was wearing, his vestments, to be hung up in cupboards. And then, if he had his coat, to hand back his coat.'

The only time Pell was left unattended in the sacristy was when someone wished to speak to him alone.

'So you stood by the door somewhere?'

'Yes,' Potter said.

'Is that the kind of occasion, you say, that he might have been alone whilst robed?' Richter asked.

'It would be a rare—on a rare occasion. I use the word rare deliberately because we made sure that he disrobed, most times, quickly.'

It must have been very confusing for the jury trying to search for the truth in the face of often conflicting evidence. As the trial went on, however, the twelve men and women would have a great deal more to unravel.

Chapter 9
War cry from Rome

As the Cathedral Trial inched forward, the windowless court-room felt like a parallel universe, suspended as it was in a curious time warp. Life outside, at least, went on as normal. A winter wind was still whipping along William Street, but one at least that now held the promise of a warm spring.

When Pell walked out of the glass doors of the court building at the end of the day, crossed the concrete concourse and went down the steps to his waiting white car escorted by Katrina Lee, a legal clerk and two police officers guiding the way, a lone news photographer might be waiting to take his picture. The odd passer-by would do a double take perhaps, or briefly pause to try and make sense of the spectacle, but largely the cardinal would go unnoticed.

On the other side of the world, however, things were far less low key. The Pope was making a tumultuous official visit to

Ireland, amid protests and confrontations over the country's dark history of clergy sexual abuse.

At an official event, Katherine Zappone, the Minister for Children and Youth Affairs, raised with the Pope the shameful case of a Catholic mother-and-baby home in Tuam, County Galway, where nearly 800 children had mysteriously died between 1921 and 1961. Run by Bon Secours Sisters, an order of nuns, the home was one of ten institutions in Ireland to which approximately 35,000 unmarried pregnant women are thought to have been sent.[1] They were places of desolation and torment.

'Pope Francis, I am responsible for the Tuam mother-and-baby home,' Zappone said in Italian. 'Children's remains were found in a sewage system there—it's important and I will write to you in detail.' The Pope thanked her and, according to Zappone, clearly recognised the name Tuam. Later, it was announced that a full forensic examination of the site would be undertaken, including excavation and recovery of juvenile remains and the use of technology to locate potential burials.

As a papal mass got underway under stormy skies in Dublin, at least 1000 people gathered in Tuam to remember victims of church scandals, while in Phoenix Park Francis asked the hundreds of thousands of faithful for forgiveness. But for those gathered in protest a few miles away down the River Liffey in the Garden of Remembrance, the Pontiff's words failed to address their anger over a long list of church-related abuses in Ireland. Protestors carried placards reading: 'Roman Catholic Church abuse has harmed all society', 'Full disclosure and jail the perpetrators'.

WAR CRY FROM ROME

Other signs remembered Dublin's Magdalen Laundries scandal. Between 1922 and 1996, the Irish government sent thousands of women and girls to harsh and physically demanding Catholic-run workhouses, where they toiled for no pay. The scandal was first brought to public consciousness when more than 130 unmarked graves were discovered at a former convent and laundry in 1993.

As the Pontiff tried to appease the anger in Ireland with prayer and apology, in Melbourne a senior Australian clergyman was taking centre stage in the Pell case.

———

Mark Coleridge, the current Archbishop of Brisbane, who lived in the presbytery at St Patrick's Cathedral as a bishop from 1995 to 1997, was giving evidence. An outspoken supporter of Pell and Philip Wilson, he seemed to have suggested in an interview in Rome just two months before Pell's trial began that both the cardinal and the archbishop had been subject to unfair witch hunts. 'In some ways, whatever the integrity of the legal process, which has to be respected obviously, but it's hard to resist the sense that there's some element of determination to make heads roll,' he told the US-based Catholic website *Crux Now*.[2] 'I wouldn't want to push that too far, but it's hard to resist that in the case of Archbishop Wilson and Cardinal Pell.'

Wearing a black suit and clerical collar, during his court testimony via videolink from Brisbane Coleridge was unable to offer a great deal of insight into the inner workings of the cathedral and the choir during the Sunday 11 a.m. mass as he never usually attended, often being needed in other parishes or churches. However, he did speak confidently and clearly of Pell as if preaching a sermon to the jury. At one point, Justice Kidd had to stop him from continuing to recount how others had reported Pell's exemplary running of mass.

But this did not stop Coleridge, who continued to praise Pell. Of the Melbourne Response he said: 'My memory of it was that the need was acute . . . the failure to deal with these matters was quite dramatic . . . and there was considerable pressure from the Victorian Government. Archbishop Pell responded very quickly and vigorously.'

A witness who had already been mentioned a great deal in the proceedings so far would soon make his way through the doors of the court. On Wednesday 28 August Monsignor Charles Portelli, the former master of ceremonies at St Patrick's who had lived in the cathedral, was back after his committal appearance earlier in the year. It was clear the defence believed he would be its trump card. Everything was at stake as the jury watched the bearded, dark-haired priest take his place in the witness stand.

———

During his time at St Patrick's, the court heard, Portelli had resided in a presbytery in the cathedral grounds with between three and six other priests. Now aged 59 and the parish priest at Keilor Downs, a suburb north-west of Melbourne, Portelli told the court that Pell would have said Sunday mass in the cathedral for the first time in late November 1996, a few months after being installed officially as archbishop. In the months in between, Sunday mass was temporarily taken in the hall within what was known as the Cardinal Knox Centre, adjoining the cathedral itself.

Portelli personally led either the 8 a.m. or 9.30 a.m. mass, and then prepared for the 11 a.m. main Sunday Solemn Mass over which Pell presided, assisting him before, during and afterwards approximately 150 times over a period of five years. He would smoke as he waited for Pell (who was 'never later or early, just on time') to arrive by car before mass.

Much was made by Mark Gibson for the prosecution that Portelli was a very heavy smoker and that he was unable to smoke inside the cathedral. Clearly keen to establish if there were any moments at all when Portelli may have left Pell's side, Gibson asked if the priest would take the chance to smoke directly after mass.

'Not at all,' Portelli said.

'Or at some stage after mass?'

'No,' he replied.

Describing a somewhat hectic scene before and after mass, Portelli told how up to seven buses would drop off as many as 350 Chinese and Taiwanese tourists to walk in and around the building. 'The reason it was the first stop is that it was free,' Portelli told the court. '. . . they were usually on a package tour.'

Gibson asked if Pell ever dropped into the choir rehearsal room to speak to the boys. 'Not at all,' Portelli said.

But the most important questions from Gibson focused on what happened directly after mass had ended.

Portelli explained if Pell decided to stay on the front steps of the cathedral to talk to people that it always took around ten minutes—unless he was in a hurry. 'If he [Pell] decided to stay at the front door I would wait with him . . . nearly always he stayed,' Portelli told the court. 'The only time he would move quickly is if we had another appointment which we were running late for . . . it was his custom to stay, but if we were in a hurry we would keep moving but that was very rare.'

With his clipped grey hair and spectacles, Gibson was softly spoken and straight-forward compared to the somewhat theatrical and volatile Richter. Measured and calm, he asked Portelli about what usually happened after he and Pell left the steps following mass.

'I would walk with him to the sacristy, I would help him remove his vestments. Max [Max Potter] would be there to put the vestments away and then we'd walk through the door, using a pass card, back down into the Cathedral presbytery,' Portelli replied.

When asked whether he would leave the room to give privacy to Pell when re-robing, he said, 'I was always there,' adding that there would also be people coming and going from the room.

Portelli explained how the vestments, which were removed, were all external to the clothes underneath and, vitally, that he could not recall occasions when he didn't accompany Pell. 'It is possible, but most unlikely as I would also remove what I was wearing . . . so that had to come off and go somewhere,' he said.

Portelli, who claimed he never once saw Pell discipline a choirboy, also claimed that he never left the archbishop's side after mass had finished. 'Since it was the beginning of our getting used to this system, I would have made sure I was always there,' he insisted from the dock.

Pressed by Gibson on whether he would always accompany Pell to the sacristy, he remained firm. 'As I said, since they were the first times that he was using the cathedral as archbishop, I would have made it my business to make sure I was with him at all times.'

As to whether the robes worn by Pell could be lifted up, he seemed to concede it was possible as they 'had to be put on'. Questioned further about the garments Pell wore, he added, 'The alb was a loose garment but the way it's worn is tight—and still to this day, we do it—it's stretched fairly tightly across the front to stop your foot catching it when you're climbing stairs, so therefore the cincture, the rope, holds it in place.'

Under cross-examination by Richter, who was keen to prove that Pell's robes were too restricting and heavy for him to carry out the attack on the boys, Portelli claimed it was even impossible for Pell to go to the toilet in the robes.

In a highly unusual spectacle, Portelli then stood up to demonstrate how the rope-made cincture was tied around the alb, the long white cotton dress-style undergarment that had already been shown to the court. Knotting the cincture five times around his suit, he showed how it would have kept Pell's undergarment in place so he didn't trip when walking up stairs. He also demonstrated how the stole, the long creamy, gold silk scarf, was worn by Pell during mass. It certainly illuminated how difficult it may have been to take off the robes in a hurry.

In later evidence, Portelli, who agreed he was a bit of a 'stickler for detail', emphasised again how during Pell's first months after being installed as the archbishop neither he nor other cathedral staff would ever have left him alone; they were working hard for things to run smoothly.

'Was there a protocol that there should always be someone with the archbishop?' Richter asked.

'Yes,' replied Portelli.

'Was it a matter of ceremony that the archbishop should never be left alone when vested? Putting aside calls of nature?'

It wasn't an explicit rule, Portelli explained. 'It's not written in the books that it's absolutely required, but the protocol has always been so.'

Richter asked why the witness recalled the first two occasions Pell led Sunday solemn mass in 1996 in particular. 'Precisely because they were the first two and we were still working out, basically working out the bugs,' Portelli replied, 'trying to work out how this was going to work properly and smoothly.'

Portelli said there would have been more reason for Pell to stand on the steps after mass to greet parishioners when he first led the services. 'People were willing, were wanting, to greet him because many of them were meeting him for the first time.'

Startling the prosecutors, as this had not been revealed before, Portelli also told the court that Pell wore a microphone. 'I would help him with the removal of the chasuble [exterior robe] and then with the removal of the microphone.'

Gibson objected. Justice Kidd instructed Portelli and the jury to briefly leave the courtroom. In a tense moment Gibson asked the judge to make Portelli's evidence regarding the microphone an 'unfavourable' witness because he had not mentioned in his four police statements that Pell had worn it during mass. If Gibson managed to strike at the credibility of this key witness, it would be a huge blow to the defence. But Kidd quickly dismissed Gibson's objection.

It was impossible to know whether the jury had taken kindly to the witnesses, like Portelli, who had had a long-standing working relationship or friendship with the cardinal. Many diligently took notes during the long days of testimony. Only later would their faces reveal any signs of emotion.

For now, only two weeks into the case, they needed as much strength and resolve as they could muster before they entered the jury room to decide Pell's fate. But first, there were more members of a large group of men in their early thirties who had some further memories to share. Memories about their days at St Kevin's singing in the cathedral choir alongside the two boys at the centre of this tangled legal maze.

———

They had contrasting, fragmented adult lives yet their common bond from the past would reunite them in their shared role in the courtroom. One by one they took to the stand.

There was a violin repairer and an air-traffic controller, an IT engineer and a marketing manager. They had different lives, but there was a common thread: as young boys, none of them particularly enjoyed donning their long red robes and singing for Sunday mass. Unimpressed by the spectacle, they couldn't wait for mass to be over, despite the pride of their families. They would have rather been playing football, watching movies or relaxing at home with their families. Many were only at St Kevin's because they were on a choir scholarship. It was a matter of sing up or ship out.

David Dearing, the first former choirboy to give evidence, was asked by Richter's junior counsel Ruth Shann about the importance of the choirboys lining up properly, hanging up robes or giving back music after mass. 'Any deviation from that would be called out?' she queried.

'Definitely,' he replied, prompting the court to laugh. Even Pell broke into a smile sitting awkwardly in the dock, as he always did, in the fold-up chair, his knees higher than his hips.

Dearing, whose father Rodney was also in the choir at the same time, described Monsignor Portelli as operating as a kind of 'bodyguard' for Pell, shadowing him at the cathedral. 'I just remember him always being with him,' he said.

The choirboys remembered the new, rather intimidating archbishop roaming the corridors and leading the processional. He'd brought in a stricter regime that meant they weren't allowed to wear their running shoes to the cathedral. The towering new boss was running the joint his way.

'It's the case, isn't it, that when you were on display for the public, for tourists, for anyone around, the expectation was that you were the face of the cathedral?' Shann asked Dearing.

'Absolutely,' he replied.

David Mayes was thirteen when he was in the choir. He explained to Gibson that the choirboys were restless after mass.

'. . . we just wanted to leave and get back home,' he said. '. . . maybe getting irritable, looking around, talking, maybe walking back and talking to the person behind you.'

While none of the men could recall R or J ever going missing, and they certainly didn't see or hear of the alleged attacks, many agreed that once mass was over there was a sense that it was time to rush off and relax. 'Some kids had it down to an art,' Dearing revealed. 'They'd be in, unrobe, ready, gone in seconds.'

As Stuart Ford, a graphic designer, explained to the court the boys felt a sense of relief once mass was over. 'We could enjoy the rest of our Sunday—you know, now our job for the day was done.' The choir was supervised, with the more senior members of the choir behind the younger ones. 'So they would see what was going on in front of them,' he said.

As for Pell's interaction with the choir, Ford said he would sometimes congratulate them after mass. 'It would be some-thing on the rare occasion in passing, like "you've sung well today" . . . and if we ever crossed paths and it was very rare, he might say "thank you, boys".'

Many of the choirboys recalled Pell greeting parishioners on the steps of the cathedral as they left the main entrance in the procession, the group of 40 boys and adult men walking two by two. Back in the choir room, based in the Knox Centre adjoin-ing the cathedral, they would change before heading out to meet their parents, who were waiting at the entrance or in cars in surrounding streets.

When they were each asked if they'd ever seen Pell alone and wearing robes after mass, this is where the evidence may have become difficult for the jury for there was a mixed response to the question. Some said categorically that they couldn't recall Pell being alone at all and that he was always accompanied by Portelli; others said they could barely remember, while yet others remembered Pell being alone on occasion. It was a 1990s mix tape of memories.

At times the defence team clashed quite dramatically with the choirboys as it tried to dispute facts and weaken the Crown's case.

Aidan Quinn, 32, a primary-school teacher, stood up for himself against the high-flying Shann when she suggested that his memory 'was not particularly clear'. 'I'd say it's not better or worse than anyone else's,' he replied firmly. '. . . I wouldn't say my memory isn't good.'

Later, the testimony of straight-talking Melbourne builder Andrew La Greca would prove to be the tipping point for Richter's wrath. La Greca had told the jury that once out of public view the choir wouldn't just relax, it would 'start going crazy', giving weight to the notion that two choirboys could well have nipped off for some mischief in the back corridors. The choristers would become noisy and the orderly line would start to break up. 'People would start speaking amongst themselves, of course people would move out of line too . . . you could see there was a bit of mischievousness.'

Richter angrily suggested in his cross-examination that La Greca had 'changed quite a few things' since giving evidence at the committal earlier in the year and that he may have discussed his testimony with others in the meantime.

La Greca was adamant that wasn't the case. He had not discussed his evidence with anyone.

The following day, as his evidence continued, La Greca recalled that Pell would sometimes actually still be in his robes when he saw him heading to the presbytery after mass had ended. Richter was livid. 'You're joking, you're making this up,' he shouted as Pell sat quietly in the dock. When Richter began questioning the witness about the role of the choir marshal Peter Finnigan, his temper flared again. 'Just answer my question,' he demanded.

Judge Kidd was not impressed, briefly halting the trial and asking the jury and the witness to leave.

He then spoke firmly to the barrister. 'I know you have a job to do but I'm not going to tolerate shouting like that . . . I'm not going to tell you off in front of the jury.'

'I'm grateful for that,' Richter said quietly.

Calling for a twenty-minute break, Judge Kidd added, 'Thus far, I must say counsel have behaved impeccably during this trial . . . so let's not see it go off the rails now.'

As Richter strolled out and greeted Pell, he didn't seem even slightly rattled by the admonishment. It was all in a well-paid few hours work for this highly experienced silk; dressing downs from judges are part of the job. What the jury was making of Richter shouting at witnesses though was another matter.

Detective Chris Reed from Sano Task Force wasn't quite as calm. 'The witness is going to kill me,' he was overheard saying.[3]

Following the break Richter, noticeably softer and calmer in tone, asked La Greca if the authority of the adults in charge was respected by the choir.

'That was respected,' he replied.

If anyone broke from a regular pattern there would be discipline, Richter suggested. The witness disagreed, however. It wasn't 'military discipline', he said. For the staff it was 'kind of hard to keep an eye on everyone'.

'It may not have been military, like . . . march, march, march,' Richter replied, dramatically stamping his feet on the thin dark carpet of the courtroom, in what appeared to be another mini judicial tantrum.

For La Greca, the experience in the witness box was intimidating. 'It was especially difficult being questioned by Richter,' he said.[4] 'I felt like he was taking my words out of context. It made me question what I said and what I thought, he made me doubt what I knew.'

He knew both the choirboys who were supposed to have been attacked by Pell. He remembered that the once happy and vibrant R seemed to change profoundly around that time. 'He became quiet and withdrawn, he would question authority. I put it down to adolescence at the time.'

R, considered by the choir staff and teachers at school as a troublemaker, would soon leave the choir and St Kevin's. He would slide into heroin abuse. As we'd heard at the committal, he'd been introduced to the drug by a friend at the exclusive school and died of an overdose in 2014.

'In life there is something that sets us on that path,' La Greca said. 'Some of us are strong enough to fight it, others are not . . . something would have had to put him on to that path.'

———

As the former choirboys were concluding their evidence in Melbourne yet another fire was burning at the feet of Pope Francis. This time it would be a matter that involved a call for his own resignation.

A former Vatican ambassador to the United States had told the media he had informed the Pope about allegations of sexual abuse against Cardinal Theodore McCarrick five years previously. Archbishop Carlo Maria Vigano called on the Pontiff to resign for one key reason—his failure to act. 'Pope Francis must be the first to set a good example to cardinals and bishops who covered up McCarrick's abuses and resign along with all of them,' Vigano said in a statement. 'He knew from at least June 23, 2013 that McCarrick was a serial predator, although he knew that he was a corrupt man, he covered him until the bitter end.'

These were damning words from a well-respected figure, but the Pope would not pass comment. CNN reported that on his flight back to Italy from Ireland he said, 'I will not say a single word about this', although he added that after some time passes, 'I may speak.'

In Melbourne, I was deciding whether or not to speak during a rather uncomfortable moment at court. Returning from a lunch break, I was briefly trapped with Pell in the small corridor leading to the main doors of the courtroom. There was something of an awkward silence between the two of us, then I held open the door for the cardinal, who seemed genuinely touched. 'Thank you so much,' he said.

There was so much I could have said or asked, but I decided it was best to stay silent. However, the chance interaction did get me thinking. Pell would normally have been followed by a guard or assisted by a legal clerk, but here he was, briefly alone. For a few minutes the usual busy routine of the building and people around him were out of place.

Pell himself would never take to the witness stand. We were never told why, but I always thought it would have been an opportunity for the defence to present Pell's human face to the jury, rather than him remaining the brooding, black-suited giant of the church sitting in the dock.

Nonetheless, the jury would soon see a vitally important response from the cardinal. On the afternoon of 3 September 2018 his explosive recorded police interview with detectives Chris Reed and Peter Sheridan was played to the court nearly two years after it was recorded in October 2016. This was the first time we would see Pell's reactions to the precise allegations against him.

The lights in the courtroom were dimmed and we were transported to a small room at an airport hotel in Rome. Pell, seated next to a dark-haired lawyer, looked fresher and younger than he did in court, but he was wearing the same black suit and glasses; his uniform for the past 50 years.

Reed started the interview by asking Pell's name.

'My name is George Pell and I live at Number 1, Piazza Della Citta Leonina in Rome,' he said, looking confidently at the two Australian policemen across the table.

Reed explained the interview was regarding allegations of indecent offences involving children under sixteen. 'Anything you say or do may be given in evidence,' Reed told Pell. 'Do you understand that?'

'I do,' Pell said. He then read the prepared statement he had told officers he wished to make. He began by pointing out that he had volunteered to take part in the interview with police.

'As I understand, allegations made against me going back decades are made in vague and imprecisely defined circumstances and time frames,' he continued, complaining it was impossible to demonstrate his innocence unless he was shown all the evidence.

'I have to rely on the law and my conscience which say that I'm innocent,' he said. 'And I have to rely on the integrity of investigators not setting out to make a case but actually searching for the truth. Despite requests which would have enabled me to gather evidence refuting these allegations, I haven't been shown statements which my accusers have made.'

He said he had been told the allegations were regarding St Patrick's Cathedral in 1996 and was deeply shocked by what he had heard. 'From what I've been told, the allegations involve vile and disgusting conduct contrary to everything I hold dear and contrary to the explicit teachings of the church which I have spent my life representing.'

He referenced how he had been responsible for creating the Melbourne Response in 1996. 'I was the first person in the western world to create a church structure to recognise, compensate and help to heal the wounds inflicted by sexual abuse of children at the hands of some in the Catholic Church.'

The cardinal said he intended to answer all the questions asked. 'In return, after having had the opportunity of considering who makes the allegations and what they actually say,

I expect to be able put together a list of people who should be interviewed, if they've not already been spoken to, and who may be in the best position to demonstrate the falsity of the accusations, so that before any decision is made whether to proceed with the allegations, a proper assessment might fairly be made about where the truth resides.'

The allegations were 'products of fantasy', he said. 'I'm told that they relate to two choirboys in '96 when I, as Archbishop of Melbourne, was in the process of actually reformulating the church's approach to allegations of child sexual abuse.'

Pell explained that he hadn't lived at the cathedral but in the Melbourne suburb of Kew, and that when he was at the cathedral to take mass he was accompanied by church officials and had nothing to do with the choir. 'I didn't know any choirboys in 1996,' he said. 'I was never present at choir practice and was never in the company of choirboys before, during or after choir practice.'

The most rudimentary interview of former staff and choirboys would confirm the allegations were 'fundamentally improbable and most certainly false', he claimed. 'I would earnestly hope that this is done before any decision is made whether to lay charges because immeasurable damage will be done to me and to the church by the mere laying of charges, which on proper examination will later be found to be untrue.'

One of the officers then said they would ask a number of questions, starting with some about St Patrick's Cathedral.

'I've heard of that place,' Pell quipped dryly. Reed responded with a slight chuckle.

The tone of the interview then became serious. Reed named the former choirboys who were at the centre of the allegations, saying they were students at St Kevin's College at the time of the alleged assaults.

The police then asked Pell about his routine when taking mass and the layout of the cathedral.

Pell described how he had his personal 'archbishop's sacristy' at the back of the cathedral where he could change. 'There was an archbishop's sacristy and we were separated from the hoi polloi. The bishops came in, if there happened to be a bishop [he] would vest with me. Priests vested next door [in the priest's sacristy].'

Reed then said they would go into the specifics of the allegations. 'I hope you do,' Pell said dryly.

Reed explained it was alleged that after catching the boys drinking sacred wine, Pell prevented them from leaving the room and moved his robes to one side, exposing his penis.

'Oh, stop it,' Pell said. 'What a load of absolute, disgraceful rubbish. Completely false. Madness. All sorts of people used to come to the sacristy to speak to the priest. The sacristans were around, the altar servers were around. They should have been on their way to change their vestments.'

Reed told the cardinal he was then accused of grabbing one of the boys and forcing his head down onto his penis.

'In the sacristy after mass?' Pell asked incredulously. 'Completely false.'

Reed then said Pell was accused of doing the same to the other boy.

'Completely false,' the cardinal repeated.

'You don't have to comment at this stage, I can continue on,' Reed explained.

'Please do,' Pell replied.

'The boys were terrified at this stage and it's been described that you were holding one boy before stopping. It's been alleged that you've then said, "take off your pants", and you've stepped up to him, knelt down and started to fondle his penis and masturbate yourself at the same time.'

Appearing angered, Pell said slowly and firmly: 'This is in the sacristy at the cathedral after Sunday mass? Well, need I say any more? What a load of garbage and falsehood and deranged falsehood. My master of ceremonies will be able to say that he was always with me after the ceremonies until we went back to the carpark or back to the presbytery. The sacristan was around, the altar servers were around, people were coming and going. They [the two boys] couldn't have dallied too long in the sacristy because the choirmaster would have been keen to get them dressed and get away.'

Pell said John Mallinson (the choir director) would tell the officers that he had nothing to do with the choir. 'He thought I wasn't interested,' Pell added.

Reed moved on to the further allegation, involving Pell pinning J to a wall and grabbing the boy's genitals. Reed explained that this was said to have taken place about a month later after mass as J was making his way back to the choir changing rooms.

'That's good for me because it makes it even more fantastically impossible,' Pell said.

Getting angrier, the cardinal said the allegation was again 'completely false' because he was out the front of the cathedral. 'I never came back with the kids.'

Asked if he had written his opening statement himself, Pell said he had written the first draft, with guidance from legal counsel.

He was then invited to comment on the allegations and the officers' questions. 'I was always accompanied by the master of ceremonies,' Pell said. 'There would be incense, solemn music, it was a big operation. 'After mass they [the choir] would line up outside. I came out at the end of the procession. I would go out the main door and stay there.'

The choirboys would go to their de-robing room and the choirmaster would make sure they had all gone home. In the meantime, the sacristy was a 'hive of activity'. 'You could scarcely imagine a place that was more unlikely to be committing paedophilia crimes than the sacristy of the cathedral after mass,' Pell said.

As the interview drew to a close, Pell commented to the two detectives that they had 'important jobs' to do even if it was 'most unpleasant'. 'You've treated me with courtesy, and I appreciate it,' he said.

'We appreciate the way you've conducted yourself here as well today, thank you,' Reed said, but he warned Pell that he may be charged with the crimes that had been discussed.

'Whatever you say or do may be recorded and given in evidence. Do you understand that?'

'Yes, I do,' Pell replied.

Asked if he wanted to say anything in answer to any possible charge, Pell said: 'I'm certainly not guilty. I believe on many, many details I've been able to prove that the charges are false, and I believe that with more work and information we'll be able to give even further information to enhance the strength of those denials.'

Asked if he wished to make any further statement, Pell said: 'No, except that I am not guilty as charged.'

This extraordinary war cry from Rome was a strong contribution to the defence case—Pell had been unwavering and confident in his denials. The police hadn't asked many questions nor had the questions been as detailed as expected; the interview was under 45 minutes long.

With Pell's future and reputation at stake, this was a case where the finest detail was argued over and where proving facts that may bring doubt to the credibility of the accuser was of the utmost importance to Pell's team. The defence may have lost some skin with the unsavoury shouting match with La Greca, but it had now gained some valuable ground.

———

The day after Pell's police interview was shown to the court, an elderly man appeared by videolink from Sydney. John Lawrence May, 89, would prove another win for Robert Richter. He had made the altar wine at a South Australian winery and confirmed evidence from the caretaker that the wine supplied to the cathedral in 1996 was white. Even though the bottle was made of 'French green' glass it would have 'definitely' been obvious that it was white wine and not red.

This was an important point because the Crown stated in its opening address the accuser had said that he and the other boy were drinking stolen red wine before being caught by Pell. Lawrence's testimony would possibly prove critical for the defence.

Later the same day, Geoffrey Ian Connor, 62, a former altar server, gave evidence that he had kept a diary in which he had recorded exactly the dates Pell took mass in 1996 and 1997. This finally established that there were only two Sunday mass dates in 1996—15 and 22 December—when Pell could have carried out the first attack and that the second attack, in the corridor, could have taken place on a Sunday the following February.

Connor, who helped clear things away after he disrobed following mass, said the priest's sacristy had to be unlocked after mass either by the sacristan, Max Potter, or another person who had the key.

'And would there be a constant thoroughfare then between cathedral and sacristy as things were being brought in and taken out?' Richter asked.

'Yes,' Connor replied, briefly touching his white beard.

Connor's testimony meant that if the boys did indeed go into the priests' sacristy and drink the altar wine, the room would have been opened by priests or altar servers who in theory would then be busy ferrying items back into the room.

Was there a time when the room would really be empty of other people long enough for Pell to carry out the high-risk brazen attack, an attack supposedly lasting up to six minutes? It would be the sliver of doubt that Richter would seize on and run with during his closing address.

Detective Chris Reed gave evidence and was questioned about whether the two victims had told any close relatives about the alleged abuse. He confirmed neither of the boys had told their parents about what happened, even R who, years before he died, was asked directly by his mother if he had ever suffered any abuse while singing in the choir. Another hit for the Crown, and a gain for the defence.

The cardinal certainly seemed relatively relaxed at this point in the proceedings, perhaps confident his expensive legal team would win the case with ease and he would be back in his apartment in Rome well before Christmas.

As Pell left the courtroom for the day, he was asked by a close friend and supporter, Anne Lastman, if the West Coast Eagles might win their forthcoming game against his former club Richmond. 'Oh God no,' he replied, smiling, clearly still loyal to his old team. When asked how he was bearing up, he turned casually and smiled, saying, 'I'm good, thanks.'

Lastman, a grief counsellor and mother of four who first met the cardinal at a conference in 1986 in Melbourne, attended many days of the trial, flying in especially from her home in Perth. She explained later that she'd kept a close friendship with the 'loyal and kind' cardinal for over 30 years, even meeting him in Rome when she visited the city.[5]

'He was surprised to see me in court the first time,' she recalled. 'He was sat in the dock right behind me and said, "why aren't you in Perth?"'

'When I said I wanted to be in court to see him and support him he looked very touched and said, "thank you". I thought he was very dignified in court under great pressure, hearing so many lies said about him.'

Whether it was 'lies' or not, the case moved forward. The day after Lastman spoke to the cardinal about the football match his legal team confirmed that it would not be calling any defence witnesses and would rely on the Crown's case alone. As the judge had told the jury at the start of the trial, it was up to the prosecution to prove Pell's guilt. He didn't have to prove anything.

The defence could not attempt, as it had done in the committal hearing, to suggest Victoria Police had acted maliciously or without integrity in terms of its investigation into Pell. 'I don't think that's fair in those circumstances,' Kidd said.

The judge also ruled the defence could not tell the jury the surviving accuser had sought counselling in the past and had suffered from depression in his twenties. The team had already failed in a subpoena bid to get the notes from the counselling sessions. Even suggesting mental-health problems invited 'speculation that there was something wrong with the accuser', the judge said. This decision wasn't good news for the defence, with its case based as it was on the argument that the accuser was lying about the attacks.

Kidd then announced that he had created a file to present to the jury to help its deliberations. He described it as a 'road-map' of key issues and key parts of witness evidence. Everything that was being presented to the jury was vital.

Richter seemed a little taken aback by this unusual development, but quickly complimented the judge on his hard work. Both legal teams would be given time to examine this file. Counsel needed to be sure there would be no taking sides from the judge himself, even unwittingly.

We would soon learn that the first charge against Pell had been reduced from orally penetrating R to committing an indecent act with a child. It emerged that the surviving accuser had been unable to say for certain that he had seen Pell force himself onto his friend, but he claimed he could see the boy's head being forced up and down.

'He said before you that he simply assumed that there had been oral penetration. And at law, I have decided that isn't enough,' Kidd explained to the jury.

It was an important change. If found guilty Pell would face less jail time as a result of the lesser charge.

The court braced for the penultimate scene in this extraordinary case; the closing addresses. It was time to take a breath and charge up laptops for the battle of the barristers—Gibson vs Richter.

Chapter 10
Play it again, Kidd

Closing submissions are vital in any trial, the last chance for both sides to summarise the evidence, passionately and forcibly where necessary. The addresses need to be memorable enough to be remembered by the jurors during their deliberations. With the high-profile nature of this case, the pressure on both Mark Gibson and Robert Richter was enormous. It was thought Richter would shine in this moment, simply through his flair for colourful rhetoric and his forceful personality.

But first it was Gibson's turn. With junior crown counsel Angela Ellis seated by his side, he rose to his feet in his black silk robe. Measured and precise, he didn't seek to create a fanfare. He began by suggesting that the jury should be 'confident' in believing the testimony they had heard from the surviving accuser in the early stages of the trial.

'You got an insight into his background, into his family's background, his personality . . . what it meant to him and his

family to be at a prestigious school,' he said. '. . . most importantly, you got to spend some time observing him . . . two
days . . . under pressure, being cross-examined and probed
extensively by an experienced member of counsel, Mr Richter.'

Gibson asked what overall impression the accuser had left
with the jurors. 'Ask yourselves: did he strike you as an honest
witness, an accurate historian as to what had happened to
him? . . . Alternatively did he come across as being a dishonest
witness, a witness who was gilding the lily, exaggerating and
embellishing at every opportunity he had, making things up,
plugging holes, putting a positive spin on things for his advantage, recounting peripheral matters that you wouldn't expect a
person to recall?'

The accuser's answers and evidence were not of someone who
had indulged in a 'fantasy or in fantasies'. 'He was simply someone
telling the truth and telling it how it was,' the barrister said.

He urged the jury to be confident in delivering a guilty verdict
'beyond all reasonable doubt'. 'The answer, we submit, not only
lies in the powerful and persuasive evidence of J but also in J's
evidence fitting with the overall evidence of the witnesses,' he
argued.

Explaining why the accuser hadn't made a complaint at the
time of the alleged first attack or told his parents, Gibson used
J's own words: 'It felt like an anomaly, so foreign and I was in
shock, I just didn't tell them. I was proud to be at that school . . .
my parents were going through a divorce at that time . . . I was
worried about anything that could jeopardise my schooling.'

Dismissing the attack on J's credibility just because he said the wine he'd drunk in the sacristy was sweet red wine and not white wine, Gibson argued a thirteen-year-old boy is not an experienced drinker. 'We were excited, feeling mischievous,' Gibson said, quoting the accuser. 'We found the bottle and we opened it and started having a few swigs out of it.'

He also revealed the accuser had explained in his evidence that he didn't 'understand' what had happened to him until later and had placed it in the 'dark recesses' of his mind until he reported it to police in 2015. 'I was young and didn't really know what had happened to me, or if it was normal,' Gibson quoted J as saying.

The barrister suggested when the jury looked at all the evidence, the 'fluidity and dynamics' showed there was nothing that detracted from the accuser's evidence. 'You should have no reservations in accepting his truthfulness and his reliability,' he said.

Due to the long passage of time an 'array' of memories had been presented during the evidence, which was understandable, Gibson said. 'So, ask yourself, do you think that choristers would really remember two choristers nicking off if nothing significant happened?' he asked.

'What we do know is there is a body of evidence showing the integrity of the procession was not always maintained as it was intended to be . . . it didn't pan out that way.'

As had been the case throughout the entire trial, there would be another unpredictable twist in this final stretch; on the second day of Gibson's summing up Richter sent a note to the court saying he could not attend that morning due to a 'family emergency'. Gibson appeared unhappy to be continuing his closing remarks without Richter being present, but Pell had instructed his counsel to proceed without the lead barrister.

Gibson stood back and faced the jury again, offering more of the accuser's testimony to explain why he had been afraid to tell his school or his parents about what had unfolded at the cathedral. 'The fact is if I mentioned something like that it would be a pretty big deal. It would be was something I thought perhaps would be dismissed or not acknowledged and I knew that a scholarship was something that could be given and taken away, even at that age I didn't want to lose that—it meant so much for me . . . and what would I do if I went forward and said such a thing about an archbishop? It's something I've carried for the whole of my life.'

As for the second incident, Gibson shared J's recollection of walking with a group down a back hallway past the sacristy after mass. 'I saw him [Pell] and he pushed himself up against me on a wall and Archbishop Pell squeezed my genitalia, my testicles, my penis—nothing was said. It was all over in a matter of seconds, 1, 2, 3 seconds . . . Archbishop Pell was in robes and I was in robes. He squeezed and kept walking. I didn't tell anyone at the time because I didn't want to jeopardise anything . . . I didn't want to rock the boat, with my family, my schooling, my life.'

Now a professional and a father, J had been asked by Richter in the closed hearing if he had cautioned his friend R after the corridor incident to watch out for Pell and what he might do. He said he didn't. 'I had no intention back then of telling anyone, ever.'

Gibson may not have shared Richter's natural preference for drama, but perhaps that didn't matter after all. His use of parts of J's testimony relayed the sense of a demolished inner life.

The jury had a lot to consider, but there was one key element it had to weigh up. Someone in this case was lying. Was it the surviving accuser? Or was it Pell?

In one of the most highly anticipated speeches in Australian legal history, Richter would soon have a great deal to say about that.

———

Like the whole Pell legal saga up to that point, Richter's closing address was predictably long, stretching over two days. He may have been in his early seventies, but he'd give the final battle everything he had and would fight bitterly to the last.

Theatrics were part of Richter's performance from the start. Picking up the wooden stand facing the judge, he moved it to the end of the bar table to face the jury directly. Wearing his round glasses, he briefly touched his short white hair and began reading from a prepared folder of notes to a packed court that included other barristers and lawyers keen to see their infamous peer in action.

Jesuit priest, human-rights lawyer and academic Father Frank Brennan was also seated in court. He seemed to be a supportive presence during the case, often shaking the cardinal's hand and speaking to him in his private interview room during the breaks. Brennan hadn't always agreed with Pell on social and political issues but had shown an interest in his legal woes. Writing in the days following publication of the allegations against Pell, Brennan joined the cardinal in calling for an investigation into its sources.

'Any government conducting a royal commission must come with clean hands, informing the commission and the public about the source of the leaks and the action taken to punish the wrongdoing and to mitigate the damage,' he wrote in the Jesuit publication *Eureka Street*.[1]

Advocate Chrissie Foster was also in court with friends, having already attended several days of the trial to observe the proceedings. Wearing a deep-purple coat, she rested her hands in her lap. Pell looked at her and sometimes nodded, clearly recognising the woman he'd had tense meetings with so many years before. The ghosts from Pell's past were in the courtroom.

Always remarkably calm and dignified, Foster looked directly at Richter as he began his address urging the jury to use its 'common sense'. The allegations were 'improbable', he said, comparing Pell to the Queen of England: 'She's not left alone and the archbishop in his kingdom is not left alone.'

Over the years Pell had unfairly come to be seen as the 'leader of the dark force', Richter claimed. 'It has come to the point where in some quarters Archbishop Pell had almost become the Darth Vader of the Catholic Church. Some people consider that he's responsible for everything that happened there.

'That's not what he is charged with,' Richter continued. '. . . the charges against him—and he is the highest Catholic official that I know of to have been charged with actually performing sexual abuse—are unique and that's what you are concerned with, not whether he is the leader of the dark force.'

Pell had volunteered to be interviewed by police in Rome, even though there was no extradition treaty between Vatican City and Australia, the court was reminded. 'He volunteered for officers to come and question him . . . as he says in the interview, he was prepared to answer any question they might ask . . . his responses appear completely genuine when he is almost taken by surprise what the allegation is really about.'

As Richter continued his strident address, a woman in her 60s sat near me in the court. Clutching rosary beads, and seemingly trying to muster the sheer will of God to help someone in the courtroom, she began whispering prayers she read from sheets of paper. Were they for the cardinal sitting in the dock? The judge? The jury? Or did she feel Richter needed a religious bunk up to help him through his marathon address? She wouldn't say.

'Please don't use your phone,' were her only words to me.

'I'm sorry, but I'm actually working,' I had to explain, as kindly and gently as I could.

The mystery woman continued praying quietly as Richter went on to discuss 'twenty key issues' in the case, including the arguments concerning whether Pell had ever been alone after mass, who had accompanied him and how the choirboys hadn't been spotted leaving the procession. He asked the jury to consider that it was 'unlikely' the two boys would not have been heard. 'If you've got a child saying, "No. Please!" someone would have heard,' he argued. The surviving accuser was 'desperately clinging to a story', he claimed.

Despite being directed by the judge not to raise mental-health issues regarding the surviving choirboy, Richter circled the issue just enough to plant a seed without facing the wrath of the judge. Such dexterous moves, of course, are why the silk commands the big bucks.'Maybe he recreated it [abuse by Pell] in some crazy way—sorry, fantastical, phantasmagorical way.'

It was a reasonable notion that the surviving choirboy had 'persuaded himself' that being abused by Pell was something that had happened, Richter would say later. 'It's that sort of possibility that we say exists in this case . . . because of the way the evidence developed.'

Richter said Pell would have needed a 'third' hand to have been able to carry out the sacristy attack. 'Here is the Archbishop in full regalia, and it's cumbersome regalia. It's not impossible altogether to expose your penis, not impossible, but it takes a fair bit of doing and you need a sort of third hand to do some of those things. And the Archbishop didn't have a third hand. The descriptions don't match the reality and they don't match what's possible.'

Richter also suggested that Pell would have to have been 'nuts' to have carried out the alleged attacks. 'There are other aspects of risk that are so great which led me to the conclusion that you have got to assume that this man was insane to do what happened . . . and these days you don't really get to be archbishop if you display characteristics of being a nutter.' The 'extreme danger' of detection is one that a new archbishop would 'at least think about'.

It was probably unsurprising that Richter's unique style would eventually fall foul of the judge's patience. He was admonished for warning the jury that if it reached a guilty verdict this could result in the 'potential destruction' of the cardinal. The judge argued with Richter that it wasn't for the jury to worry about the sentencing of the cardinal, or the impact on his life that a conviction could bring, only whether he was guilty or not.

Richter was also told to apologise to the jury for suggesting the verdict itself would have no impact on the surviving choirboy who had given evidence. 'Forgive me as I got slightly carried away by the enormity of the situation . . . saying things that were emotional in some sense,' he said in his defence.

In arguing it was bizarre that J had said in his testimony the two choirboys had never discussed the attack by Pell, Richter was again forced to apologise, this time for using the example of concentration-camp survivors who may choose not to talk to others alone but would possibly do so in a group of those who had also suffered the same experience. If the boys truly had shared a brutal attack by Pell, he tried to suggest, they surely would have spoken of it together.

During Richter's two-day long closing address, news broke of an unprecedented announcement from Rome: in February 2019 Pope Francis would be summoning the presidents of every bishops' conference around the world for a summit to discuss the prevention of clergy sexual abuse and the protection children.[2] The move revealed that Francis had realised the scandal was a major global problem, and that inaction would threaten to undermine his legacy. It was certainly curious timing, however, considering what was unfolding in a courtroom in Melbourne.

Continuing his closing address, Richter referred to a video of the surviving choirboy doing a walk-through of the cathedral with police officers. This was the first time the existence of the video that had been played to the jury in the media's absence had been made public.

During the video, Richter said, the man pointed to the vault in the sacristy, saying it was unchanged from 1996 when, as the court heard, the area had been remodelled around eight years later. 'Another aspect of how the mind plays tricks on those people who have persuaded themselves that something has happened,' he told the jury.

Using the philosophical principle of Occam's Razor—if there are two explanations for an occurrence then the simpler one is the one to be preferred—Richter concluded for the defence. Speaking slowly and casting his gaze at each member of the jury, the crimes allegedly committed by Pell 'didn't happen', he said.

He'd done his best, Richter told the jury, and he trusted it to do its duty. 'If your state of mind is "we're not sure"—the verdict is not guilty. If your state of mind is "he probably did it"—we say it won't be—but if your state of mind is he probably did it—your verdict, the law says, must be one of not guilty. It's with these words I leave you for the last time . . . I know you will take your task as seriously as the law expects you to and return a verdict of not guilty, we would say. Thank you.' The words 'not guilty' were said so many times it felt more like hypnosis than a closing address.

Clearly exhausted by the two-day marathon, Richter joked as he left the court on 12 September 2018 that he needed to lie on his sofa in his chambers and have a 'double whiskey' to recover. 'Doing these cases is like doing a PhD, I was up a couple of nights in a row.'

———

The last day and a half of the trial was taken up with legal directions from the judge, who stressed the key principle that if the jury was to find Pell guilty it had to be 'beyond reasonable doubt'. Each juror was then asked to swear an oath or make an affirmation before leaving the box for the jury room—at least four chose to swear on the Bible.

Their deliberations had begun. A rattling trolley of freshly cut sandwiches was rolled into the court for their lunch, a low-key offering considering their mammoth task ahead.

Speculating on the outcome, reporters were divided. Half believed the deliberations would be quick—Richter had presented so many elements of doubt, one said, how could they possibly convict? The rest of us weren't so sure. We hadn't been party to the most important piece of evidence of all: the surviving choirboy's testimony. This could change everything we had heard and witnessed.

Either way, the finish line seemed to be in sight as we settled into the small interview rooms next to the room for Pell and his supporters. We busied ourselves with writing up notes, working on other stories, talking, snacking and speculating.

We could hear Pell thanking the legal clerk from Galbally & O'Bryan for the hot sausage rolls she'd delivered for his lunch. 'They're delicious,' he said. How many more take-away lunches would the cardinal need before the jury made its final decision? And how long would it be before the jury pressed its buzzer and handed down its verdict? We sensed that the deliberations might take some time. Adam Cooper from *The Age* started an informal book on when they'd be back. It was a light-hearted distraction.

After lunch the jury had a request. Could it be given a copy of the video recording of the testimony of the surviving choirboy? We knew he had been questioned by the Crown and the defence over at least two days, so was the jury planning on watching the whole recording? Or just parts of it to monitor his body language and choice of wording? We would never know, but it was clear it would be watched very carefully with one question in mind: Was he telling the truth?

We waited into the following day, before the jury were dismissed for the weekend. Pell now seemed a little shaken. His previously relaxed face became furrowed, and he looked down at his feet.

His concerned demeanour wasn't surprising; after all, he'd engaged a top legal team at great cost, a team he clearly believed would easily convince a jury to make a quick decision to acquit. The fact that these deliberations were now going to go over a weekend and into the following week was a matter for concern.

'Don't worry, just relax at the weekend,' Richter told the cardinal reassuringly, patting him on the shoulder as he left the courtroom. Richter could try and comfort his client as much as possible, but there was undoubtably enormous strain on the Vatican's treasurer.

Monday passed without a word from the jury.

Tuesday played out as another long day of waiting. Retired lawyer Rosemary O'Grady, who had attended the case on behalf of American abuse-advocate group SNAP and had become a knowledgeable legal presence for the Pell pack, waited on a chair near the courtroom door. A male abuse survivor had become so exhausted by the long hours that he went to sleep across four chairs. His snoring could be heard echoing along the corridors.

Pell sat in his small interview room reading a book when Richter and Shann appeared in his room from their nearby chambers, as usual, just before 4 p.m., when the jury was dismissed for the day. The defence and crown teams both agreed with the judge that it was the right moment to ask the jury, for the first time, if it was making progress.

'Yes we are,' the forewoman quickly replied, pushing her long ginger hair away from her face, giving nothing away.

The following day, after the lunch break, Judge Kidd received a 'question from the jury'. 'We have reached an impasse, please can you advise further instructions,' the note read. Thanking them for their hard work, the judge simply urged the jury to keep deliberating. They looked tired and a little despondent.

This could only mean one thing—a hung jury and a retrial. Worn down by the previous five weeks and the long hours of waiting outside the courtroom, I didn't think I could do it again. 'I'm not doing it,' I told the other reporters.

This story had already consumed so many years of my life, at one point smashing both my well-being and my career to pieces. The idea that it could be extended was hard to comprehend. I was due to go on a long-planned road trip with my family; maybe we could just keep driving so I'd never have to return to this gruelling legal saga.

But repeating the trial would be far more arduous and traumatic for the legal teams, the judge and police informant, let alone the accuser. I had to keep moving forward. The friendship and support from the Pell pack would help greatly. I'd also survived the bows and arrows so far, and I couldn't give up now—this case mattered too much for so many people, let alone for the truth of my being.

———

The next day, Thursday 20 September 2018, we arrived at court to be told one juror was missing as his son was unwell. As a result, the jury could not deliberate until midday. The delay added to the rising tension. I came across Mark Gibson pacing the corridor. He looked pale and tired. Always generous to reporters with his guidance and expertise, he told us that whatever happened, today would be the last day of the trial. 'It will be over by the end of the day,' he said with certainty.

The jury had been deliberating for only half an hour before the judge called it in and asked about progress. They were still 'essentially at the same position' he was advised, without being given exact numbers as he had previously directed. He then gave a majority-verdict direction, which meant an 11-1 verdict in agreement could be given instead of a unanimous verdict. It was immediately obvious that this wasn't going to help. A male juror sitting in the front row of the jury box grimaced and shook his head, his expression revealing that the division ran deep.

For the rest of the day there was an ominous silence from the jury. There were no questions. There was no buzzer. There was no verdict.

At 4 p.m., Judge Kidd again asked the jury the million-dollar question: had it reached a verdict with the majority direction?

The forewoman shook her head. 'No, we haven't,' she said quietly.

Judge Kidd then asked if one more night to 'think things over' and to come back fresh in the morning would help.

The jury briefly went back into its room.

'If she comes back and says no, then I just think we're at the end, aren't we?' the judge said, looking down at the bar table.

'The end of the line,' Richter agreed.

'Regrettably, yes, your honour,' Gibson said.

As the court stood for the judge to leave, the buzzer rang. The jury filed back in, faces pallid and drained.

Again, the judge asked whether the jury would benefit from more time the next day. The forewoman shook her head and simply said 'No, we wouldn't, your honour.' Silent tears rolled down her cheeks.

The jury would be dismissed.

Judge Kidd thanked the jury for its hard work in the 'difficult case'. He reassured them that they would be exempt from jury duty for ten years, and that they could access services such as counselling if they felt the need. A two-week all-expenses paid trip to a spa hotel in Bali would have been more appropriate for these twelve souls. They had been through a mentally and emotionally challenging ordeal, sitting in judgement over this intricate, repetitive and often harrowing case for little more than the cost of their tram fares.

As Kidd spoke, two women jurors began crying. It was a sorrowful sight. A man in his early sixties also wiped his eyes. A court tipstaff offered a box of tissues. It was the tipstaffs' role to keep order in the courtroom for the judge. Today their job was to keep a river of tears at bay.

'I can see that you're finding it very difficult,' the judge said. 'I don't think you should be hard on yourselves.'

Here were people whose lives had been unexpectedly dominated by this case and, in the end, there was no result. They'd spent weeks listening to shocking and challenging evidence, unable to even discuss it with their friends, families or colleagues.

'I think I can make this observation . . . that the burden in this case was going to be greater than most,' Judge Kidd added. 'And I know you've taken your task very seriously.'

Later it would be wrongly speculated, largely among Pell's supporters in the media, that the jurors had voted 10-2 in favour of finding Pell not guilty, thus suggesting the jury had been unfairly described as a hung jury. (In criminal cases in Victoria juries cannot be split below 11–1.) But the votes were never revealed to anyone outside the jury room including the judge, at his request.

There wasn't even a chance to pause to take a breath after the jury left the courtroom before Judge Kidd began to discuss potential dates for the retrial with the legal counsel, which would take place in November—starting on the date that had been allocated for the Swimmers Trial. That trial would now be heard, the judge ruled, in March 2019. As had been predicted on the day Pell was charged, this case would indeed take years to conclude. The cost of covering this case would also soar for the Pell pack's news organisations.

Paradoxically, the cardinal himself seemed to be the only one upbeat. 'Well, we gave it our best shot,' he said loudly to his legal team as they left the courtroom. Richter, Shann and the rest of the team may well have given it their all, but they'd just had a very close call. They now had seven weeks to regroup and work out a new strategy. It was time for Richter to spearhead round two of the Cathedral Trial.

———

Travelling through vast landscapes, waterfalls, rugged escarpments and sandstone outcrops of the Top End of Australia on my family's road trip proved the perfect escape from five weeks in an airless courtroom. The huge skies of the Kimberley and the endless, glistening sands of Broome's Cable Beach were a beautiful 2000-kilometre detox from the darkness of the preceding weeks and months.

The ancient rock galleries at Ubirr in Kakadu offered much-needed perspective; the Pell case was a moment in time. It had to be recorded, but it would eventually be over. My job was to help paint a detailed picture of what was unfolding for future generations. To look back on. To learn from.

I arrived back home in time to report on another highly important matter—the long-awaited national apology to victims of child abuse in institutions by Prime Minister Scott Morrison on 22 October 2018. He fought back tears as he gave the powerful speech to a packed House of Representatives.[3] Broadcast live across the country and at special local screenings for survivors, Morrison had a strong message—that the abuse was not the fault of the victims and that action needed to happen to ensure the future safety of Australian children.

'Whether you sit here in this Chamber, the Great Hall, outside elsewhere in the nation's capital. Your living room. In your bed, unable to rise today or speak to another soul. Your journey to where you are today has been a long and painful one, and we acknowledge that and we welcome you today wherever you are,' Morrison began.[4]

Mr Speaker, silenced voices. Muffled cries in the darkness. Unacknowledged tears. The tyranny of invisible suffering. The never heard pleas of tortured souls bewildered by an indifference to the unthinkable theft of their innocence. Today, Australia confronts a trauma—an abomination— hiding in plain sight for far too long. Today, we confront a question too horrible to ask, let alone answer. Why weren't the children of our nation loved, nurtured and protected?

Why was their trust betrayed? Why did those who know cover it up? Why were the cries of children and parents ignored? Why was our system of justice blind to injustice? Why has it taken so long to act? Why were other things more important than this, the care of innocent children? Why didn't we believe?

Today we dare to ask these questions, and finally acknowledge and confront the lost screams of our children.

He recognised how thousands of victims abused in institutions, from schools to church-run orphanages and scout groups,

had been 'crushed, disregarded and forgotten' by their perpetrators. 'As a nation we failed them, we forsook them and that will
always be our shame. It happened week after week, decade after
decade . . . unrelenting torment.'

Morrison urged all institutions to adhere to the recommendations of the royal commission, vowing that the government was
already taking action on 104 of the 122 final recommendations.
He also announced that the newly created National Office of Child
Safety would report directly to him, and that there would be a new
museum honouring those who had been abused as children.

'We honour every survivor in this country, we love you, we
hear you and we honour you,' he said. Overcome with emotion,
he spoke about the tragic experiences of Chrissie and Anthony
Foster's daughters. 'As a father of two daughters I can't comprehend what she [Chrissie] has faced,' Morrison continued.

The apology was largely welcomed by survivors and advocates, hundreds of whom had been allocated tickets in a special
ballot to attend the event in person. For Chrissie Foster, however,
the apology wasn't the end of the issue, or a line in the sand.
Children are still at risk, she said, in church-run schools and
choirs, while victims need more funding for extensive, life-long
counselling. 'It's not the end. We're not done,' she said.[5]

She'd told Morrison personally of the abuse inflicted on
her daughters at a special meeting in Sydney with him and
the apology advisory group just ten days before. 'He clearly
connected with me as a father himself, which is important, as he
gets it. When people get it there is action and he's in a position
to do something.'

Later, taking to the stage in Parliament's Great Hall, Morrison was heckled by several of those attending the event: survivors angry the recommended $200,000 redress compensation had been capped at $150,000. They were also making their views known about the application process, which was proving to be difficult to navigate, while questioning why the government was also giving extra funding to Catholic schools.

Labor leader Bill Shorten also spoke to those gathered in the Great Hall. 'To all of you who have suffered it was never your fault, it was not your fault . . . and I terribly apologise for the fact you were not believed, I'm so, so sorry.'

As with Kevin Rudd's apology to the stolen generation on 13 February 2008, being acknowledged by the nation's government was a largely welcome but symbolic gesture. Words could never come close to healing the life-long mental scars of terror, shame and betrayal experienced on a daily basis by the thousands of Australians who had suffered institutional abuse. Many had tragically already found they could not continue to live with those memories. Saying sorry would never be of use to them. It was too late.

———

Returning to the County Court of Victoria for the first day of the retrial on 7 November 2018 was like 'Groundhog Day'. Everything seemed the same as it had on the first day of the first trial back in August: the same lawyers, identical video screens and for the next five weeks the same trial—reloaded.

With a sprightly step, Richter came into court, seemingly

well rested and ready for the task ahead. A court clerk asked him how he was. 'Well, we're alive,' he joked. 'Where's his Eminence?' The silk was pointed outside the courtroom to the private interview room where Pell was waiting.

When the cardinal himself walked into court a few minutes later, wearing a brown jacket, white shirt and his clerical collar, he took his seat in the dock. Long-time supporter Peter Westmore walked over and shook his hand. Westmore, former head of a Catholic lobby group set up by the high-profile anti-Communist B.A. Santamaria in the 1950s, had been a regular fixture at most of Pell's court hearings. He would sit diligently typing up the proceedings on a laptop perched on his knees.

Judge Kidd was fresh from an appearance on the ABC's TV's *Four Corners* on which he'd spoken about the unfair media coverage of what was being dubbed the 'African gang problem'. He went downstairs to the jury room for the empanelment.

The video screens flickered into life in the courtroom, revealing rows of potential jurors, a mix of ages and backgrounds. We watched as 248 members of the public were informed by Judge Kidd that they faced selection for a trial regarding the 'Director of Public Prosecutions versus Pell'.

'That is Cardinal George Pell,' Kidd clarified, as subtle expressions of surprise flickered across the faces of many of the assembled men and women. It was explained that if any of them had a reason they could be biased in the case or were not able to attend for the full five weeks, they should offer their excuses in a questionnaire.

The cardinal was asked to stand to enter his plea for the five charges. 'Not guilty,' he said in a loud clear voice with a hint of annoyance and incredulity.

The fact that this 'arraignment', the formal name for the moment a criminal defendant is formally advised of the charges against him and is asked to enter a plea, was carried out without the final selection of jurors present in the same room would later become a highly debated point.

Judge Kidd firmly told the potential jurors that Pell was entitled to a fair trial, saying, 'Cardinal George Pell is a very senior member of the Catholic Church, he is in fact a cardinal of the Catholic Church . . . just because you are of Catholic faith does not disqualify you from sitting on this jury. But if because of your Catholic faith, or identifying with the faith, you can't bring a fair or impartial mind . . . you must seek to be excused.' What mattered, Kidd said, was that the jurors were able to bring a fair mind, notwithstanding any particular 'religious identity you might have'.

Fourteen jurors were chosen; nine men and five women. If they were all in place by the time the jury came to deliberate two would be voted off by ballot. The law prevents jurors from being publicly identified, but they represented a cross-section of Melbourne society and had a variety of jobs.

'More men is good for the defence,' a court reporter muttered. 'Apparently men rely less on their emotions.' Could a male-heavy jury make a difference and lead to Pell being acquitted? Would men really be more sceptical about the accuser's testimony than women—or less compassionate in regard to trauma and suffering? I wasn't so sure.

Before releasing the jury members for the night, the judge sternly warned them not to research Pell on the internet or tell friends and family what case they were sitting on. 'I know that by the end of this trial—you will be thinking here he goes again, here goes the trial judge, he's lost his mind, he's giving us this direction for the 15th time, but that really just demonstrates or illustrates just how important this direction is.'

'Do not talk to anyone about this case, do not conduct any research of any kind. Do not get on the internet . . . do not engage with social media,' Kidd said.

I completed my re-framing of the situation in my mind. The court could very well hear the same evidence heard in the first trial, but it would be considered by this brand-new set of jury members—a fact that could make all the difference to the verdict. Each juror would be informed by their own life experiences, values, beliefs and backgrounds.

As I braced myself with the rest of the Pell pack for the re-run of the case, I knew there would be nothing predictable about the result. There were fourteen new kids on the block.

Chapter 11
Beyond reasonable doubt

Dr Sarah Jane Pell unobtrusively took her seat in court the next day. When asked during the committal earlier in the year if she was supporting the cardinal she had replied, 'Of course,' refusing to answer any more questions.[1] Up close, Pell's 43-year-old niece bore his same striking features: large eyes, similar bone structure and jaw line, and the tall stature. An academic and an artist and the daughter of Pell's brother David, she is also described as an 'intrepid astronaut candidate and commercial diver' who performs astronautics with space agencies around the world.[2]

It was little wonder then that she had become a strong and intelligent supporter of her uncle. They seemed to have a close bond. In her early years growing up in Ballarat she'd run to the presbytery at St Alipius asking for 'Uncle George' to play with her. Now she served as a nurturing and feminine presence in the courtroom, offering caring words and keeping him company during the breaks.

Before the day's hearing began, the cardinal's legal team and court officers rearranged a chair in the dock to accommodate the cardinal's 'painful knees'. He needed more space, so he could stretch out and not be constrained by the waist-height dock in front of him.

Explaining that Pell would be having knee surgery before Christmas, Richter asked the judge if Pell could be excused from standing each time the jury came into the courtroom. He also requested the court security officer in the dock be directed not to stand, so it wasn't 'obvious' that the cardinal was unable to get up himself.

Giving initial directions to the jury, Judge Kidd explained they were the 'judges' of the case, that they occupied 'one of the most important institutions in our community'. 'You sit in judgement of the accused man, it's your role to decide which facts to accept,' he said. 'And it's your role to decide if Cardinal Pell is guilty or not guilty of the charges.' There was 'no special skill involved' in being on a jury, 'you just use your common sense', he told them.

Mark Gibson, also looking rested, made his opening address for the Crown. As in his initial remarks in the first trial, he went into fine detail about the nature of the alleged attacks on the two choirboys. It wasn't any less disturbing to listen to the second time around.

'The issue really is . . . you accepting the evidence given by J,' he said. '. . . the burden rests with the prosecution from start to finish and it must prove these charges beyond reasonable doubt based on the evidence.' Emphasising the importance of fairness towards the defendant, Gibson also pointed out it was vital that the jury judged Pell on the evidence alone. He also explained it was the duty of the Crown to call all relevant witnesses whether they are helpful or unhelpful to the Crown case.

While we sat in secret in the courtroom, in the heart of darkness, across the other side of the city the Spring Racing Carnival's Kennedy Oaks Day—Ladies Day—was taking place at Flemington racecourse. The city's trains were speckled with brightly coloured fascinators and dresses and carefree and happy racegoers. They were all unaware of what was unfolding regarding Australia's most senior Catholic cleric.

When Gibson closed his remarks, Robert Richter moved the wooden lectern to face the jury, as he had done in the first trial. Gaining eye contact and making a strong impact was clearly his aim. 'It's better standing sideways,' he said, smiling. Would the jury find his style endearing? Or would his often lengthy arguments alienate them?

Opening with what he described as the 'elephants in this courtroom', Richter reminded the jury of the Tim Minchin song calling on Pell to come home. 'Well, he came back and came back of his own accord to clear his name.

'Although he had diplomatic status at the Vatican, and as we know there is no extradition treaty with the Vatican and Australia, he came here voluntarily. So the notion that he had to be brought here to face justice has to be clear, because that song . . . was a toxic song.'

It was clear that Richter had reworked his opening speech. The silk told the jury that the evidence in the case made the allegations by the surviving accuser 'practically impossible, and in other incidences highly improbable' and that there was 'no opportunity' after a busy Sunday mass for the alleged abuse to have occurred. He also argued there was a lack of motive. 'We have no evidence, other than the notion that he somehow gets sexual gratification [from the alleged attacks].'

He emphasised that Pell must not be on trial over whether he knew about 'paedophile clerics' in the Catholic Church and didn't do enough to stop them. 'That is not the trial here,' Richter said. 'The trial here is of the most senior Catholic cleric charged with actually, let's call a spade a spade here, actually orally raping a child of 13 and doing some other disgusting things with two children, with a child of 13. That's what this trial is about. It's not about what he knew about whether some other priest 20 years even before then had been doing things to little boys and failed to report.'

The accuser's evidence would again be presented to the jury—this time as a recording from the first trial, sparing him from another tough cross-examination by Richter—and again the media was barred from hearing his testimony.

Keen to at least try and remain in the courtroom, I organised a joint submission with several media outlets, including *The Guardian* and the *New York Times*. It would almost immediately be rejected by Judge Kidd. We were also denied access to the transcripts. This was highly frustrating and not a little troubling. This evidence was the key part of the case. Without identifying the witness, wasn't it in the public's interest to share the allegations? And aren't the courts based on the concept of open justice?

Legal expert Jeremy Gans understood the reluctance of an accuser being watched while giving evidence, but he shared my view that the transcript should have been made available. 'I think making the transcript available as much as possible is crucial in a case like this,' he said, 'where it's the only source we have about what is actually alleged against Pell.'

Just an hour after the first day of the accuser's video evidence had ended, a shocking event unfolded in the city a few streets away from the court. In a horrific Islamic State-inspired terror attack, Hassan Khalif Shire Ali, 30, drove a ute packed with gas cylinders to near the top of the Bourke Street Mall and set them alight. He stabbed two men and also fatally stabbed Sisto Malaspina, the well-known owner of Italian cafe Pellegrini's. Confronted by police, Ali was shot by an officer and died in hospital that night. Police later said they believed Hassan had tried to create a deadly explosion that would have spread shrapnel across a 100-metre radius. A shrine of flowers, candles and cards grew outside the doors of Pellegrini's.

As news organisations focused on reporting the incident, the Pell case quietly opened to media again on Wednesday 14 November. After being shown the video testimony of two of the group of men who were choirboys at the cathedral, surely the jury must have guessed it was participating in a retrial. 'It makes you wonder, doesn't it?' Gibson said.

As with the first trial, the jury was taken to St Patrick's Cathedral for an official 'viewing', accompanied by the judge, legal counsel, court staff, two 'jury keepers' (who usually worked as the judge's tipstaff) and Detective Chris Reed. It was clearly a huge undertaking. The Cathedral had to again be closed to other visitors, and filming of the parts of the building had to be undertaken without any of the jurors being identified.

Asked how he was bearing up, 'I'm alive,' Richter replied, in what was becoming his personal mantra. He was happy the jury had watched the accuser's evidence on video. 'They are not being distracted by anything else in the courtroom, they can see his every facial movement and gesture,' he said. At one point the accuser was shown laughing, only to become serious when told the video was live once more. 'It's good for us,' Richter said confidently.

It was of course his role to show confidence in his case, but Richter's relaxed demeanour was seductive. If this experienced silk was so confident, would Pell find himself exonerated and soon flying back to Rome in time for the traditional midnight mass in St Peter's Basilica?

———

Considering that the Vatican's treasurer was still fighting for his future, the media's investment in the story was noticeably subsiding. In a decision they would perhaps come to regret, some editors had come to the conclusion it wasn't worth the cost of sending a senior reporter to a trial that might well end up a hung jury again, or at the very most with a not-guilty verdict. Even *The Australian*, which had earlier declared the case to be the 'Trial of the Century', hadn't sent any reporters back to the case. Was it the cost? Or was it because some of its high-profile commentators such as Gerard Henderson were strongly supporting the cardinal? It was certainly viewed as rather an odd decision by the other reporters at court, considering the global importance of the case.

The remaining members of the Pell pack all agreed the cardinal didn't appear to be in good shape. The physical and mental strain of the retrial seemed to be catching up with him. Using a crutch to walk into court, he looked in pain from his ailing knees and was also suffering from a deep, chesty cough. It couldn't have helped that local and international media, as well as high-profile advocates, were all witnessing his degrading position as an accused man in the dock.

One of those advocates who quietly took a seat in the back of the courtroom alongside her friend Chrissie Foster was Joan Issacs. Accompanied by her husband Ian, Issacs was the author of *To Prey and to Silence*, a powerful book about being cruelly abused from the age of fourteen. She wrote of how it had almost destroyed her, leaving her with a permanent trail of shame.

Father Francis Derriman was a priest of the Archdiocese of Brisbane and chaplain of Brisbane's Sacred Heart Sandgate in 1967 and 1968 when he began his campaign of grooming and persuaded Issacs to join his cult-like group of four children, using the *Peanuts* comic to bond them. Highly manipulative, he called himself and the children Brown, after the comic's main character Charlie Brown.

Issacs desperately tried to erase the shattering experiences from her memory, until one day she noticed a young woman in her late teens holding a baby on a beach near Brisbane. She was with an older man. To her horror, Issacs realised the man was the clergyman who had abused her all those years before.

It would be another six months before she had the strength to go to the police and it wasn't until 1998 that Derriman was finally convicted of indecently assaulting her. He was sentenced to one year in prison, which was suspended after just four months.

Issacs was attending the Pell trial because as a survivor it was a 'healing experience' and not because she regarded the cardinal as responsible for the clergy-abuse scandal as a whole.[3] 'To see someone of that stature within the church be in a position where they were being held accountable, like any normal citizen, and also had no power, sitting there in the dock, was a really big experience as a survivor,' she said.

Yet there was something about the replayed videoed evidence of the elderly former wine maker from the first trial that left her feeling somewhat confused. 'What he said baffled me,' she said. 'He insisted the wine supplied to the cathedral was white wine. But that just didn't make sense. This is the main Catholic cathedral in Melbourne and red wine is hugely symbolic of the blood of Christ and has been for centuries. If the dean had an allergy to red wine, why didn't they reserve a white bottle for him, and allow everyone else to continue the tradition of drinking red?

———

Tension rose as the days went on. After the weekend break Judge Kidd would have to admonish Richter yet again, this time regarding his questioning of the cathedral's former assistant choirmaster and organist Geoffrey Cox. The judge said it was 'impermissible' that the barrister had asked Cox to speculate whether 'elevated children's voices' would ever be able to be heard from the sacristy.

Richter, however, defended his questioning, saying Cox was a 'lay expert'. 'I suppose it's a retrial, one tries to improve,' he said, shifting insistence to repentance in just a few words.

The same general pattern of witnesses in the first trial followed, although slightly reduced to 'streamline' the Crown's case.

Many of the original witness testimonies were shown on the video screens, while those witnesses who attended the retrial in person were asked again in careful and forensic detail about the main issues: the routine of the choir after mass; whether they'd ever seen the cardinal alone and wearing his robes after the Sunday service; and, crucially, whether it would have been possible for two little boys in red robes to nick off and run into the southern part of the cathedral unnoticed.

As much as the testimonies would mostly repeat evidence from the first trial, there would be two unforeseen twists.

The first would occur during the evidence of Max Potter, the former sacristan of the cathedral. It was soon evident his answers seemed more favourable to Pell than they had been in the first trial. In particular, he stated Pell was 'never alone' after mass—despite telling police in 2016 that he could not be certain. He then adamantly declared that it would have been 'impossible' for Pell to move his robes to expose his private parts. 'They were long and heavy, and he sometimes would wear another vestment,' Potter told the court.

In a break without the jury present, Gibson complained to the judge that Potter seemed to have 'shifted his evidence' and that he was being overly favourable to Pell by trying to 'assist the accuser in being found not guilty'. As a result, Gibson argued, Potter was an unreliable witness who'd been possibly trying to 'enhance the chances of acquittal', but by confronting the witness, or suggesting he was lying, there may be later legal ramifications.

Judge Kidd advised Gibson that he could 'invite' the jury in his closing arguments not to accept Potter's evidence. Richter conceded Gibson's concerns were 'legit' as long as he didn't go to the jury at the end of the case saying the witness was 'telling lies'. It was also argued that Potter's advanced age could be influencing his changing testimony.

Scoring this vital point for the Crown, Gibson later asked Potter with what frequency would Monsignor Charles Portelli not be there to help Pell after mass and accompany him to the sacristy. 'It would be a very rare occasion because he was very close and worked with the Cardinal constantly. But sometimes Monsignor Portelli would be required to say a mass later . . . it would be rare occasions.'

The word 'rare' was important—he wasn't saying 'never'.

As Potter left the court he looked at Pell in the dock, but the cardinal just put his dead down, writing in his notebook.

———

And so the drama continued. In the second unexpected turn of events, we learned that Melbourne barrister Daniel McGlone had come forward to Pell's defence team after reading about the allegations raised during the committal hearing earlier in the year. An altar server at the cathedral from 1987 to 1997,

McGlone believed that the abuse 'could not have happened' in the sacristy after mass as it was such a busy and public place.

Questioned by Gibson, McGlone was asked if he'd served Pell during mass. He had but could recall only one occasion which he said was in December 1996, the month of the alleged first attack. Describing the priest's sacristy, McGlone told how it was generally not locked during mass. He also explained that he and his mother had spoken to Pell on the steps of the cathedral after the service, giving weight to Pell's assertion that he didn't go back to the sacristy for some time.

Gibson then re-examined McGlone regarding his assertion that the first time he had served Pell was in December 1996. He presented him with a photograph taken of him and other altar servers at an evening mass in November 1996 where he had served Pell.

'Do you see yourself depicted?' Gibson asked.

'Well, it does appear to be me,' McGlone replied quietly.

The witness seemed surprised by this development, and it immediately cast doubt on the veracity of the rest of his evidence.

McGlone then confirmed he had sought some 'eternal verification' of his memory, before giving a statement to police, from another witness—former altar server Geoffrey Connor—who he knew kept detailed diaries at the time. The credibility of witnesses is everything, so this was not a good look.

If the defence thought it had pulled a rabbit out of a hat by asking the Crown to call McGlone as a witness, it had just been eaten for breakfast with a side dish of toast.

The Crown was nearing the end of the prosecution case.

Impressively, the jury still seemed engaged and interested. This appeared a bonded group. They showed a respectful friendliness to one another not seen with the first jury. Would this affect their deliberations and the outcome of the case? We would have to see.

Geoffrey Connor, former choirboy Andrew La Greca and Sano Task Force detective Chris Reed were again the final witnesses to take to the stand before Gibson informed the judge, 'So Your Honour, that concludes the evidence to be called on behalf of the Crown.'

As he had done in the first trial, Richter confirmed the defence would not be calling any witnesses of their own. 'We rely on the evidence heard before the jury and call no further evidence,' he said.

Before allowing the jury to leave, the judge emphasised the case wasn't yet over. He urged them to 'keep an open mind'. 'The case isn't finished, don't reach any conclusion yet,' he said. '. . . try to perhaps put a lot of this out of your mind and come back fresh next week for an important week.'

Gibson and Richter, on the other hand, were likely to get little sleep as they prepared their vital closing addresses. The end was in sight, but there was still a towering, judicial mountain to climb. These would be the most important submissions of their entire careers.

———

When the closing addresses began on Monday 3 December all the seats in the courtroom were filled by advocates, supporters, reporters, lawyers and law students eager to witness round two of the show down of the silks. They would need patience. Gibson would spend the entire day, longer than his closing address in the first trial, arguing that the jury should find Pell guilty on all five counts against him.

The 'critical issue', he explained, was whether the jury accepted that the surviving choirboy was telling the truth. There was an important difference between 'no opportunity' and a 'reduced opportunity'. Simplifying the main points of his argument, Gibson broke them into three parts. First, had Pell remained on the steps of the cathedral after mass for an extended period of time, removing the opportunity for him to be back at his sacristy when the offence occurred? Second, had there been an opportunity after mass for two choristers to separate from the procession? And finally, had Pell entered the sacristy alone, as opposed to being in the presence of someone else, and remained in that room uninterrupted?

Gibson urged the jury to think back to their impression of J after he finished giving his evidence. 'He was not a person indulging in fantasy or imagining things as was suggested to him by my learned friend [Richter] and suggested in the record of interview by Cardinal Pell. He was not a person indulging in fantasy or imagining things to a point where he believed his own imaginative mind, but rather simply telling it as it was—and is.'

There were some key reasons, along with the testimony of the surviving choirboy, why the jury should find Pell guilty, Gibson continued. First, there was an opportunity for the abuse described [by J] to have occurred. 'The opportunity in terms of the mass; there being a mass on 15 December and 22 December 1996 and 23 February 1997 in the time period J said the abuse occurred,' he said. Second, the procession line of choristers was not of 'military precision'. 'It broke down at times, especially the further it got to the iron gates and the toilet corridor.' Third, Gibson argued, the boys' re-entry via the south transept of the cathedral would not have brought attention to the pair given the 'throng' of people leaving after mass.

Explaining his next point, Gibson said the first double door leading to the sacristy door was in fact open and therefore accessible to the two choristers. The sacristy door itself was also open and there was a period of 'inaction' in terms of ferrying items from the sanctuary into the sacristies. The wine and wood panelling in the priest's sacristy, as described by J, did exist at the time. Gibson also reminded the jury that it had also been heard in court that Pell was using the priest's sacristy at the time as his own sacristy was undergoing renovations.

Finally, Gibson said, the second incident against J in the corridor should be believed as there would have been a reason for Pell to have been presiding over mass and to have been returning via the corridor where the alleged attack occurred. 'And so for all those reasons, Mr Foreman and members of the jury, I ask that you return verdicts of guilty on each of the five charges.'

The following day, in another packed courtroom that included former deputy prime minister Tim Fischer, who had served as Ambassador to the Holy See, Richter would respond with a reloaded array of impassioned statements delivered with his unique flair. 'This story is made up and you've been given a very un-tasty dish to digest, and you have to as that is your sworn duty,' he told the jury bluntly.

Richter's closing address had been extensively reworked in both content and structure. It had to be. His famous client was in the last-chance saloon; in a few days' time he could either be sitting in a comfortable business-class seat on an A380 headed to Italy or on the achingly hard surface of a prison bed. The stakes couldn't be higher.

Not only had Richter's arguments been carefully revised, with new layers of detail and explanation, but he also added a lengthy PowerPoint presentation—something the experienced regular court reporters covering the case had never seen before. He used over 30 pages of diagrams, maps and bullet points to explain in forensic detail why the allegations against the cardinal were 'impossible'. The presentation also included three pictures of the surviving accuser on the police tour of the cathedral's sacristy. Wearing a beige jacket and red jumper, it was the first time the media present had seen any images of the man at the centre of the case.

Accusing the jury of assuming the cardinal was guilty when they first saw him in the dock, Richter claimed: 'When you came to take your seats . . . and you looked at the accused . . . George Pell the man, Cardinal Pell, third most important person in the Vatican, minister of the economy—that's like the treasurer—did you say to yourselves "I bet this man is innocent"? I bet you didn't.'

The comment prompted the fury of Judge Kidd, who asked the jury to leave the court briefly. Richter would also be ticked off for mentioning Sano Task Force's appeal in December 2016 for any other victims of abuse in the time of Pell's tenure as archbishop to come forward. 'I'm furious, Mr Richter,' the judge said, staring down at him from the bench. 'Given that the issue was debated and I ruled against you on that . . . I can't believe you've done it.'

Richter, who no doubt prepared himself well for the likely fallout, made what he described as a 'grovelling apology' to the jury—phrased, as ever, with a dose of self-deprecating charm. 'The fact is I suppose I have been practicing law for some time . . . but practising means practise, you never get to be perfect,' he said, pushing his round spectacles to the top of his nose.

As Tim Fischer left the courtroom, he walked over to the dock and shook Pell's hand. It was a notable display of support from the man who a month earlier had publicly announced he was being treated for 'acute leukaemia'.[4] Afterwards, outside on the court steps, Fischer lifted his hand and covered his face as reporters took photos of him with their phones. 'I don't want to say anything,' he said as he walked off across Lonsdale Street.

Pell may well have been enduring the lowest point of his life and career, but he certainly still had friends in high places. Even if they didn't always want the world to know about it.

———

Continuing his closing address, Richter went back into combat the next day. Of the Crown's case, he said it only had 'a sequence of possibilities' but no firm evidence. 'You wouldn't hang a chicken on that . . . let alone decide a man's fate.'

He then made an announcement that would briefly halt proceedings and surprise both the judge and the prosecution team. He wanted to play a video, a 'visualisation of our argument'. In a reminder of the 1980s' video game Pac-Man, it depicted the layout of St Patrick's Cathedral with coloured dots representing each person involved in Sunday Mass in December 1996. Overseen by Ruth Shann and a young tech guru, Pell's legal team had outsourced the video's production. It must have taken hours and cost thousands of dollars to make.

If Pell's team thought the video would greatly assist them, they would be disappointed. Both the Crown and the judge took time to watch the video, but after lengthy legal argument it was finally ruled it could not be played in court. The judge pointed out that there was no CCTV footage from the era of the allegations and that the video attempted to suggest a reconstruction of where people were at certain times when there wasn't supporting evidence for this. It would be wrongly 'seductive' in regard to where everyone was at the cathedral after mass, the judge said. The banning of the video would become a handy weapon in Richter's armoury for later.

Richter calmly soldiered on. His address lasted a day and a half. The legal system 'depends on jurors like you', he told the court. 'I ask for a verdict of not guilty, thank you.'

Pell's solicitor Paul Galbally smiled at Richter as he sat down. He would later pat the barrister on the back. Congratulating him outside the courtroom, the pair broke into laughter. The defence team seemed to be extremely confident. It could not be denied that Richter had injected new and multiple layers of uncertainty regarding the allegations. Was a guilty verdict now even possible? Surely the jury was drowning in doubt? Or had the testimony of J been so convincing and powerful on its own, it would override everything Richter had said and argued?

In summing up, Judge Kidd said the 'real issue' for the jurors was whether they were satisfied beyond reasonable doubt that the events described by the surviving accuser happened. 'If you're not satisfied beyond reasonable doubt you must acquit.'

Kidd presented the contrasting arguments heard regarding the fact that the deceased choirboy had been asked by his mother in 2001 if he had been 'interfered with or touched up' when he was in the choir. 'R replied he had not been, he said "no" to his mother . . . the defence rely upon this evidence and ask you to act on it, they in fact asked you to keep this steadily in mind,' Judge Kidd said.

'On the other hand you heard from Mr Gibson,' the judge continued, 'and he puts an argument to you . . . that there may be many reasons why a 17 or 18 year old male would not want to tell his mother that he was sexually abused as a child . . . he gave some possible reasons such as embarrassment and shame.'

The judge also gave legal directions to the jury regarding the fact the surviving choirboy didn't come forward to police with a complaint against Pell for nearly 20 years. 'Experience shows that people react differently to sexual offences and there is no typical, proper or normal response to a sexual offence. Some people may complain immediately to the first person they see, while others may not complain for sometime, and others may never make a complaint.'

The defence placed greater weight on the fact the two choir-boys had apparently never discussed the alleged sacristy attack, the judge reminded the jury. Richter had said if the attack had really happened it would have been expected for the boys to have talked about it together. 'Mr Gibson put arguments that they were two 13-year-old boys and he put the arguments to you that you would not expect 13-year-old boys to discuss such matters . . . you will consider all of those arguments,' the judge said.

Judge Kidd then turned to the evidence of J, saying it was a matter for the jurors to decide using their 'common sense' whether his evidence was honest 'in the sense that the complainant believes it to be true but also whether it is in fact true'.

The ballot for two jurors to leave in order to reduce their number to twelve took place just before lunchtime on Thursday 6 December. The first to be called out was the foreman. Everyone in the court laughed, even the cardinal: only the foreman was exempt from being balloted off.

The rapid-fire clicking of the handle of the ballot box being turned echoed around the court again.

A middle-aged man and a woman in the middle row of the jury box were called up and left the box with no time to say goodbye to their fellow jurors who remained behind. It was a reminder that serving on a jury could be a tough business; these two jurors had invested four weeks of their lives in a case they would now not be deliberating on.

The remaining twelve jurors, eight men and four women, were instructed to leave the court to begin their deliberations.

The cardinal took his seat in a small interview room directly opposite the courtroom door. He seemed relaxed, putting in his favourite order with the legal clerk of a diet coke and sausage rolls.

The reporters settled into nearby interview rooms. As with the first trial, a betting sheet was drawn up. Those hoping to fly back home in time for the weekend were optimistically pitching for a result by the following day. But taking my cue from the long deliberations in the first trial, I settled on 4 p.m. the following Tuesday.

———

In identical timing with the first trial, the jury requested a copy of the recording of the accuser's testimony almost immediately. It was clearly as essential to deliberations as it had been for jurors in the first trial. The jury also asked for a recording of Monsignor Portelli's evidence.

If Pell had been disheartened by these requests, he would surely have received a morale boost from the breaking news that the former Adelaide archbishop Philip Wilson was set to walk free from his home-detention sentence after his conviction for concealing child sexual abuse had been quashed. At a hearing in the same Newcastle court where he'd been sentenced five months earlier, Judge Roy Ellis said Father Wilson was an 'honest and consistent' witness and he had reasonable doubts that he had been told about the abuse.[5]

Survivors and advocates were outraged by the decision. Steven Smith, a survivor of sexual abuse in the Anglican church, told the ABC victims continued to be 'smacked down' by the legal system. 'All we've seen today is if you throw enough money at something, which the Catholic Church has done here, you'll eventually find a judge that will see things your way,' he said. 'We've got the police who encourage us to come forward and speak up and we've got the judges who slap us back down again. Seriously, why would you bother?'

As the deliberations continued in Melbourne, Pell ensured he fitted in some gentle exercise by walking up and down the corridor. Asked by a court security guard if everything was okay, Pell replied breezily, 'Battling along.'

With his door often left open, a female supporter could be heard reading out messages of encouragement. There would be sporadic laughter, and at one point Pell could be heard loudly discussing the evidence regarding the sacramental wine.

By 4 p.m. it was clear that no verdict had been reached and that the jury would have to return the following week. Had the jury reached a stressful deadlock, or did they just need more time to go through the thousands of pages of court transcripts?

———

At 3.45 p.m. on Tuesday 11 December we were back in the court. 'Bring in the jury,' Judge Kidd said.

The jury filed in, looking serious yet relaxed and certainly not giving any indication of what their decision might be.

'Mr Foreman, I understand that you have a verdict,' the judge said.

'We have,' the grey-haired man replied.

Judge Kidd's young senior associate, Bridie Kelly, then stood and read out the first charge to the foreman. It concerned Pell committing an indecent act with or in the presence of the now deceased choirboy when he was thirteen.

'Do you find George Pell guilty or not guilty?' asked the law graduate.

There was a brief pause.

'Guilty,' he said, firmly yet calmly.

The word ricocheted around the room like a hand grenade. I'd never known a single word to carry so much weight. Was this even real? Did I hear it correctly? The foreman had set off the equivalent of a global atomic bomb that would soon reach the heart of the Holy See 16,000 kilometres away.

'Oh my God,' I whispered, as a collective gasp was heard around the courtroom. The whole scene seemed to be playing out in slow motion.

Pell pursed his lips and looked down at the carpet. His large hands gripped his thighs as if he needed to steady himself. He turned so pale his skin looked almost alabaster against his black suit. He suddenly appeared older, lost and fragile.

Two female abuse advocates started crying. As I tried to write notes my own tears began falling onto my laptop. My emotions stemmed from the fact the former choirboy wasn't alive to know the verdict, but he and his family were getting their vindication. It felt like a voice from the grave.

George Pell had been found guilty of an evil deed against an innocent young boy in his own holy cathedral. The betrayal of those who had trusted him—the victim, his parents, cathedral staff, the Catholic community—was immense. The hypocrisy of every sermon, every prayer and every word he'd written on faith, duty, homosexuality and celibacy was overwhelming.

The foreman would calmly say 'guilty' four more times regarding the charges of assaults on J. A muffled but shocking verbal gunshot echoed around the courtroom, and eventually around the world. What would the Pope say? The ramifications were endless.

Judge Kidd leaned forward, hands clasped together. Even he looked startled. He knew that Pell's future had taken a sharp turn away from career recovery and a return to Rome to years inside a Victorian jail cell and his name being marked on the Victorian Register of Sex Offenders. Pell's red robes carefully pressed by nuns for mass at the Vatican would soon be replaced by an itchy prison-issue green tracksuit and the sound of locks turning in iron-clad doors.

Pell would have known in that instant that at the age of 77, and with his bad heart and other ailments, he might not see the other side of a jail term alive.

Paul Galbally put his head in his hands and shook his head in despair. It was clear he couldn't face meeting his client's devastated eyes.

Sarah Pell, who had briefly left the court, returned and reached out to hold her uncle's hand. He angrily shooed her away. 'Sit down,' he said. The little girl who knocked on his door in Ballarat had now knocked at the wrong time. This was the first time Pell's infamous temper had shown itself publicly in the gruelling eighteen-month long case, his mask of poise and inner calm dropped as he struggled to comprehend his new reality.

'Thank you very much, members of the jury, for the work you have done on this case,' Judge Kidd said, getting on with business. 'I make no comment whatsoever about your verdicts. It wouldn't be appropriate for me to do so. That's your decision and yours alone.

'The work that you have done over the last several weeks has been noticed by us all, and in particular over the last few days you have obviously all worked diligently towards your verdicts in accordance with your oath.'

Kidd conceded the case been 'onerous' for the jury, '. . . in terms of the length of the trial and in terms of the issues which you had to grapple with. I for one strongly believe in the jury system. I think it's a terrific system, it's really important that our fellow citizens are ultimately judged by their fellow citizens like you have done in this case no matter what their station is in life . . . On behalf of the court and behalf of the community of Victoria, I cannot express our thanks enough for the time and dedication you've brought to this case.'

Richter addressed the judge in uncharacteristically low tones. He applied to have the cardinal's bail extended into the new year so he could proceed with knee surgery in Sydney. Kidd agreed, remanding Pell into custody at his plea hearing.

'I have had the opportunity throughout the course of the last several months to observe Cardinal Pell move and it's clear that he is a man labouring under a disability . . . this is no way a sign of the sentence Cardinal Pell will face,' the judge added. 'It is simply a sign of the court's humanity in recognition of an elderly person who has been found guilty of serious offences to attend what is an obvious need for significant surgery to his knees.'

For Richter, this high-profile case was perhaps to be one of the glorious swan songs to a successful career. Standing up, he walked over to his client, who was sitting motionless in the dock, reached out and held the cardinal's hand. He just stood there, clearly struggling to find words to comfort the man whose reputation was lying in ruins. Ruth Shann also walked over and reached out her slim hand to rest on the cardinal's pale wrist.

What could either of them say? They'd given two trials every ounce of their experience and expertise. They'd spoken a million words and spent endless nights preparing, writing submissions and determining questions. Yet this was the result: never had two Melbourne barristers been such winners and losers at the same time. Pell was to be remanded to jail in the city where he had once been such a power player. As he walked out of the glass doors of the court into the early-evening summer sunlight, he pulled off what might be described as a mini-miracle; he managed a small smile. Despite everything, the proud church-man wasn't going to allow himself to crack in front of the breathless, jostling media pack as it squeezed around him from all directions. Flanked by about twenty police and protection-service officers, hanging on to his crutch he kept walking to his waiting silver Volkswagen.

The tough former ruckman would be jailed awaiting a certain appeal. And even Richter couldn't stop that. Pell had fallen. Fallen from a height so great, it would surely be impossible to rise again.

As the convicted cardinal began his long car journey towards Sydney and a date with a knee surgeon, the Pell pack posed for some group pictures to mark what we realised was an important moment in history. We were all exhausted. We had survived eighteen months of hearings and the two intense trials. It was time to go home to recharge.

None of us had broken the suppression order. As frustrating as it was that we couldn't report on the story, at least we had time to rest, write up our notes and start preparing for Pell's sentencing, a possible appeal and the Swimmers Trial.

But there was trouble ahead, serious, complicated trouble none of us could ever have predicted.

Chapter 12
The world's worst kept secret

Just as reporters were saying their goodbyes on the concrete concourse of the County Court of Victoria, the *Herald Sun*'s chief court reporter Shannon Deery was glancing down at his phone looking concerned. 'I'm sure this is going to leak,' he said with an edge of certainty. 'I'm already getting texts.'

I'd also received several messages from people who had somehow heard the news, even though at that stage it hadn't been reported by a single media outlet anywhere in the world. Chrissie Foster, holidaying in Uluru, had heard the news from a friend, while an entertainment and sports PR sent me a text saying he'd heard about the verdict too. Both asked the same question: 'Is it true?'

Deery was right. This juicy, jaw-dropping one-fact piece of news was just too explosive in the age of smart phones and social media not to spread like wildfire. How could it even be expected to be contained in 2018? The third most powerful man in the world's most powerful church was facing jail. The trial of the century had just resulted in the verdict of the century and it couldn't be reported.

The county court, in a move which I suspect it later regretted, issued the verdict with a copy of the suppression order to all registered media outlets, including those overseas. It had trusted the media organisations would abide by the order. The news of the hung jury back in September had gone mostly unreported, bar for a couple of vague mentions on rogue blogs that the court soon had removed. It had no reason to believe the suppression order would be breached with this development; after all, suppression orders aren't a 'suggestion' by a judge. Breaking them can lead to heavy fines and up to five years in prison.

'So we definitely can't publish it today?' Patrick Elligett, the editor of *The New Daily*, asked me in a version of the same call being received by reporters from their bosses. In truth they already knew the answer, but the frustration of sitting on a story of such important public interest that would boost subscriptions, web traffic and readers was clearly immense.

The angst felt by the Australian editors would soon be challenged. While they remained tied by the gag order, news of the verdict was spreading through offices, buses, cafes, hairdressers, homes and gyms throughout Australia and much of the world. It was a runaway train racing along the world wide web bearing the words 'Pell' and 'guilty' that couldn't be halted. Its originating station wasn't Melbourne, however—its starting point could be precisely pinpointed to the desk of one ambitious, hungry reporter sitting in an office 16,600 kilometres away in New York.

––––––

Lachlan Cartwright, a journalist with left-leaning online news website the *Daily Beast*, which prides itself on exposing secrets in politics in particular, had made his name working for *The Sun* in London and the *New York Post*. He rang me early on the morning following the verdict to give me the 'heads up' that the site was planning to be the first media outlet in the world to run a story about the guilty verdict.

Cartwright had been sniffing around the story of the retrial for a few weeks. I'd been friendly but had politely declined helping him with court reports, worried it could harm the proceedings and put me at risk of breaking the suppression order. 'It's okay though, we've geo-blocked Australia,' he said confidently about the potential legal impact of the story.

'But you can't geo-block people tweeting it,' I replied, warning him that the story was almost guaranteed to go viral and cause all sorts of problems for the court and Australian media. 'I'm telling you now you could be responsible for the Swimmers Trial collapsing. Do you and your website really want to be known for that in the long term?'

The website was aware of the legal situation and had taken advice from lawyers, he said. 'There's huge interest in this.'

'I know there is,' I replied, my voice rising. 'I've just spent years on this story and the last few months sitting through two trials along with other reporters who have invested their lives in this at great cost to their employers. Your website didn't invest anything, yet now you're claiming it's suddenly so important. And it's going to cause massive problems down here.'

I didn't blame him for wanting to break a bold exclusive story—that's the goal of every good journalist—and part of me felt a sharp pang of jealousy, but I knew this situation was different. The *Daily Beast*'s one story could put the future of the entire legal proceedings in another country in jeopardy.

Like many of the reporters in the Pell pack I had begun to care deeply that the next trial would run as planned, for the sake of the men who deserved their day in court. After initially being sceptical about the suppression order, I'd now come to strongly support it. I'd witnessed first hand how fragile and delicate this legal case was: dealing with allegations against a defendant of such status and fame while also trying to maintain a fair and unbiased jury. It was like juggling an eggshell.

But over in the offices of the *Daily Beast* in New York it was clear it was too distant, both geographically and emotionally, to either fully understand or care about what was at stake. The world would eventually know the important news about the conviction—it just had to wait. I continued doing my best to try and persuade Cartwright not to run the story. 'You know my work,' I said. 'In any other situation I'd say go for it and say good luck to you but this is not the time.'

Despite these conversations, the website soon published the story anyway—of course it would, how could it resist? The beast had roared. It had its dream scoop. The story went live early on 12 December Melbourne time, around seventeen hours after the guilty verdict was handed down. And, predictably, within minutes the details had spread on Twitter at lightning speed. Helplessly, I watched the story being picked up in media circles in New York, retweeted across the United States and then around the globe. It was the modern-day version of the 'shot heard around the world'.

'We understood there could be legal, and even criminal, consequences if we ran this story,' said Noah Shachtman, editor-in-chief of the *Daily Beast,* of the scoop.[1] 'But ultimately this was an easy call. You've got a top Vatican official convicted of a horrific crime. That's major, major news. The public deserves to know about it.'

While there were few actual details of the court proceedings in the story, it quickly gave confidence to many other platforms to publish. Radar Online, Slate.com and several Catholic news sites and blogs soon ran their own stories, all fuelled by retweets on Twitter.

I alerted CNN and *The New Daily* that the story was leaking online and that I was also hearing rumours that some Australian outlets were planning to challenge the suppression order at a court hearing in coming days. If it was spreading on the internet, they would argue, then further publicity wouldn't make a difference.

For the Pell pack the situation would play out the same way: we had to furiously write up as much as we could as quickly as possible in case the order was successfully challenged. Articles we previously thought we had months to carefully write and prepare might now be needed a lot sooner.

The mental and physical strain of being in the centre of this bizarre vortex was intense. My stomach locked in a spasm of pain that felt so severe they reminded me of labour contractions. I writhed in agony at my desk late at night and found myself vomiting on the floor. I wanted to do justice to all the months spent working on the trials, especially for those for whom it meant so much. And I wasn't alone. Another reporter was experiencing the same symptoms.

The situation was officially out of control. The guilty verdict was breaking the internet—and breaking some members of the Pell pack as well.

———

Amid the unfolding online chaos, I wondered if Margaret had heard the news in Gippsland? What had she felt in that moment? Was it of comfort to her or had it served to trigger painful, unwanted memories? Whatever I was feeling would be nothing compared to the suffering this bomb would cause her and many other survivors.

Among those also hearing the news through friends or Facebook would be the distressed jurors from the first trial. Surely it would have been a shock to hear not only that there had been another trial—but that the jury had agreed on a guilty verdict.

The verdict would certainly prove to be a lightning bolt that would strike the heart of the Vatican. Journalist Christopher Lamb remembers when the news of Pell's conviction reached Rome it caused 'a form of PTSD' for the church. 'As a result, there was a lot of denial among some Catholics,' he said later.

'I thought to myself, "This is all going to take a long time to process."'

The conviction also underscored there were no more free passes for bishops, and everyone was accountable. 'It did huge damage to the church as an institution and the morale of Catholics, and was a big moment in the abuse crisis, reshaping the relationship between the church and state,' Lamb explained.

Lamb's colleague in Rome, Gerard O'Connell, Vatican correspondent for *America Magazine*, also recalls the seismic shock the guilty verdict caused.[2] 'Almost everyone I knew in Rome was stunned at the verdict,' he said. 'It was rumoured that the first jury had tended 10–2 in his favour, but nobody knew this for certain.

'I personally was very surprised that he was convicted in the cathedral case. In fact, almost nobody in Rome that I know had expected him to be convicted, the charges against him seemed so improbable and difficult to sustain.

'The verdict must surely have come as a blow to Pope Francis, who had put so much trust in the cardinal, who always protested his innocence.'

In a telling signal, the Vatican chose the immediate aftermath of the conviction to announce that it had removed two cardinals from a powerful small council of advisers known as the C9.[3] One was Pell, the other was Francisco Javier Errázuriz of Chile, who had been accused of covering up abuse. Members of the council had asked the Pope to reflect on the 'work, structure and composition of the council, taking into account the advanced age of some members'. Old age, it seemed clear in this case, was a polite excuse for being sacked for causing scandal of the most shocking order.

The *Washington Post* then boldly joined the rogues' gallery by tweeting its own story on the verdict to its 13 million followers. 'The story is, indeed, a blockbuster, especially for Australian citizens,' wrote the *Post*'s media columnist Margaret Sullivan.[4] '. . . the secrecy surrounding the court case—and now the verdict—is offensive. That's especially so because it echoes the secrecy that has always been so appalling a part of widespread sexual abuse by priests.'

Sullivan quoted a survivor who suggested the wildly false idea that the media blackout was part of a wider conspiracy to protect the church. It was a view that was gaining traction. 'It's hard to know if there are any shenanigans going on—things the church did that are illegal themselves,' said Steven Spaner, Australia coordinator for the Survivors Network of Those Abused by Priests. 'There is always suspicion when you don't know what is going on.'

The fact one of the world's most highly respected newspapers was running a story that could be read online in Australia turned up the temperature in other newsrooms. It quickly prompted a conference call with my hyperventilating CNN editors in Hong Kong and the United States.

'We still can't run anything on any platform that can reach Australia,' I strongly advised. 'If you run it and use my reporting I could get jailed for contempt of court and breaching the order. The judge has already said as much this morning.'

Would CNN decide to sacrifice its local freelancer in order to break news of the verdict to 200 countries it broadcast into?

In the infamously dog-eat-dog world of journalism it wouldn't have surprised me, but CNN held back.

As the story picked up speed online, media outlets in Australian remained cautious, at least at first. But their frustration was reaching boiling point. It seemed everyone in the country—and the world—knew about the verdict. It was one of the worst kept secrets in history.

Radio and TV presenters were discussing the story without mentioning Pell by name. I'd overheard people on trains and mums at school gates talking about it. Knowing I had broken the first Pell story, I was excitedly asked for details. Fearful I would be quoted on social media and fall foul of the court order, I told anyone who asked that I couldn't discuss it.

Andrew Dodd, the Director of the Centre for Advancing Journalism, wrote that he hoped the farcical situation would re-energise the push to reform the use of suppression orders. 'As familiar and trusted TV anchors pretend the stories they're presenting are the best or only ones to report, viewers could be forgiven for questioning whether the media is party to a perverse form of fake news,' he said.[5]

Australian editors were becoming increasingly exasperated at being gagged. By the morning of 13 December newspapers across the country carried thundering front pages and editorials criticising the suppression order. This would prove to be a high-risk move with serious and drawn-out consequences.

Unlike overseas media the Australian papers didn't name Pell, but with the cardinal as the second-highest trending subject on Twitter, and being widely discussed on Facebook, it was alleged later it wouldn't be hard for readers to guess what the headlines were referring to.

'The world is reading a very important story that is relevant to Victorians,' wrote the *Herald Sun*, below a headline 'Censored'. Sydney's *Daily Telegraph* described it as the nation's biggest story: 'An awful crime. The person is guilty. Yet we can't publish it.'

The determined hack from the Big Apple had kickstarted a huge, complicated mess. The sheer scale of the bizarre situation had never before been experienced in Australian journalism.

Melbourne's *The Age* ran the headline, 'Why the media is unable to report on a case that has generated huge interest online'. The paper also informed readers that 'A year-long review of Victoria's 2013 Open Courts Act by retired judge Frank Vincent called into question the function and efficacy of suppression orders in an internet age. So far, none of the 18 recommendations have been implemented.' Vincent had found that of the 1594 orders made between 2014 and 2016, 22 per cent were blanket bans that either failed to say what was being suppressed or simply stated that the 'whole or any part of the proceeding' could not be reported at all. A further 12 per cent did not give any grounds.

While the newspapers may have genuinely believed their cryptic front pages and accompanying debates about suppression orders would not fall foul of the court order, Judge Kidd didn't see it that way. Far from it. On short notice, he called the legal teams for both the Crown and the defence to court on 13 December (the same day as the hysterical Australian newspaper front pages were published) for an emergency mention hearing. The media was not informed—we were all apparently in the judicial doghouse.

What was evident from a transcript issued shortly afterwards was that Kidd wasn't just annoyed about the coverage of the case—he was livid. 'Some of the media that has occurred overnight at the very least raises a serious question as to whether my suppression order has been breached in the most egregious way possible,' he told the assembled barristers. 'The media coverage overnight also raises a serious question, quite independently of that, of contempt of the court, namely bringing inappropriate and improper pressure upon me to vary or revoke my suppression order application.'

Kerri Judd, QC, the newly installed Victorian Director of Public Prosecutions, was also present in court and seemed equally as alarmed. She suggested to Kidd that she would take over the matters regarding the possible media breaches. 'Can I add into the mix of other possible offences a contempt in the sense of potentially prejudicing the next trial?' she asked. 'So you have got the suppression order breach . . . you have got the contempt you mentioned . . . but there is also . . . the sub judice contempt.'

Known in legal circles as a force to be reckoned with, Judd suggested the starting point was to draft a letter to the media outlets that may have breached the order. Reporters and editors overseas could face prosecution. 'There are some considerations and I don't want to elaborate on those at this point in time but there's issues in terms of jurisdictions, extradition,' she said.

The usually measured and unemotional Kidd didn't hide his anger over the media coverage. 'It's just breathtaking,' he said. 'You are supposed to leave the bench when you are angry, but I'll stay for a bit longer to finish this hearing off.'

As paparazzi photos were published of the cardinal hobbling with his crutches to a waiting car at a Sydney hospital following his knee operation, it was clear a hearing the following day involving newspapers and broadcasters applying to revoke, or vary, the suppression order could well be a volatile affair indeed.

———

Representing multiple media clients languishing in a crowded sin bin was never going to be an easy task for barrister Sandip Mukerjea. On Friday 14 December, in the same courtroom where Pell had been convicted just three days earlier, the barrister attempted to persuade Judge Kidd why the press should be able to report the guilty verdict. It was soon obvious why he was recognised as being one of the country's leading media lawyers. Despite a strong pushback from the judge, he never gave up trying.

Engaged on behalf of a number of media outlets including the Herald and Weekly Times, the ABC, Nine Network, *The Age* and Nationwide News, Mukerjea told the judge it would be 'fair' and in the public interest for the verdict to be reported in Australia considering the extensive reporting online from overseas outlets.

'Fair to who?' Kidd immediately shot back red-faced. 'To the accused person? What about the complainants, they are entitled to justice too?' He reminded Mukerjea that no media outlets had opposed the suppression order in regards to publication in Victoria when it was handed down earlier in the year.

At one stage Kidd admonished the barrister for pointing at him with his finger, discussing with Mukerjea that the media clients had come to the court with 'dirty hands', alleging they had attacked the court and pressured him for 72 hours. 'They engaged in the court of public opinion without having made a single submission to me.' He argued that now Pell had been convicted it was all the more reason to 'quarantine the next jury' from coverage in Australian media. If the order was lifted, that coverage would be at 'saturation'.

Mukerjea conceded that his task applying for the media to be allowed to report the guilty verdict 'wasn't an easy application'.

'You are in a difficult situation today, it has to be said,' Kidd replied smiling.

Richter contributed to the otherwise tense hearing when he was asked to make his submission. He urged the judge to maintain the suppression order as it stood, saying that even though the 'cat's head was out of the bag it didn't mean you had to release the body'.

Having lost trust in journalists, Judge Kidd made a further order preventing reporting of the hearing itself. 'Given I have no faith in the media at the moment to apply the most basic form of common sense I make a suppression order over these proceedings.'

Not a single member of the Pell pack had broken the suppression order, yet Judge Kidd had decided he couldn't trust anyone in the media at all, including us. I immediately wrote a personal note to the judge making that point in case there had been any misunderstanding. Another reporter did the same. We had all worked incredibly hard to abide by the order and had respected both Judge Kidd's rulings and the court process. We didn't want to be grouped with the other journalists who allegedly hadn't. We also wanted to make sure we'd be allowed to return for the next trial.

When a noticeably calmer Kidd returned to court at 4 p.m. to announce his decision, no one was surprised that he refused to lift the suppression order. For 'proper procedure of justice' he needed to contain what would otherwise be an extreme level of publicity. 'Whilst I've got real concern of conduct of some interveners,' he continued, 'I want to recognise there are a number of journalists out there who have behaved responsibly and ethically and have not engaged in this kind of conduct and I congratulate you for that.'

His words were much appreciated and with them came a sense of relief. Not only did the Pell pack have more time to work on our extensive trial reports for a later date, but our group had also survived. We'd successfully distanced ourselves from those now facing potentially serious legal action.

It seemed like our own Christmas miracle. It would be a brief reprieve, however, from yet another spot fire.

———

The following afternoon I discovered that *Crux Now*, a US-based website that reports on Catholic-related news stories, was running a story on the Pell verdict together with unreported details of what had been heard at the trial. What alarmed me most was the site, sponsored by the world's largest fraternal service organisation, Knights of Columbus, was edited by John L. Allen Jr, a fellow CNN freelance contributor and Vatican expert.

I'd checked with my editor and agreed to Allen's emailed request to be copied into my daily confidential internal CNN court memos several weeks before. It had been made clear on every memo that the information was strictly suppressed—and subject to a court order.

When I questioned Allen, he immediately took down the story and admitted he had been 'guided' by my memos. I also pointed out to him that he'd published an earlier story about the suppression order itself. He also claimed to have used other Australian legal sources to compile the reports. I felt shocked and let down.

Allen and his platform *Crux Now* were fully aware of the legal consequences of reporting on the case and the verdict and how it could affect both my position as a journalist and the next trial. What was the presiding motivation?

I couldn't afford to take any chances; nor could I ignore a possible crime. I decided my priority had to be to the jurisdiction of Victoria, where I lived with my family, and to the court, where I worked. It was a difficult decision, but I had to trust my instincts. There was no other option. I informed the court about the *Crux Now* stories and decided to withdraw my freelance services for CNN.

I felt I'd been caught up in a parallel universe of yet more media treachery and questionable agendas. It was also plain to see what I had already suspected from my News Corp experience—this global story was almost too hard and too deep to handle for even the largest news organisations. CNN was so vast, it couldn't prevent its own staff or a contributor from interfering with the story. In the thin and mysterious membrane between sleep and wakefulness, memories were triggered of the intense turmoil I endured after breaking the original *Herald Sun* story on the abuse allegations. Yet again, I was paying a personal price in my quest to simply report the truth. And for not giving up against the odds.

I had to prevent myself from falling over the precipice; I was already teetering on the edge. I asked CNN to delete all the suppressed court content I had filed in case it was misused elsewhere. I also warned friends and contacts to delete any comments I may have made about my experience reporting on the Pell story. I also put my laptop and notebooks, containing all my notes from the suppressed trials, in a safe place and hid the key. My priority was just to make it to the finish line without being prosecuted or crumbling into a heap. But I'd keep moving forward and would focus on preparing my extensive court diaries and stories about the case for *The New Daily*.

I was also quietly proceeding with an incredible opportunity that had arisen: the chance to write a book on the history-making case. My tumultuous journey was now starting to make sense. There had been something important waiting for me at the end of the twisting, murky tunnel after all.

I soon gained a welcome sense of assurance about my tough stance on the *Crux Now* stories when I received a personal invitation to attend an unexpected hearing on the Pell matter just five days before Christmas. The court had become so concerned about the leaks that it selected only a handful of trusted members of the Pell pack to be present for a mention on plans for the Swimmers Trial.

Just seven journalists were present; it felt as if we were the last survivors standing after the media charge through the china shop. After the messy hysteria of the previous week, the court was back in control. The storm had passed.

The *Herald Sun*, knowing its 'Censored' front page had been mentioned disparagingly by the judge, didn't take any chances. It sent a black-suited lawyer to sit with journalist Shannon Deery like a protective bodyguard.

During the hearing Richter confirmed what we had all suspected: Pell was planning on launching an appeal. The defence, he told the judge, would be taking the overall approach that the conviction was 'unsafe and unsatisfactory'. Richter's deputy, Ruth Shann, was already working 'furiously' on the matter, which would be lodged with the Court of Appeal on the other side of Lonsdale Street.

After setting dates for a pre-hearing for the Swimmers Trial in mid February, and also deciding that the trial itself would commence in April, Judge Kidd encouraged us all to take a break. 'We are all entitled to look after our well-being,' he said, looking down at the legal counsels seated at the bar table. 'Merry Christmas and happy new year and see you in a few weeks' time.'

Kidd's words certainly brought a much needed although temporary full stop. This time we really would be going home for Christmas. Everyone, that is, except for Cardinal Pell.

Home for his Eminence was now a basic room in the Sydney seminary, recovering from his operation, with the dire prospect of a Victorian jail cell being his new abode in the new year. While Christmas candles flickered in Rome's churches, Pell's apartment on Piazza Della Citta Leonina stood locked, cold and empty.

Chapter 13
Friends in high places

During the festive season news of the guilty verdict started to dis-appear and fall silent on the internet. Silence was a positive force, Pope Francis said as he delivered his New Year's Day Homily Mass in St Peter's Basilica. 'To set aside a moment of silence each day to be with God is to keep our soul,' he told worshippers.[1] 'It is to keep our freedom from being corroded by the banality of consumerism, the blare of commercials, the stream of empty words and the over-powering waves of empty chatter and loud shouting.'

As the cardinals, bishops and abbots stood in formation around the Pontiff under towering arrangements of deep-red flowers and candles, he spoke of the importance of maternal love, while also encouraging believers to start afresh. 'At the beginning of the year, we too, as Christians on our pilgrim way, feel the need to set out anew from the centre, to leave behind the burdens of the past and to start over from the things that really matter,' he said. Francis may well have been referring to his desire to move forward from his church's past troubles and accusations in the previous year of his own failures dealing with allegations against clergy.

Early in February he acknowledged that the sexual abuse of nuns, by priests and bishops, was a past and present problem 'we've been working on for some time'. During a press conference aboard the papal plane on a return flight to Rome from the United Arab Emirates, Francis spoke of the sexual abuse of nuns in France and the action his predecessor Pope Benedict had tried to take only to be thwarted by Vatican insiders.[2] 'Must something be done? Yes,' Francis told reporters. 'Do we have the will? Yes.'

The Pope's hardline attitude on matters of sexual abuse increased after the controversy around his initial response to the Chile scandal. This was evidenced just after Christmas when it emerged that a long-promised investigation into the alleged crimes of disgraced ex-cardinal Theodore McCarrick had begun.[3]

Back in Melbourne, it emerged that a group of 50 to 100 reporters, editors and outlets had received a letter from Kerri Judd, the Victorian Director of Public Prosecutions, advising they may face prosecution for possible breaches of the Pell case suppression order. This was unprecedented. Judd had been wholly serious about taking action over the cryptic headlines about the case. Media lawyers were busy fighting back aggressively in tone, denying any wrongdoing and rejecting the accusations.

Either way, the Pell case was back in motion and the reporting pack was reunited. On 13 February 2019 we returned to court for the pre-trial hearing for the Swimmers Trial.

The trial would centre on allegations that Pell had separately touched two boys while playing with them in a pool between 1977 and 1979. One boy was aged eleven or twelve, and the other was said to have been aged nine or ten.

We heard in the opening hours of the pre-trial hearing how the older boy told detectives many years later that he felt one of Pell's fingers touch his testicle when he was lifted and thrown out of the water. The other boy reported that on several occasions Pell 'deliberately' groped him on the genitals and backside while under the water.

We listened as prosecutor Fran Dalziel, SC, applied to Judge Kidd to grant the use of 'tendency and coincidence' evidence in the trial. She referenced an incident that had been raised in the committal proceedings. At a family picnic at Lake Boga, a third boy was playing in the water with Pell when he slipped off the priest's shoulders and made accidental contact with his apparently erect penis. Dalziel needed the judge to allow her to argue that Pell had a tendency to indecently touch boys under the guise of playing in the water, and that it was improbable that the men's allegations were coincidental.

The evidence of all three men would need to be heard by the jury if both charges were to be proven, the barrister conceded, in what seemed a very complex scenario. Robert Richter and Ruth Shann, naturally, argued forcefully against Dalziel's application.

Judge Kidd would hand down his decision the following week, he said.

The Pell pack had been left somewhat confused by the possible ramifications of this delay. Kidd hadn't seemed convinced by the tendency evidence; he'd drilled deep holes into what had been presented by the Crown. If Kidd ruled against the evidence being used, it was very likely the Crown would not proceed with the Swimmers Trial.

The collapse of the case would have two outcomes: the media suppression order would be lifted, and the accusers, who'd spent years in a judicial holding bay, would not have their day in court after all.

As we grappled for some certainty in the complicated judicial maze, it emerged the Vatican had made a firm decision regarding Theodore McCarrick—he'd been defrocked.

———

In the United States, church officials said allegations McCarrick had sexually assaulted a teenager five decades before were credible.[4] The 88-year-old had resigned from the College of Cardinals, becoming the first cleric in more than 100 years to do so, but claimed he had 'no recollection' of the alleged abuse.

'No bishop, no matter how influential, is above the law of the church,' said Cardinal Daniel DiNardo, president of the United States Conference of Catholic Bishops.

But just as Pope Francis was preparing for his eagerly awaited summit with the world's bishops on the child-abuse crisis, the *New York Times* published a story exposing the Vatican's secret rules for priests who have children. The Vatican confirmed, apparently for the first time, that its department overseeing the world's priests had general guidelines on how to act when clerics break their celibacy vows and father children. This drew attention to the question of whether it was time to make celibacy optional—as already recommended in the final report of Australia's royal commission into the sexual abuse of children.

There would be another embarrassing hurdle for the Pope to face before he took centre stage at the 'Meeting on the Protection of Minors in the Catholic Church'. An explosive book, *In the Closet of the Vatican* by French journalist Frédéric Martel, claimed homosexuality was rampant in the city state of supposedly celibate clergy. Martel claimed to have spoken to 1500 sources, including 41 cardinals, 52 bishops and 45 current and former Vatican ambassadors, or nuncios, during his four years of research.

'The timing of this book is tremendously problematic,' Reverend James Martin, an American Jesuit priest, told CNN. 'It will distract from the summit and raise in people's minds the idea that all gay priests are breaking their vows and are linked to abuse.'[5]

Whatever the fears surrounding the book's impact, the summit went ahead. It was attended by 190 mostly male delegates, and watched with great anticipation by the world's media, survivors and advocates.

Francis opened the four-day summit by warning that constituents were expecting concrete actions—not just empty promises and words. 'The holy people of God are watching and expect not just simple and obvious condemnations,' he said, 'but efficient and concrete measures to be established.'

Sitting in stunned silence, the delegates watched videotaped recordings of searing, raw interviews with five child sexual-abuse victims from around the world.[6] In heartbreaking detail, they described the attacks they endured at the hands of clerics. A survivor from Africa told of a priest who had beat her from the age of fifteen if she refused to have sex, and then forced her to have three abortions when she became pregnant.

Manila's cardinal, Luis Tagle, fought back tears as he watched the video testimony. Afterwards he demanded his fellow bishops and superiors no longer turn a blind eye to the harm caused by clergy who rape and molest children. 'Our lack of response to the suffering of victims, yes even to the point of rejecting them and covering up the scandal to protect perpetrators and the institution, has injured our people,' Tagle said. It had caused a 'deep wound in our relationship with those we are sent to serve'.

For his part, Francis proposed a path of practical reform, offering 21 proposals for the church to consider. Calling for specific protocols to handle accusations against bishops, he also suggested protocols to govern the transfers of seminarians or priests to prevent predators from moving freely to unsuspecting communities. Other ideas included calls for bolstering child-protection laws in some countries by raising the minimum age for marriage to sixteen, and the preparation of a handbook telling bishops how to investigate cases.

While Francis may have tried to set a conciliatory tone at his summit, by the evening of day three he couldn't prevent the pointed fury of Valentina Alazraki, the woman considered to be the doyen of the Vatican press corps. 'If you do not decide in a radical way to be on the side of the children, mothers, families, civil society, you are right to be afraid of us,' she said forcibly in Spanish. 'Because we journalists, who seek the common good, will be your worst enemies.'

The summit was certainly being used to speak truth to power. And for those close to hand, it was recognised as an important moment in the history of the church's response to the abuse crisis.

'This was the first time the bishops collectively heard from survivors and addressed the matter from a global perspective,' Vatican journalist Christopher Lamb explained.[7] 'It shifted the internal debate and awareness in the church—and that's how things change.'

While the summit itself was welcomed by advocates for facing the problem of abuse within the church, there was also a sense of disappointment that there had been no clear policy decisions. It wasn't the concrete action the Pope had promised at all.

It would take time, Mark Coleridge, the Archbishop of Brisbane, pointed out.[8] 'It's like turning around . . . an enormous ship,' he said. 'Now the ship has begun to turn quite some years ago, but it is still turning, and I do think that this meeting was quite a significant moment in the turning of the ship.'

If Pope Francis held any hope that the summit would be a public-relations success, there was bad news in store. We were about to be back in court in Melbourne for the final decision about the Swimmers Trial.

———

Judge Kidd had made the ruling we had predicted: he would not allow the tendency and coincidence evidence to be used in the Swimmers Trial. The crown wanted time to consider its options, Dalziel told the judge. If the trial collapsed, the cloak of secrecy over the whole Pell matter could finally be lifted for good. The latest news on the Pell scandal was about to strike the Holy See.

It had been a tense wait of over a week, but on 26 February 2019, as the cardinal sat in the dock in his clerical suit looking strained and anxious, Fran Dalziel stood and announced very simply the news we had been expecting: the Crown would not proceed with the Swimmers Trial.

Pell didn't show any emotion except to gulp and fiddle with the large episcopal gold ring on his finger. It was a bittersweet moment. On the one hand it was certainly a victory not to face another trial, but he would have been well aware the decision also meant the news blackout would immediately be lifted. Reporting of the guilty verdict in the choirboy case would dominate the news around the world. What was left of his already damaged reputation would soon be destroyed so completely that nothing could be salvaged.

After lengthy legal argument about whether Richter would pursue an extension of the suppression order in the court of appeal, he eventually decided he would not argue further.

Judge Kidd stiffened and declared the order was lifted.

Reporters quickly sent messages to their editors telling them to publish the stories they had first written in haste in the viral storm before Christmas. We tweeted the news of this important story that we had wanted to share since December. The truth was out at last. It was a huge relief after being constrained by the court order for so long.

By the time Pell left the court a few minutes later, an ugly scene was already playing out on the concourse. Some members of the public who'd received the news alerts began shouting obscenities at him. 'You're a monster' and 'scum', they yelled as he was led through a huge media scrum to a waiting car.

Police officers held back furious onlookers pushing towards the cardinal. Two photographers were punched in the crush. Katrina Lee, the executive adviser for the Archdiocese of Sydney who had been by Pell's side from the start, protected the cardinal as best she could.

The nasty crush served as a reminder of the importance of the suppression order for this unique legal case. If these heated displays had occurred in front of the jury, there could have been constant disruption and consequences for a fair trial.

The collapse of the Swimmers Trial was certainly difficult for the men involved. Ingrid Irwin, the Ballarat solicitor who had represented Lyndon Monument and the late Damian Dignan, was close to tears outside the court. She was devastated the case had been discontinued. 'The men, who have gone through a gruelling legal process to this point lasting years, will no longer get their day in court,' she said.[9]

Surrounded by reporters and cameras, Viv Waller, the specialist clergy-abuse lawyer who represented the surviving choirboy, read out a statement from her client. The invisible accuser suddenly felt very present.

Thank you for your interest in this case.

Like many survivors I have experienced shame, loneliness, depression and struggle. Like many survivors it has taken me years to understand the impact on my life.

At some point we realise that we trusted someone we should have feared and we fear those genuine relationships that we should trust.

I would like to thank my family near and far for their support of me, and of each other.

I am a witness in a case brought by the State of Victoria, I have put my trust in the police and the criminal justice system.

The process has been stressful and it is not over yet.

I need space and time to cope with the ongoing criminal process.

I understand this is a big news story but please don't reveal my identity.

I ask that the media respect my privacy. I don't want to give any interviews. Please don't come to my home. I want to protect my young family and my parents. I don't want them swept into the spotlight.

I am not a spokesperson about child sexual abuse. There are many other survivors and advocates who bravely fill this role.

I am just a regular guy working to support and protect my family as best I can.

Thank you for your support and understanding.

As quickly as the accuser's emotional words were reported, Pell's supporters in the right-wing media began their thunderous attacks in response.

The fightback had begun.

———

'He is a scapegoat, not a child abuser,' wrote my former colleague Andrew Bolt for a piece published in the *Herald Sun* the following day. Even though he had not attended a single day of the trial, and like the rest of the media had not heard the accuser's evidence, Bolt described the guilty verdict as a wrongful conviction, saying he didn't believe the 'gothic story' of the abuse in the cathedral. 'On top of that, the man I know seems incapable of such abuse,' he continued, 'but so intelligent and cautious that he would never risk his brilliant career and good name on such a mad assault in such a public place.'

Miranda Devine, writing in the *Daily Telegraph*, another Murdoch-owned tabloid, also appeared to base her assessment of the verdict on a belief the cardinal was incapable of the crimes. 'It's devastating because I don't believe that Pell, who I know slightly and admire greatly, could be guilty of sexually assaulting two choirboys in a busy cathedral after Sunday mass,' she wrote.

The Australian, which hadn't sent a single reporter to the retrial, published a number of articles on its front page by critics who argued the victim's testimony was false. Father Frank Brennan and Professor Greg Craven cast doubt on the conviction, suggesting media pressure and the court of public opinion had influenced the outcome. 'George Pell: a case in which fair justice never had a fair chance', was the headline on Craven's article.

Peter Westmore, the former Catholic lobby-group leader who had attended much of the trial and been a supportive presence for the cardinal, even appeared alongside Bolt on his Sky News Australia program as they slammed the jury's decision.

The general consensus among the right-wing critics, largely

working for News Corp, was that a grave miscarriage of justice had occurred akin to the infamous case of Lindy Chamberlain, who was wrongfully jailed for killing her baby Azaria while camping at Uluru in 1980. Bolt, in particular, faced a strong public backlash regarding his outspoken defence of Pell. Most prominently, Clare Linane, the wife of well-known Ballarat survivor and advocate Peter Blenkiron, wrote a frank and blunt open letter that soon went viral on Facebook and was published in the *Sydney Morning Herald*.

Condemning the way Bolt claimed that Pell had been falsely convicted due to 'overwhelming evidence', she said he was 'misleading, irresponsible and ignorant'. 'Your lack of insight into the issue makes a mockery of survivors and all they have endured,' she wrote.

Forensically pulling apart Bolt's claim that Pell was of good character, she pointed out paedophiles can be 'otherwise lovely, intelligent, charismatic people'. 'We know from history they include successful politicians, celebrities, judges, teachers, priests. They are from all walks of life and run the gamut from stupid to brilliant, charming to repulsive.'

Lyndon Monument's sister echoed Linane's views.[10] She praised the work of the jury and revealed Catholic clergy abuse had affected her family for 40 years, culminating in the loss of another brother ten years before. 'The decision to come forward with allegations against George Pell, almost four years ago, set my brother, myself and my family on a journey that has had equally dark times and inflicted stress that I did not, at times, think we would survive,' she said.

She slammed Father Frank Brennan for using his position in the media to promote the cardinal's innocence and explained how Bolt's 'continued tirades' were depicting the victims as unreliable 'and worse'. 'What dampens my rage and instead restores my faith in being human is how the public has sent the strongest of messages to these men of white privilege and power. You no longer rule our world.'

As the backlash continued, journalist and author Richard Cooke, writing for *The Guardian*, pointed out that Pell's defenders had not sat in on the trial or read the unsuppressed media reports before 'weighing in'. The options of saying nothing or waiting for more information, he said, were not taken and instead the cardinal's supporters 'began with Pell's position and his politics and reverse engineered his innocence from there'.

'Here's my question,' Cooke wrote. 'Where have these people been? Did these past decades of institutional child abuse never happen? Were they looking away the whole time? Has everything we learned—painfully—about the damage it does, and its shame, been unlearned?'

For some survivors of clergy abuse the dismissal of the accuser's testimony by these powerful right-wing commentators proved highly damaging, both psychologically and emotionally. Georgie Burg, who had been abused by a male relative as a small child and raped and abused by an Anglican priest multiple times between the ages 13 and 15, posted a graphic photograph of her fingernails on her Twitter account. She had pulled them off completely. The reason, she said, was due to the 'despair and frustration' she felt amid the male-led rejection of

Pell's conviction.[11] 'If these powerful people were questioning one victim, they're questioning all victims.'

Burg's post certainly seemed to strike a chord; she received 234 comments, many of which were made by fellow survivors who stated they were also feeling devastated by the attacks on the credibility of the alleged surviving accuser. 'It seems like other survivors related to the honesty I was showing,' Burg said. 'I got the feeling many were also hiding impacts like my nails— it's part of the secrecy and shame of both the abuse and allowing people like Bolt to get to us.'

While Pell's long-time supporters steadfastly continued to fight his corner, their words couldn't stop the wheels of justice turning. Within 24 hours their admired man from Rome would be settling himself into a jail cell in Melbourne.

———

The very next morning, on 27 February 2019, the cardinal was overwhelmed by an even larger and louder angry crowd as he arrived for his pre-sentencing hearing, which he knew would conclude with him being remanded in custody. The 15-metre walk from his car to the door of the court, the last time he would be seen in public before going to prison, took over a minute as he hobbled on his crutch, constantly halted by the media and the angry protestors who squeezed around him.

'Hope you've packed your pyjamas,' one man jeered. Another man, a survivor of abuse who goes by the name Michael Advocate to protect his identity, shouted a litany of insults as the cardinal shuffled slowly through the baying crowd. 'You freak, you paedophile, you monster, you criminal . . . you deserve to be executed,' he screamed. All the while, Pell remained silent.

It was a wretched start to a day that had already borne the news from Rome that the Vatican was opening its own investigations into the accusations against Pell. The move would mean he could be dismissed from the priesthood if the Vatican's doctrinal office also found him guilty. 'After the guilty verdict in the first instance concerning Cardinal Pell, the Congregation for the Doctrine of the Faith (CDF) will now handle the case following the procedure and within the time established by canonical norm,' Vatican spokesman Alessandro Gisotti said. Gisotti also confirmed that Pell was no longer the Vatican's treasurer; his five-year term had expired several days before.

All in all it was a hellish morning for the cardinal, and it would soon get a lot worse.

Inside courtroom 3.3, the level below where the trial had unfolded, over 100 people crowded the public benches. Those left standing were asked to move to an overflow court to watch the proceedings by videolink. Reporters who missed out on seats leant against the empty jury box. A request to sit in the box itself was refused. The court did not want to give the impression this was a 'trial by media', rightly foreseeing what Pell's supporters would say.

Chrissie Foster sat in the front row alongside fellow advocate Eileen Piper, whose daughter Stephanie committed suicide in 1994 after being abused by a priest in the 1970s. In her hand Foster clutched a badge that featured a quote from Pell from when he gave evidence to the royal commission from Rome in 2016.

'It was sad, but of little interest to me,' he had said in reference to the prolific offender Father Gerald Ridsdale.

Mark Gibson spoke first. His submission for the Crown would last most of the day. Pell deserved to be jailed immediately, he argued. 'As we know, five or six minutes of abuse can last a lifetime.' Referring to the cardinal as 'the prisoner' for the first time, Gibson said Pell had carried out a 'humiliating and degrading' attack on 'vulnerable children'. 'In his mind, he thought he could get away with it . . . he possessed a notion of impunity.'

Gibson presented victim impact statements, including from the father of the deceased choirboy. Kidd ruled, however, the heroin overdose had not been caused by the abuse by Pell.

Robert Richter continued for the defence, telling the judge Pell would be 'extremely vulnerable' in jail due to his well-known status and the type of crime he had been convicted for. His fight for his client was ceaseless and impassioned.

Asked by Judge Kidd why his client had committed the crimes, Richter said he was in a difficult position as Pell's lawyer because his client maintained his innocence. 'The cardinal's position is that he is innocent. I'm not in a position to say why he did something he says he didn't do,' Richter said.

There was no evidence Pell had mental-health issues, the judge determined. He could only accept, therefore, that Pell thought he would escape justice over the attacks because he considered himself as the 'king of the castle'. This reflected evidence given by experts during the royal commission that clericalism—an assumption by clergy of authority—was a contributing factor to child abuse.

Working hard to mitigate the sentence, Richter then made what would prove to be one of the biggest missteps of his legal career. Attempting to argue Pell's offending was spur of the moment, and not of the type of severe sexual depravity seen in other cases, he told the judge, 'This is no more than a plain vanilla sexual penetration case where a child is not volunteering or actively participating,' he said.

A flicker of shock crossed the faces of the reporters and advocates in the courtroom. Judge Kidd wasn't impressed either. 'He engaged in some shocking conduct toward two boys,' he said. 'At the moment, I see this as callous, brazen offending. Blatant.'

Social media went into overdrive, with survivors voicing outrage and dismay. Richter would later issue a formal apology, saying no offence was intended during what was a 'long and stressful process' in court. He vowed never to repeat such 'carelessness' in his choice of words.

It wasn't only Richter's clumsiness that would prompt controversy. The court heard that ten glowing references for the cardinal had been submitted to the court. Among them was one from former prime minister John Howard.

It was clear that Howard's reference had been written after the cardinal was convicted in December.[12]

I am aware he has been convicted of those charges; that an appeal against the conviction has been lodged and that he maintains his innocence in respect of these charges.

None of these matters alter my opinion of the Cardinal.

I've known Cardinal Pell for approximately 30 years. We first became acquainted when he was, I think, an Assistant Bishop in the Archdiocese of Melbourne.

Inevitably we became better known to each other after he became Archbishop of Melbourne and, later still, Archbishop of Sydney.

Cardinal Pell is a person of both high intelligence and exemplary character. Strength and sincerity have always been features of his personality. I have always found him to be lacking hypocrisy and cant.

In his chosen vocation he has frequently displayed much courage and held to his values and beliefs, irrespective of the prevailing wisdom of the time.

Cardinal Pell is a lively conversationalist who maintains a deep and objective interest in contemporary social and political issues.

It is my view that he has dedicated his life to his nation and his church.

We would learn more about Pell's loyal circle from their character statements. It emerged he had been staying at the home of friend Anne McFarlane when he was in Melbourne for the legal proceedings. She revealed the cardinal's needs were 'very simple' and he was always 'very grateful for any kindness or help at all'.

Australian Catholic University vice-chancellor Greg Craven had also stepped forward in Pell's hour of need, infuriating some of the university's students. He wrote that Pell's 'public presentation does not necessarily match his private persona'. 'Publicly, he is businesslike, and can appear gruff and intensely determined . . . privately, he is a deeply sensitive person: thoughtful, considerate; and notably charitable.'

Pell's other seven character witnesses were his cousin Chris Meney, Sydney lawyer Terence K. Tobin, QC, and past and present loyal staff from the Archdiocese of Sydney including Daniel Casey, Michael Casey, Katrina Potter and Ellie Heiss. Sue Buckingham, the founder of religious group David's Place, also supplied a witness statement.

'He relates to everyone from a prime minister to street beggars,' Richter said of his client. 'He is a person of the highest character, putting aside the convictions that were recorded.'

While Richter may have simply been doing his job as Pell's lawyer, protestors and advocates outside, many of whom had been abused in Catholic orphanages as children, made their negative feelings towards him known when he left the court for the lunch break. As the barrister crossed over William Street towards his chambers, they shouted, 'dirty money' and 'paedophile protector'.

It was behaviour that Judge Kidd strongly condemned. He threatened to have anyone who committed any further abuse prosecuted for contempt. 'This is not a game,' he said angrily. 'The system requires defence counsel to defend people.'

No one jeered Richter when he left court for the day—and they didn't have a chance to jeer at Pell either. For the first time in court hearings spanning twenty months, he wasn't leaving by the front door. Originally, Pell was due to have a bail hearing at the Supreme Court of Appeal, in a last-ditch attempt to avoid jail, however, the bid was abandoned.

It was time.

'Take him away,' Judge Kidd nonchalantly told the three guards sitting with Pell in the dock.

The cardinal was led out towards a door to the left of the dock. He paused, turned slowly and bowed to the judge. If he was going down, it was clear he was determined to go down with dignity.

This was the last moment he would be in control. The authoritarian, ambitious and dogmatic Prince of the Church then walked through the door and was quickly out of sight. He would descend in a lift to be held in a cell in the basement, before being led to an underground carpark and the doors of a prison van.

The senior churchman of Rome was now officially a prisoner of Corrections Victoria.

Chapter 14
Solitary retreat

It's only a short drive from the county court to Melbourne Assessment Prison, commonly known as MAP, on nearby Spencer Street. But seated in the back of a white Mercedes prison van, the prospect of what awaited inside the high-security compound must have been nothing less than terrifying for Cardinal Pell. Never before in his 77 years had his personal Latin motto *Nolite timere*—be not afraid—been more needed as he faced what lay ahead.

The facility, opened in 1989, has a capacity of 305 male prisoners and the cardinal would soon find out that he would be spending 23 hours a day in a cell in a unit dubbed by the staff 'sep, sep'. 'It's like a segregation unit within a segregation unit, it doesn't get more isolated that that,' a source explained.[1] The cardinal would be allowed only one official visitor a week but could have as many legal visits as was necessary.

When he arrived on the evening of 27 February 2019, he was taken to his cell with its basic bed, thin mattress, TV and a metal toilet in the corner. He was met by senior staff and a prison psychologist to check his mental state. 'They gathered around him for some time, explaining the rules and routine. One of their prime concerns with a new prisoner is whether they are at risk of self-harm, which is common,' the source said.

'Pell was told he wasn't going to be mixing with any other prisoners at all, as it was too high risk. He would only mix with staff, but mostly he'd be in his cell.'

The fear Pell could be harmed was justified. In the past decade high-profile prisoners in Victoria's prison system have been attacked, most notably murderer and drug trafficker Carl Williams, who died from a head injury in April 2010. Fellow inmate Matthew Johnson was later sentenced to 32 years in jail for using part of an exercise bike as a fatal weapon against the notorious underworld figure.

Corrections staff were also still on high alert after infamous Victorian drug dealer Tony Mokbel was knocked unconscious before being stabbed up to seven times in a frenzied assault with a makeshift knife at Barwon Prison, a maximum security jail outside Melbourne.[2] The brutal attack by two fellow prisoners happened just 16 days before Pell was remanded in custody.

Ostensibly Pell may have been kept safe from attack by being unable to mix with the general prison population, but his new 'housemates' in neighbouring cells would turn out to be some of the most notorious criminals in the state. Bourke Street killer James Gargasoulas, who was jailed for life for committing one of Australia's worst mass murders when he drove his car into pedestrians in the centre of Melbourne, was in a cell directly next to the cardinal. In other neighbouring cells terror suspects languished on their beds watching television. No phones or internet access are allowed.

'Usually, once all the publicity calms down around a high-profile prisoner they are allowed to mix with other crooks in more open units but I don't think that's ever likely with Pell,' the source said. 'It's just too risky that someone might take him out or harm him.'

The nights in MAP, when prisoners can hear the vivid yet unreachable sounds of inner-city life from surrounding streets including the sharp horns of taxis and rattling trams, can be long and brutal. 'Inmates sometimes shout out in the darkness, they cry and verbally abuse each other, but generally Pell's row of cells was calm.'

Despite the constraints of his new abode, Pell apparently settled in without much fuss, co-operating with the guards and doing as instructed. He would spend the long hours alone in his cell reading books, praying and writing letters to friends who were sending regular dispatches of hope and support. He wouldn't be able to have wine, so taking communion on a Sunday was out of the question.

A grace period exists for the first seven days of a prisoner's arrival at MAP during which anyone with suitable ID may drop off property or money for a prisoner. After this time, this is limited only to people registered on the prisoner's visit list.

'I tried to visit several times but I was turned away,' says Anne Lastman, Pell's close friend from Perth who had attended much of the court proceedings.[3] 'It broke my heart knowing he was in there, locked up and alone.'

For a man once in charge of balancing billions of euros as the Vatican's treasurer, he was now restricted to having a maximum of just $140 Australian dollars a month to spend on prison issue snacks and toiletries.[4] The cardinal would also have to get by with fewer clothes and effects than he was used to. Prisoners at MAP have to abide by strict rules regarding personal items. Pell had been informed through his legal team that he was only allowed to bring the following clothes and items into the prison:[5]

6 pairs of jocks or boxer shorts

6 pairs of socks

2 singlets

2 windcheaters or tracksuit tops or jumpers or jacket [no hoods, camouflage or quilted/puffy items accepted]

Professional court clothing [trousers, jacket, shirt, tie, dress shoes]

4 tops [t-shirt, polo top, long sleeve]

4 bottoms [tracksuit pants, trousers, jeans, shorts]

1 pair of pyjamas

1 pair of shoes/runners

1 belt [small buckle—subject to prison discretion]

1 pair of scuffs/slides/thongs

2 pairs of prescription glasses & soft case

1 cap

6 books

6 magazines

6 photographs (laminated/polaroids not accepted)

Every aspect of his life was now controlled and restricted—right down to his underwear. Dignified it wasn't.

Former priest Eugene Ahern sent his close friend Pell a pop-up card covered in bright flowers almost as soon as he was remanded to try and 'cheer him up'.[6] 'I'm loyal to George because he sent me a wonderful letter himself when I was going through a hard time myself, after I left the priesthood,' he explained. 'I left for the sake of my mental well-being, I was clinically depressed and my doctor felt I would be better out of the ministry.'

It seemed Pell would have no shortage of other correspondence from loyal friends and requests to visit. He reportedly told friends he had come to view his incarceration as an 'extended retreat'. That was certainly an optimistic way to look at his new life in solitary confinement.

If his legal bid for freedom failed, a correction source predicted it would be 'highly likely' that Pell would be moved to Hopkins Correctional Centre, a medium security prison 200 kilometres west of Melbourne in Ararat. It is here that a large proportion of approximately 700 inmates are serving sentences for child sex offences and are kept apart from the general prison population for their own protection.[7] If the court decides it's not safe to release paedophiles at the end of their sentence, they are then sent to live in small units of approximately 50 men in an outer, minimum security section called Corella Place, dubbed locally as the 'village of the damned'.

Waiting to greet Pell at the facility would be his former house-mate Gerald Ridsdale, who isn't eligible for parole until 2022 after pleading guilty in 2017 to abusing 12 more children.[8] He might also recognise Robert Claffey, a peer from his days in the seminary in Werribee, who is likely to die in jail after three convictions for child abuse. On 8 July 2019, perhaps thanks to the courage of survivors who came forward to the police and royal commission, two new male victims came forward and made complaints that Claffey had indecently assaulted them while working as a priest in Ballarat in the 1980s. One was just seven years old at the time. The 76-year-old pleaded guilty to four more charges.[9]

With the very pressing possibility of an unwanted reunion with disgraced former clergy associates on the horizon, Pell's powerful friends in high places were continuing to rally around him. The newly installed Archbishop of Melbourne, Peter Comensoli, vowed to visit his friend in prison, and former prime minister Tony Abbot, himself a former seminarian and high-profile Catholic, had personally called the cardinal on the day the suppression order was lifted.

Food cooked fresh daily by fellow prisoners in the kitchens for a small wage was delivered to prisoners' cells. Pell would have enjoyed curries with rice and vegetables, roast dinners and chilli con carne, all popular menu items in the prison. Nevertheless, when we saw Pell again two weeks later for his sentencing hearing he appeared pale, gaunt and noticeably thinner. After fourteen long nights spent in a tiny cell in solitary confinement, his Eminence had apparently lost his appetite.

———

Before dawn on the morning of 13 March, I passed St Patrick's Cathedral in East Melbourne on route to court to ensure I had a seat inside for the sentencing hearing. The grand, gothic-style spires loomed out of the drizzly sky, and dozens of colourful ribbons adorning the metal gates near the grand front steps fluttered in the wind. The word 'loud' was marked in silver foil on the main gate. The night before, a group called 'Guerrilla projection' and lighting brigade activist group EvoLens projected the words 'crime scene' on the cathedral itself. Their aim, stated on Twitter, was 'to let the Catholic Church know we are watching them'.[10] The support group Loud Fence had organised the spectacle, which had become a familiar sight in Ballarat.

Outside court advocates were already waiting. Roy and Rhonda Janetzki, who were both abused in Catholic orphanages, stood sipping coffee with Leonie Sheedy, the CEO of Care Leavers Alliance Australia, an advocacy group for children brought up in orphanages and foster homes. The Janetzkis had driven for four hours from their home in Wodonga to be at court. They carried placards calling for greater redress for victims. 'But we are here mostly to mark the fact that it's really good one child is being believed against the third highest Catholic in the world,' Roy said.[11]

As the cardinal was ushered into the dock just before 10 a.m., all 120 people gathered in the court—reporters, advocates and relatives of the two choirboys at the centre of the case—turned and collectively gasped. Pell hadn't just lost weight behind bars, he'd also been stripped of two precious items he'd never been seen without for over 50 years—his clerical collar and his gold ring. These items were considered part of a 'uniform' by the prison authorities, so they had been taken away from him.

With the top few buttons of his black shirt open, he appeared tired and dishevelled. Profoundly altered from the man who had been led away from the court a few weeks before, it was a pitiful sight in many ways to witness how far this once formidable churchman had fallen. If anyone was uncertain whether prison would be enough of a punishment for his conviction, his appearance told another story. Within 65 minutes Pell would learn he would also be stripped of his liberty for quite some time.

Via a sole ABC cameraman in the jury box, Chief Judge Peter Kidd broadcast his sentencing remarks live to the world. They would prove to be a balanced mix of fair and brutal. 'In my view, the first episode in the priests' sacristy involved a brazen and forcible sexual attack upon the two victims,' he said early in his reasons for sentencing. 'The acts were sexually graphic.'

The judge accepted that the offending was opportunistic and spontaneous, rather than pre-planned or premeditated conduct. However, he told Pell, who sat emotionless looking straight ahead, that his conduct was 'permeated with staggering arrogance' and his status as archbishop at the time cast a 'powerful shadow' over the offences. 'The authority you carried within the cathedral setting in relation to the choirboys, carried with it a significant responsibility of trust, not to do anything to the detriment of the boys,' he said.

Kidd explained in detail how he had taken into account the cardinal's health problems, age and the stress he had endured from being publicly 'pilloried' and from receiving verbal abuse whenever he arrived or departed from court. He didn't consider him as a risk to the community. He was also conscious of the 'heavy reality' of a prison term, conceding the cardinal was a man of advanced years who had led an otherwise blameless life.

'Cardinal Pell, will you please stand,' the judge said. 'All things considered I impose the following sentence on you.'

For charge one—the indecent act against the since deceased choirboy—Kidd sentenced the cardinal for two years and six months in prison. For charge two—the sexual penetration against the surviving accuser—he was sentenced to four years in prison. On charge three—the indecent act against the same boy where he touched his genitals—he was sentenced to two years and six months.

On charge four, where he touched his own private parts in the presence of the surviving accuser, he was sentenced to fifteen months. Finally, for charge five, regarding the moment he accosted the accuser in the corridor two months after the sacristy assault, he was sentenced to 18 months.

The sentence totalled eleven years and one month. However, the judge directed the total effective sentence would be six years imprisonment, with a non-parole period of three years and eight months. 'I declare the fourteen days imprisonment you have already served in pre-sentence detention, is reckoned as time already served against the sentence I have just imposed,' Kidd said.

But Pell's ultimate public humiliation was still yet to come: the cardinal had to sign his name on the Victorian Register for Sex Offenders.

It all felt like the modern-day equivalent of a public hanging. There was no jeering or sense of triumph or jubilation—it was a depressing and uncomfortable sight.

'Take him away, please,' were Kidd's final words as Pell got up, briefly bowed, turned and walked out of the dock with the guards.

Until we learnt a date for his appeal, we knew this could be the last we would see of him for possibly a very long time. That's if, with his various health problems, he even made it through the long drawn out days and nights in solitary confinement alive.

———

In the front row of court, two women sat crying. One was the distraught mother of the choirboy who had passed away. Sano Task Force detective Chris Reed was warmly hugged and congratulated by the women. 'I told you it was best to wait to come to court for this hearing,' he told the family.

The choirboy's sister, a young mother based in Melbourne, told me the family had 'struggled greatly' during the legal case but had been very relieved when they first heard about the guilty verdict in December, describing it as 'great news'.[12] 'It's been a terrible, tense time,' she said, 'My mother has found it very hard in particular . . . every day we think about him and miss him . . . I wish he was still here to be an uncle to my children.'

Outside, protesters holding placards and pictures jeered at Pell's legal team as they left court. 'Happy days,' one shouted. 'You helped a paedophile!' another screamed.

For Stephen Woods, who'd been abused by two Christian Brothers and then Gerald Ridsdale in Ballarat, it was a significant moment. 'It's quite amazing to see him go to jail,' he said.[13] 'Never in my life did I think this day would come.'

'We heard rumours years ago in Ballarat, and so when the charges were brought through, I thought "yes, finally some justice", as there are so many of us who are still suffering as a result of clergy abuse and many still don't come forward.'

As Dr Vivian Waller, the lawyer for the surviving accuser, walked out of the revolving court doors, advocates, many of whom were past and present clients, turned towards her chanting, 'We love you, Viv.'

'A ripple of applause broke out,' the lawyer explained later.[14] 'It made me smile, just a little. I played no role in the conviction of Pell. I represented the complainant in dealing with the significant media interest in the criminal case in an effort to protect his identity and privacy.'

Surrounded by dozens of reporters, photographers and cameras, she read a statement from her client, who had been watching the live broadcast at home. It was clear he had been wounded by the critical commentary about his accusations from Pell's media supporters.

> It is hard for me to allow myself to feel the gravity of this moment. The moment when the sentence is handed down. The moment when justice is done. It is hard for me, for the time being, to take comfort in this outcome. I appreciate that the Court has acknowledged what was inflicted upon me as a child. However, there is no rest for me.
>
> Everything is overshadowed by the forthcoming appeal.
>
> I am aware of a lot of the public comment by people who are critical of my evidence. But only the judge, the jury, Pell and the legal teams have heard my evidence.

Regardless of the outcome of the appeal, a few facts will always remain.

I gave evidence for several days. I was cross-examined by Pell's defence counsel. A jury has unanimously accepted the truth of my evidence.

Pell chose not to give evidence. The jury did not hear from him. He did not allow himself to be cross-examined.

I have played my part as best I can. I took the difficult step of reporting to police about a high-profile person and I stood up to give my evidence. I am waiting for the outcome of the appeal like everybody else.

Being a witness in a criminal case has not been easy. I'm doing my best to hold myself and my family together. I would like to thank the media for respecting my wish to keep my identity private and to keep my loved ones out of the spotlight.

The words were damning, but the accuser had touched on an important, remaining truth: the appeal was looming. This case wasn't finished.

And neither were Pell's ambitions to clear his name and release from prison.

———

A new, very expensive and well-respected Sydney barrister—Bret Walker, SC—had been recruited to run Pell's appeal. His case would rest on three main points of contention. The first was centred on the argument that the jury erred in relying on the evidence of only one victim. 'The verdicts are unreasonable and cannot be supported, having regard to the evidence, because on the whole of the evidence, including unchallenged exculpatory evidence from more than twenty Crown witnesses, it was not open to the jury to be satisfied beyond reasonable doubt on the word of the complainant alone,' the appeal document said.

The second ground alleged there was a fundamental irregularity in the trial process that prevented Cardinal Pell from entering a not-guilty plea in front of the jury; they were still downstairs in the empanelment room, having not yet been officially sworn in. The third ground was that the judge erred in not allowing the defence to show the 'Pac-Man' video, the controversial 'moving visual representation' of Pell, the staff and the choirboys in the cathedral.

Three judges of the Court of Appeal would preside over the hearing in early June—the Chief Justice of the Supreme Court of Victoria Justice Anne Ferguson, President of the Court of Appeal Justice Chris Maxwell and Justice Mark Weinberg. The hearing, set to be heard over two days, would be live streamed on the internet by the Supreme Court.

While Richter would not be leading the appeal for Pell himself, he said he was still very much part of Pell's core legal team. 'I am very angry about the verdict,' he told *The Age*, 'because it was perverse.'

Pell would be better served by someone 'more detached', he said. 'I think the man is an innocent man and he's been convicted. It's not a common experience.'

Pell's other staunch supporters would also continue their defensive rhetoric in the weeks leading up to the June appeal.

Andrew Bolt allocated ten minutes of his Sky News program and his weekly *Herald Sun* column to a story I had written earlier in the year about a conversation between Pell and Charles Portelli, the former master of ceremonies of the cathedral. Pell, I reported, had apologised to his close friend Portelli for embroiling him in the legal case.

Bolt conjured up the bizarre and false notion that I had been supplied the contents of the conversation by Victoria Police, who had possibly 'bugged' the cardinal's phone. His evidence-free assumption was laughable. And wrong. And I told him as much in a statement. But his behaviour didn't shake me in the least. It simply served to give me closure on any lingering upset I had following my brutal experience at the hands of News Corp. Pell's acquaintance was continuing to be allowed to use his influential platform to launch vicious, unfounded attacks on the work of the reporter who had first uncovered the allegations of abuse for the company that paid his salary. It was nonsensical.

I realised I'd been exactly where I was meant to be at all times, including all the detours and smackdowns. I'd discovered my true self and personal values simply by being the author of my own life, following my intuition and surrendering myself to the journey. Journalists, I now believed for certain, were only doing their jobs properly if they questioned everyone at every turn, even if it meant probing their own colleagues, editors and media organisations. Transparency and truth in the name of public interest had to prevail.

I also had a new-found appreciation of the humble, unsung heroes of the clergy and institutional abuse scandals: the advocates and survivors sharing their difficult personal stories to bring about change, not to mention the unwavering, dedicated work of the Sano Task Force detectives who to this day keep investigating new allegations and making arrests. These brave people would continue to get criticised after Pell was remanded, being accused of waging some kind of unjust war against the cardinal.

But Pell's allies weren't just rallying around him in Australia. In what was beginning to feel like a carefully co-ordinated PR campaign, his close friend George Weigel, Senior Fellow of the Ethics and Public Policy Center in Washington DC, argued that the 'unsafe' verdict in the case is one a jury could not rationally have reached.[15] 'Friends of truth must hope that the appellate judges, tuning out the mob, will begin to restore safety and rationality to public life Down Under in June,' he wrote. He also made the bizarre and unsubstantiated claim that the complainant's description of the sexual assault he alleged Cardinal Pell had committed bore a striking resemblance to an incident of clerical sexual abuse described in *Rolling Stone* in 2011, insinuating the man made up the complaint from what he may have read.

As some members of the media were busy fighting Pell's conviction, a group of 30 news outlets, journalists, presenters and editors were beginning their own fight against the early stages of a prosecution based on allegations that they had broken the suppression order and were in contempt of court over the cryptic reporting of the guilty verdict back in December. As the case involving outlets including the Herald and Weekly

Times, *The Age* and the *Australian Financial Review* moved through the courts one thing was for certain: the Pell matter was so important and complicated it had tested everyone involved. It had tested systems, loyalties, laws, rules, newsrooms and ethics. It wasn't just the cardinal who had been on trial; lawyers, the courts and the media had effectively been on trial too. This saga of epic proportions would cause drama, debate and angst for some time to come.

It was now highly possible that, like Pell, not everyone would emerge unscathed.

———

When the appeal began on 5 June 2019 in a crowded, tense courtroom in the Supreme Court on William Street, we saw a surprisingly smarter cardinal in the witness box. His collar was back on. So too was his neat black suit. His combed hair completed the high-ranking clerical look. Had his Eminence been prepped to make sure he appeared more cardinal than convict? Would a smart appearance give subconscious weight to the idea that he had been wrongfully imprisoned?

Whatever the reason for his much-improved sartorial presence, wildly different from his dishevelled appearance at his sentencing hearing nearly three months before, it still seemed to be a difficult scene to witness for some members of Pell's family seated together in the front row. His brother David, ten years younger than his stricken sibling, was there alongside his daughter Dr Sarah Pell and several family friends, some of whom had driven great distances to show their support.

Pell's barrister Bret Walker addressed the three judges for the whole of the first day, passionately arguing that the jury had delivered an 'unsafe' verdict. His key points included the fact there were no witnesses to the attacks on the choirboys and that it would have been 'physically impossible' for Pell to have been alone and in the sacristy at the time of the first alleged assault. He stressed that Monsignor Charles Portelli, Pell's close friend for decades, was his key 'alibi' because he said the cardinal always lingered on the steps after mass and that he was always by his side.

The next day, despite all that was at stake for Pell and most of all for the surviving complainant, the Crown prosecutor Christopher Boyce stumbled, mumbled and fumbled through his appearance, struggling to answer questions from the judges and even causing a brief panic when he accidentally said the name of the accuser in court.[16] Advocates expressed their upset in the corridors during the breaks, while commentators wrote scathing appraisals of the barrister's handling of the situation. 'On the surface the day was a train wreck,' David Marr said of Boyce's submission. '. . . the barrister whose job was to defend the jury's verdict, Christopher Boyce, SC, found himself lost for words.'[17]

Boyce may not have demonstrated a judicial style as eloquent and slick as Walker's but his key argument was made loud and clear to the judges, who are well used to barristers' differing styles: the surviving choirboy should and must be believed.

As the judges closed the hearing to begin considering the arguments and Pell was sent back to prison in time to celebrate his 78th birthday behind bars the following day, one thing was for certain: Catholics across the country were in grief over the fall of their senior churchman. They'd been so proud he'd made it to Rome and now he was languishing in a Melbourne jail. 'For weeks I have been unable to bring myself to attend Sunday Mass,' Anne O'Donovan wrote in the *Sydney Morning Herald*. The book publisher and former director of Jesuit Publications said every story of abuse of children by Catholic clergy created a 'deadening of the heart'. 'Internationally, Catholics like me are in grief,' she said, but she would still keep connected to the faith through her love of ritual and knowledge that there are 'good people' working among the Catholic education and health system.

For many of the shaken faithful it was clear that no matter what happened with Pell's appeal, the model of Catholicism he was associated with, a finger-wagging church of power and status, was dying. 'The whole Pell case gives a chance for ordinary Catholics to take a hard look in the mirror and ask about what kind of Church they want to be part of,' journalist Christopher Lamb said frankly from Rome.

Change, in some form at least, seemed to have started. Two weeks before Pell's appeal began, Pope Francis announced the first law obligating officials in the church globally to report cases of abuse, and any attempts to cover it up, to their superiors.[18] To the anger of advocates, however, the new law does not require church officials to report accusations to police, but it does say that church officials should not interfere with investigations by civil authorities. Laid out in a document titled

'You Are the Light of the World', the law will be re-evaluated after three years.

As the Vatican's correspondent for *America Magazine*, Gerard O'Connell says, the Pell case and the summit with the senior bishops heralded important change in Rome.[19] 'It brought home even more clearly both the global dimensions of the problem and the urgency of coming to strong decisions to deal decisively with it. Pope Francis has issued important universal norms and procedures to help eradicate the plague of abuse from the church worldwide, and further steps in this direction are likely.'

While allowing the breaking of the seal of confession to report abuse, or making celibacy optional for the clergy of the Roman Catholic Church, seemed unlikely in the near future, the Pope was not excluding the possibility that married men could be ordained in some isolated communities around the world. There are also already many married men who are Catholic priests in the Eastern Rite Churches and in the Greek-Catholic Churches, O'Connell points out, but they decided to get married before being ordained deacon. Between 200 to 300 former married Anglican priests who joined the Catholic Church in England are now working as married Catholic priests. There are other such married priests in the USA.[20]

As for a greater role for women in the church, it seems some long-held traditions run too deep. 'Pope Francis has excluded the possibility of ordaining women as priests, saying John Paul II took a definitive decision on this subject,' O'Connell says.

As those inside the faith continued to find new ways of moving forward, the cardinal himself was doing his best to keep his mind, body and spirit alive, holding out hope that the three appeal judges would decide to set him free, although winning an appeal would not be the end of the matter. The Crown's final option is to apply for a hearing before the High Court to decide the final outcome.

Also, at some point, Pell will have to face the release of the redacted findings of the royal commission. He could still emerge badly tarnished. There are also several civil suits against him potentially looming as a result of his conviction.

If exonerated, could Pell ever pull off a return to Rome after everything that has happened in his home country? 'Nobody expects him to be given a new position in the Vatican,' says O'Connell. 'So the only role he could have as cardinal, and this only if acquitted both by the civil justice and the Vatican investigation, would be to participate in the board meetings of the Vatican Congregations to which he was appointed. His mandate expires on reaching the age of 80.' He still has personal belongings in his Rome apartment.

'He may also wish to come and meet Pope Francis again,' O'Connell says. 'But ... given this situation, most people in Rome do not expect him to return to the Vatican any time soon, if at all.' At the very least, freedom from prison would allow him to declare himself a victim of a grave injustice at the hands of a biased jury, a baying media mob and a lying accuser.

As Pell awaited his appeal outcome, he shuffled out to the small concrete exercise yard for the one hour he was allowed out of his cell each day. Slowly pushing his walking frame in one direction, but unable to turn, he carefully trod backwards to repeat the process again. Back and forth. Back and forth. His every move watched carefully by prison officers.

The elderly cardinal had found himself trapped in his own living hell, incarcerated in the very city where he once wielded so much power, the city where he proudly wore his elaborate mitre and carried his crosier in the procession with his choir out of the main doors of his cathedral. This was the choir from which one small, powerless, adolescent soprano walking in his red-and-white robes would eventually find the strength to speak up.

His allegations may eventually be discredited and ultimately rejected. But he has been heard. His voice has set a course of profound change, contrition and much needed inner reflection within the Holy See and the Roman Catholic Church around the world.

He may have given hope and a call to action to many voiceless survivors still struggling in the darkness, too frightened to tell, too damaged to share their experiences. He may also have brought courage to a woman in Gippsland who should have been saved, not ignored as a tiny girl trapped in Ridsdale's ruthless grip.

For those many legacies, his voice will never be forgotten.

He'd proved to the world the meek really can inherit the earth.

———

On Wednesday 21 August 2019 at 9.30 a.m. Chief Justice Anne Ferguson took her seat alongside Justice Mark Weinberg and Justice Chris Maxwell in court 15 at the Supreme Court of Victoria to hand down the cardinal's much awaited appeal decision. Ferguson glanced up at the tense and silent courtroom packed with reporters, advocates, legal teams and supporters of the cardinal. Pell's younger brother David sat in the second row accompanied by his daughter Dr Sarah Pell. Former news reader Katrina Lee was front and centre, her loyalty and stoic court attendance unwavering to the last.

Ferguson nodded to the male guard standing to her right. He turned and opened a wooden door near the judges' bench. Pell, the former Vatican powerhouse turned elderly prisoner, was slowly escorted into the courtroom accompanied by five armed guards. His black suit hung loosely around his once athletic shoulders as he walked awkwardly into the dock. His hair was noticeably thinner and balding. After 175 long nights in solitary confinement his clerical collar was in place but loose around his shrunken neck.

Ferguson was blunt and to the point. 'By majority (2–1) the Court of Appeal has dismissed Cardinal George Pell's appeal against conviction for the commission of sexual offences,' she said. 'He will continue to serve his sentence of six years imprisonment. He will remain eligible for parole after he has served three years and eight months of his sentence.'

Pell reached out his left hand to grip the side of the dock. As Ferguson began to read out the summary of the decision his head fell forward and he stared down at the floor.

The cheers of victims and their advocates outside the main steps of the court echoed along the ground floor corridors and reached into the courtroom itself to those listening inside, including his eminence who glanced towards the door.

In a powerful statement Ferguson told the court: 'The Chief Justice and Justice Maxwell accepted the prosecution's submission that the complainant was a very compelling witness, was clearly not a liar, was not a fantasist and was a witness of truth.' She went on to declare that Pell's official robes were 'not so heavy nor so immoveable as the evidence of Monsignor Portelli and Mr Potter had suggested'.

Justice Weinberg, on the other hand, found in his dissenting judgment that at times the complainant was inclined to 'embellish aspects of his account' and that his evidence contained discrepancies. But he was over-ruled.

As for the two further grounds of the cardinal's appeal— that Pell was not properly arraigned in front of the jury and that it was wrong that the defence was not allowed to play the infamous 'Pac Man' video—both were scathingly dismissed.

While the cardinal was driven back to prison a few minutes away handcuffed in the back of a white transit van, a statement was read by his legal team. He was 'obviously disappointed with the decision', it said and that his team would be examining the possibility of a special leave application to the High Court.

Whatever the future held for Pell's on-going fight, focus turned to the poignant and harrowing reaction to the appeal decision by the surviving choirboy, J. In a statement read by his lawyer Viv Waller, he said he would take the moment to express his hopes that it was 'all over now' four years after making his first statement to police. 'The journey has taken me to places that, in my darkest moments, I feared I could not return from,' he said.

'After attending the funeral of my childhood friend, the other choirboy, I felt a responsibility to come forward. I knew he had been in a dark place. I was in a dark place . . . I had experienced something terrible as a child, something that marked my life. I wanted at least some good to come of it.'

He was 'grateful for a legal system that everyone can believe in, where everybody is equal before the law and no one is above the law.'

And rightly so.

Acknowledgements

Towards the end of the Pell re-trial late in 2018, I took a phone call from Elizabeth Weiss, a publisher at Allen & Unwin. She had read my pitch, but needed more. The one-hour conversation that unfolded was nothing less than a masterclass. I noted down every word. Elizabeth's wisdom, honesty, enthusiasm and guidance for this project proved exactly why she is a respected powerhouse in the book industry. I'm hugely grateful for her help and also for her obvious care for the importance of this story and all that it represents.

Thank you to Rebecca Kaiser, the brilliant editorial director at Allen & Unwin, who edited the manuscript along with the wonderful copy editor Lauren Finger. They were across every small detail and complexity.

Many thanks to all the staff at Allen & Unwin involved in this book, including Louise Cornege, the head of publicity.

I'm also very grateful to agent Alex Adsett to providing her excellent consulting services in the early stages of the project.

I'm incredibly honoured and thankful that Chrissie Foster AM kindly agreed to write the foreword for this book. She is a remarkable individual, mother and advocate and an inspiration to everyone for her fearless pursuit of truth and justice.

I will always treasure memories and friendships made with the world-class journalists I worked with on a daily basis on the Pell matter. In particular, I want to thank the dedicated core of the 'Pell pack' for your collaboration, humour and generous spirit: Melissa Davey, Emma Younger, Amber Wilson, Karen Sweeney, Shannon Deery, Adam Cooper, Robb M. Stewart and Sonali Paul.

I also thoroughly enjoyed the company of other great reporters and writers working on the Pell story at different points, including Livia Albeck-Ripka, David Marr, Tessa Akerman, Damien Cave, Rod McGuirk, Chris Reason, Eliza Rugg, John Ferguson, Lane Sainty, Rick Goodman, Megan Neil, Jacqueline Le, Adam Baidawi, Stefanie Waclawik and those from international outlets who flew in for key stages of the case including Subel Bhandari and Till Flanders.

Many thanks to the CNN staff and freelance team members who I worked with at different points including, Hilary Whiteman, Anna Coren, Peter Morris, Delia Gallagher, Bex Wright, Sandi Sidhu and Ben Westcott.

I will be eternally grateful to Bruce Guthrie, the co-founder and editorial advisor of *The New Daily*, for investing in me to comprehensively cover the case for the outlet even when the suppression order meant that publication would have to be postponed.

I also want to thank the publishers and directors of *The New Daily* with a special thanks to the editorial staff, both past and present, who edited, produced and designed my work, especially the lengthy 'Pell Diaries' series published early in 2019. Thomas Hunter, Patrick Elligett, Jackson Stiles, Mike Bruce, Zona Black and Neil Frankland all played a vital part in helping the Pell coverage make its mark from the very first court appearance in July 2017 and throughout.

Many thanks to lawyers Sharon Kermath, David Barrow and Ingrid Irwin for their insight, support and humour along the way. Also to Professor Jeremy Gans of the Melbourne Law School for always providing such quick and comprehensive answers to questions.

I'm so grateful to two leading journalists based in Rome— Gerard O'Connell and Christopher Lamb—who were generous in sharing their insider expertise from the Vatican.

Thank you to the many survivors, clergy, lawyers, academics and advocates who gave me their time in interviews for this book and during the course of my work as a journalist investigating and reporting on Pell. And a special thanks to the confidential sources who I cannot name, but who gave me their insight and trust.

Thanks for the support and help from the dedicated court media officers and advisors, including Sharon Rainsbury of Melbourne Magistrates Court, Ed Gardiner from the County Court of Victoria and Andre Awadalla of the Supreme Court of Victoria. They all dealt with the Pell matter at different points with incredible grace and professionalism, often under siege from a media army.

I also want to thank Julie Cameron (AKA Joolsmagools®) a highly-skilled former librarian who subsequently helped me source a mountain of media articles and transcripts for my research.

Thank you to my dear friends and family in the United Kingdom who have shown their support from afar including Julia and Kurt Newman, Jenny and Peter Marr, Ruth, Paul, Sam and Alexis Irvine, Matthew, Simone and George Morris, Sarah Morris, David and Paula Rolfe, Natalie Galsworthy, Kate Moore, Kirsty and Mark Boyle, Graham Johnson, Emma and Gideon Dewhirst, and Samantha Welford.

A special mention to my uncle, John Lanham OBE in Portugal, remembering his late wife Suzi, my inspiring warrior aunt who sadly passed away during the trial.

Thanks to my mother Julia, in particular, who walked me into the offices of *The Lymington Times & New Milton Advertiser* in Hampshire, England at the age of 15 and encouraged me to ask for work experience from the late owner and editor Charles Curry MBE.

Thank you to my close friends in Melbourne who supported me during this journey. A particular thanks to Sharon and Denis Bourke, Nick and Ella Piggott, Sarah and Andy Barker, Kim and Jay Harper, Tessa and Brendan Sullivan, Clare Stephens, Romain Ohlmus, Ray and Jennie Devereaux.

Finally, thank you to my husband Michael, son Nathaniel and daughter Talia. They have supported me at every turn, even when it meant long hours, days, and weeks away from them reporting at court or hidden away writing the book. They are my everything.

This book is a tribute to all those affected by clergy sexual abuse in Australia and around the world, and those who have spoken truth to power, sought justice and used their voice to make change for future generations.

And in memory of those who never made it through.

Lucie Morris-Marr
Melbourne
July 2019

Notes

Chapter 1   A whisper in the dark

1. Quote from speech by George Pell, 15 July 2008, World Youth Day, Barangaroo, Sydney. Published in Pell, Cardinal G., *Test Everything: Hold Fast to What is Good*, Connor Court Publishing, Brisbane, 2010
2. Gerard O'Connell, *The Election of Pope Francis: An inside account of the conclave that changed history*, Orbis Books, NY, 2019
3. *Catholic Herald*, 31 May 2013
4. The name has been changed to protect the identity of the victim

Chapter 2   Big George from Ballarat

1. The eulogy for Pell's father in Cardinal G. Pell, *Be Not Afraid*, Duffy & Snellgrove, Sydney, 2004
2. R. Dixon, *The Catholic Community in Australia*, Openbook Publishers, Adelaide, 2005
3. From the eulogy for Pell's mother in Cardinal G. Pell, *Be Not Afraid*
4. T. Livingstone, *George Pell: Defender of the Faith Down Under*, Ignatius Press, San Francisco, 2005

5. Interview with the author, March 2019

6. Quotes from speech in Cardinal G. Pell, *Be Not Afraid*

7. T. Livingstone, *George Pell*

8. This and following Cahil quotes, interview with the author, March 2019

9. Interview with the author, March 2019

10. Opening address, senior counsel assisting, Case Study 28, Royal Commission into Institutional Responses to Child Sexual Abuse, May 2015

11. www.brokenrites.org.au/drupal/node/74

12. Interview with the author, March 2019

13. www.parliament.vic.gov.au/images/stories/committees/fcdc/inquiries/57th/Child_Abuse_Inquiry/Transcripts/Michael_Parer_25-March-13.pdf

14. Interview with the author, March 2019

15. Interview with the author, March 2019

16. T. Livingstone, *George Pell*

Chapter 3   Silencing the lambs

1. www.theage.com.au/national/victoria/churchs-suicide-victims-20120412-1wwox.html

2. www.abc.net.au/news/2015-05-27/paedophile-gerald-ridsdale-unable-to-control-sexual-urges/6500598

3. This and following Scala quotes, interview with the author, March 2019

4. www.theguardian.com.au/story/3110629/i-had-a-breakdown-in-swan-hill/

5. Peter Ellingsen, 'Ballarat's good men of the cloth', *The Age*, 14 June 2002

6. Interview with the author, March 2019

7. Interview with the author, March 2019

8. Interview with the author, April 2019

9. David Marr, *Quarterly Essay*, 'The Prince: Faith, abuse and George Pell', September 2013

10. edition.cnn.com/2017/06/29/world/timeline-catholic-church-sexual-abuse-scandals/index.html

11. Interview with the author, March 2019

12. Witness statement of Cardinal George Pell, Case Study 16: Melbourne Response, Royal Commission into Institutional Responses to Child Sexual Abuse, May 2015

13. www.ad2000.com.au/archbishop_pell_installed_in_sydney_june_2001.html

14. www.smh.com.au/national/pell-lashes-out-after-gays-refused-communion-20020520-gdfakf.html

15. Even though this accuser has been named, he no longer gives interviews and doesn't want to be identified

16. Report of an inquiry into an allegation of sexual abuse against Archbishop George Pell, October 2002

17. www.abc.net.au/worldtoday/stories/s701136.htm

18. Comment to author, March 1019

19. Anthony Barnett, 'Vatican told bishops to cover up sex abuse', *The Guardian*, 17 August 2017

20. www.abc.net.au/7.30/archbishop-pell-reacts-to-abuse-inquiry/4370042

21. www.abc.net.au/news/2014-03-24/$5,000-for-abuse-compensation-grotesque,-pell-tell-inquiry/5341294

22. Saffron Howden, 'Cardinal George Pell gives final mass before leaving for Vatican', *Sydney Morning Herald*, 27 March 2014

23. Transcript from the Melbourne Response case study, 21 August 2014

24. *The Saturday Paper*, 14 November 2015

Chapter 4   Winter Gail

1. Lucie Morris-Marr, 'The forgotten find a voice', *Herald Sun*, 20 May 2015

2. www.stpats.vic.edu.au/en/news/article/cardinal-pell-visits/

3. Statement of Timothy Green, in Case Study 28, Royal Commission into Institutional Responses to Child Sexual Abuse

4. Lucie Morris-Marr, 'Haunted by his voice', *Herald Sun*, 28 May 2015
5. 'Sex abuse victim slams Pell's $100k legal costs', *Ballarat Courier*, 27 October 2015

Chapter 5   Wake up the cardinal
1. Interview with the author, November 2015
2. www.smh.com.au/national/cardinal-pell-associate-banned-from-preaching-in-ireland-over-abuse-allegations-20161007-grwxlh.html
3. www.abc.net.au/news/2015-12-11/george-pell-too-unwell-to-give-evidence-at-child-sex-inquiry/7021846
4. Lucie Morris-Marr, 'Wake up the Cardinal', *Marie Claire Australia* and *The Sunday Times*, July 2017
5. www.theguardian.com/media/2016/feb/22/andrew-bolt-lashes-out-at-herald-sun-reporter-over-george-pell-story
6. www.cjr.org/analysis/covering-child-abuse-in-the-catholic-church-under-a-court-gag-order.php
7. www.theAustralian.com.au/commentary/opinion/cardinal-george-pells-enemies-sneer-as-police-leak-smears/news-story/c4f0a24b4aaa673508824f26867798e7
8. www.independent.co.uk/news/catholic-anger-at-murdochs-papal-knighthood-1145252.html

Chapter 6   Courting controversy
1. Interview with the author, April 2019
2. www.abc.net.au/news/2018-05-07/denis-ryan-victorian-detective-police-pension-booted-force/9645982
3. www.dailymail.co.uk/news/article-3470903/What-kind-fresh-media-hell-Sky-News-fire-sending-harsh-child-sex-abuse-royal-commission-critic-Andrew-Bolt-report-Cardinal-Pell-s-testimony-Rome.html
4. www.dailymail.co.uk/news/article-3470903/What-kind-fresh-media-hell-Sky-News-fire-sending-harsh-child-sex-abuse-

royal-commission-critic-Andrew-Bolt-report-Cardinal-Pell-s-testimony-Rome.html

5. Interview with the author, April 2019
6. www.abc.net.au/news/2016-05-10/david-ridsdale-accused-of-downplaying-abuse-past/7401022
7. Interview with the author, March 2019
8. Tim Elliot, 'Defending George Pell', *Good Weekend*, 17 February 2018
9. www.heraldsun.com.au/blogs/andrew-bolt/pell-witch hunt-new-conspiracy-theory/news-story/208089094a8c684b3cc7 f66bb1722c98
10. www.smh.com.au/public-service/human-resources-allegiance-is-to-the-organisation-not-the-boss-20170202-gu43o4.html
11. www.bbc.com/news/world-australia-38877158

Chapter 7 Belinda's burden

1. www.theguardian.com/australia-news/2018/mar/09/robert-doyle-accuser-tessa-sullivan-all-i-want-is-the-truth
2. Interview with the author, December 2017
3. edition.cnn.com/2018/01/10/asia/australia-pell-seminary-sydney-intl/index.html
4. Lucie Morris-Marr, 'Cinema abuse allegations, Pell case starts to ring louder', *The New Daily*, 19 March 2019

Chapter 8 The Cathedral Trial

1. www.nytimes.com/2018/04/25/world/europe/pope-chile-sexual-abuse.html
2. Speech by James Peters QC, president of the Victorian Bar, upon Kidd's appointment to the bench, indaily.com.au/news/2019/02/28/who-is-the-adelaide-lawyer-at-the-centre-of-the-pell-trial/
3. www.theherald.com.au/story/1289651/gillard-talks-about-child-sex-abuse/

4. edition.cnn.com/2018/08/14/us/pennsylvania-catholic-church-grand-jury/index.html

Chapter 9   War cry from Rome

1. BBC News digital report, 27 August 2018
2. cruxnow.com/interviews/2018/06/20/Australian-prelate-laity-could-have-prevented-catastrophic-abuse-crisis/
3. Comment overheard by the author in court
4. Quotes from La Greca from post-court interview with the author, April 2019
5. Interview with the author, July 2019

Chapter 10   Play it again, Kidd

1. www.eurekastreet.com.au/article/an-unholy-mess
2. www.nbcnews.com/news/world/pope-calls-february-meeting-key-bishops-sexual-abuse-n908751
3. thenewdaily.com.au/news/national/2018/10/22/hear-morrison-apologies-child-abuse-victims/
4. www.theguardian.com/australia-news/2018/oct/22/scott-morrisons-national-apology-to-australian-survivors-and-victims-of-child-sexual-abuse-full-speech
5. thenewdaily.com.au/news/national/2018/10/22/advocate-chrissie-foster-speech/

Chapter 11   Beyond reasonable doubt

1. Comment made to the author, April 2018
2. www.abc.net.au/radionational/programs/sciencefriction/2019-02-03/10732646
3. Interview with the author, April 2019
4. www.9news.com.au/national/tim-fischer-diagnosed-with-acute-leukaemia/b148e6db-20a4-4c11-96e2-36339a39a3cb
5. www.abc.net.au/news/2018-12-06/philip-wilson-former-archbishop-conviction-quashed/10589198

Chapter 12 The world's worst kept secret

1. www.washingtonpost.com/lifestyle/style/a-top-cardinals-sex-abuse-conviction-is-huge-news-in-australia-but-the-media-cant-report-it-there/2018/12/12/49c0eb68-fe27-11e8-83c0-b06139e540e5_story.html?utm_term=.666534251aee

2. Comment to the author, June 2019

3. www.nytimes.com/2018/12/12/world/europe/pope-cardinals-pell-abuse.html

4. www.washingtonpost.com/lifestyle/style/a-top-cardinals-sex-abuse-conviction-is-huge-news-in-australia-but-the-media-cant-report-it-there/2018/12/12/49c0eb68-fe27-11e8-83c0-b06139e540e5_story.html?utm_term=.666534251aee

5. 'Contempt and suppression', *Meanjin*, 13 December 2018

Chapter 13 Friends in high places

1. www.vaticannews.va/en/pope/news/2018-01/pope-homily-new-year-2018-mother-of-god-full-text.html

2. CNN digital, 'The Pope for the first time, calls the sexual abuse of nuns "a problem"', 6 February 2019

3. www.washingtonpost.com/religion/2018/12/28/vaticans-investigation-into-theodore-mccarricks-alleged-crimes-is-underway/?noredirect=on&utm_term=.bd9cb72de92b

4. BBC, 'US ex-cardinal Theodore McCarrick defrocked over abuse claims', 16 February 2019

5. CNN, 'Salacious new book says homosexuality is rampant in the Vatican', 14 February 2019

6. www.apnews.com/5085e970462c4a5aa12cb5dab86127ae

7. Interview with the author, March 2019

8. Gerard O'Connell, '"We dare not fail": Australia's top bishop on the church's sex abuse crisis', *America Magazine*, 26 February 2019

9. Interview with the author, 26 February 2019

10. Melissa Cunningham, 'You no longer rule our world', *The Age*, 1 March 2019

11. Interview with the author, May 2019

12. www.theage.com.au/national/victoria/none-of-these-matters-alter-my-opinion-john-howard-s-character-reference-for-george-pell-20190227-p510pn.html

Chapter 14   Solitary retreat

1. Interview with the source who was the basis for the prison information, April 2019

2. Karen Sweeney, 'Duo behind attack on drug kingpin Tony Mokbel plead guilty', AAP/news.com.au

3. Interview with the author, July 2019

4. www.corrections.vic.gov.au/melbourne-assessment-prison-map-visitor-information

5. www.corrections.vic.gov.au/melbourne-assessment-prison-map-visitor-information

6. Interview with the author, March 2019

7. 700 statistic supplied by a spokesperson for the Department of Justice and Community Safety, Melbourne

8. Emma Younger, 'Gerald Ridsdale gets three more years in jail for new sexual abuse cases', ABC, 31 August 2017

9. The author present in court for the plea hearing of Robert Claffey, 8 July 2019 10.   www.mamamia.com.au/george-pell-st-patricks-cathedral/

11. Interview with the author, 13 March 2019

12. Comment to the author, 13 March 2019

13. Interview with the author, 13 March 2019

14. Interview with the author, May 2019

15. www.firstthings.com/web-exclusives/2019/05/the-pell-case-developments-down-under

16. Lucie Morris-Marr, 'George Pell to spend birthday behind bars awaiting appeal decision', *The New Daily*, 6 June 2019

17. David Marr, 'After a train wreck of a day, George Pell's date hinges on alibi evidence,' *The Guardian*, 6 June 2019

18. www.nytimes.com/2019/05/09/world/europe/pope-francis-abuse-catholic-church.html
19. Comments to the author, June 2019
20. Gerard O'Connell, *America Magazine*

9/10/20